ANSI FORTRAN IV and FORTRAN 77
Programming with Business Applications

ANSI FORTRAN IV and FORTRAN 77
Programming with Business Applications

Third Edition

Nesa L'abbé Wu
Eastern Michigan University

wcb

Wm. C. Brown Company Publishers
Dubuque, Iowa

wcb group

Wm. C. Brown Chairman of the Board
Mark C. Falb Corporate Vice President/Operations

wcb
Wm. C. Brown Company Publishers,
College Division

Lawrence E. Cremer President
Raymond C. Deveaux Vice President/Product Development
David Wm. Smith Vice President/Marketing
David A. Corona Assistant Vice President/Production
Development and Design
Marcia H. Stout Marketing Manager
Janis M. Machala Director of Marketing Research
Marilyn A. Phelps Manager of Design
William A. Moss Production Editorial Manager
Mary M. Heller Visual Research Manager

Book Team

Nicholas Murray Associate Developmental Editor
Lisa Bogle Designer
Bob McGuill Production Editor

Contents

Preface   ix

1: Introduction to Computers 3
1. A Brief History of Computers 3
2. Programming Languages 4
3. Computer Time-Sharing 5
4. How does the Computer Work? 6
   Exercises 12

2: Introduction to Fortran Programming 14
1. Processing a FORTRAN Job 14
2. The Source Statements 17
3. FORTRAN Coding 17
   Exercises 20

3: Flowcharting 23
1. Use of Symbols for Program Flowcharting 24
2. Example 1. Computing the Tuition for One Student 30
3. Example 2. Monthly Payments for a Car Loan 34
4. Example 3. Homeowners' Real Estate Tax 35
5. Checking the Logical Flow 36
   Exercises 39

4: The Arithmetic Assignment Statement 42
1. Variable Name 45
2. Arithmetic Expression 46
3. Arithmetic Rules 47
4. Examples of Arithmetic Assignment Statements 52
5. FORTRAN 77 Character Constants and Assignments 53
   Exercises 55

5: Input/Output Statements 59
1. Input/Output Statements 59
2. Format 60
3. READ/FORMAT Specifications 60
4. WRITE/FORMAT Specifications 65
5. FORMAT Rules 75
6. FORTRAN 77 Additional INPUT/OUTPUT 77
7. Summary of Format Specifications 78
   Exercises 79

6: Some Elementary Business Programs 82
1. Halt Statement 83
2. Simple Business Examples 84
   Exercises 94

7: Transfer and Decision Statements 97
1. GO TO Statements 97
2. The Arithmetic IF Statement 99
3. The Computed GO TO Statement 102
4. The Logical IF Statement 105

5. FORTRAN 77 Additional Control Statements   115
6. Good Programming Style (continued)   118
   Exercises   119

8:   **DO Loop**   129
1. The DO Loop   129
2. DO-Loop Rules   134
3. FORTRAN 77 Additional DO Loop Considerations   144
4. Good Programming Style (continued)   145
   Exercises   145

9:   **Use of Subscripts**   152
1. Single Subscripted Variables   152
2. Double Subscripted Variables   167
3. FORTRAN 77 Additional Subscript Considerations   180
   Exercises   181

10:   **More Advanced Business Programs**   187
1. Calculating the Monthly Payment of a Loan   188
2. Updating the Inventory Stock   191
3. Term Revolving Credit Plan   196
4. Savings Accumulation: Single-Premium Life Insurance Policy   204
   Exercises   211

11:   **Subprograms in Fortran**   216
1. Built-in Functions or Library Functions   217
2. Arithmetic-Statement Functions   219
3. The FORTRAN Function Subprogram   220
4. The FORTRAN Subroutine Subprogram   223

5. The Common Statement and Variable Dimensions   227
6. Good Programming Style with Subprograms   228
   Exercises   230

12:   **Type-Declaration and Date Statements**   234
1. Integer Declaration   234
2. Real Declaration   235
3. Double-Precision Declaration   235
4. Logical Declaration   240
5. The IMPLICIT Statement   240
6. Rules in Using Type-Declaration Statements   241
7. Data Statement   241
   Exercises   243

13:   **Sorting Data**   244
1. The First Program: The Selection Sort   244
2. The Second Program: The Bubble Sort   247
3. Other Sorting Techniques   250
   Exercises   250

14:   **Simulation**   252
1. The Random Number Generator   252
2. Simulating the Inebriated Individual Crossing the Bridge   254
3. Computation of π Through Simulation   258
4. Transportation Cost Analysis: A Simulation   262
   Exercises   269

15:   **Business Analysis**   270
1. Moving Averages of the Dow Jones Industrial Stocks   270
2. Goodness-of-Fit Test for the Random-Number Generator   276
3. Network Analysis: PERT-Program Evaluation and Review Technique   282

16: **Three Case Proposals** 291

1. Case Study #1: The Payroll Case 291
2. Case Study #2: Asset Depreciation Case 293
3. Case Study #3: Analysis of an Advertisement 296

Appendix A
Flowcharting Symbols 302
Appendix B
Summary of FORTRAN Statements 304
Appendix C
List of Flowcharts 308
Appendix D
The IBM 29 Card Punch 309
Appendix E
File Processing 314

Preface

Written primarily as a textbook for business students, this book may also be used by those taking their first computer course. It may also be used as a text in both Industrial and Systems Engineering. In developing the content, the author has striven for clarity, practicality, and simplicity; therefore, the book can also be found very useful in both industrial and business organizations as a ready reference source.

The programming language used is FORTRAN. The unique contribution of this text to the gallery of FORTRAN publications can be summarized briefly. It is a pioneer approach to the teaching of the FORTRAN programming language through practical applications.

Recognizing that flowcharting is a powerful tool for logic programming, the author uses it to demonstrate the logic solution procedure for all examples and cases used throughout this book.

It has not, however, been the intention of the author to cover, in detail, all facets of the FORTRAN programming language.

The input from my colleagues here at Eastern Michigan University, and the valuable input from reviewers is reflected in this edition. The three major additions and changes are: the introduction of the FORTRAN 77 standard; the discussion of good programming style, and a revised presentation and discussion of cases.

Because FORTRAN 77 does not conflict with the standards set by FORTRAN 1966, and because not all users have such a compiler, each chapter on FORTRAN concludes with some Fortran 77 features. Readers may then, at their discretion, decide whether or not to use this additional information.

Because there is a need for teaching good programming practice and structured programming, major emphasis is placed on these concepts throughout this new edition of the text.

The final chapter introduces the user to three cases, analyzes them in great detail, and then encourages students to flowchart and program the solutions procedure as discussed for each case.

Students and faculty who have used this text before have indicated that this text "does not waste words" and "teaches with plenty of examples"; that it is "good to place emphasis on flowcharts throughout the text" and that "the chapters are in a logical sequence".

Chapter 1 introduces the students to Computers. Chapters 2 through 12 present FORTRAN principles that are illustrated through problems and exercises at the end of each chapter, and it is necessary to follow these chapters in sequence. A complete chapter, Chapter 13, is devoted to Sorting Data, an essential subject, whereas Simulation is present in Chapter 14. Three Business Analysis Cases are developed in Chapter 15. They are: 1. Moving Averages of the Dow Jones Industrial Stocks, 2. Goodness-of-Fit Test for the Random-Number Generator, and 3. Network Analysis: PERT-Program Evaluation and Review Technique. The final chapter proposes three cases for the students to work on.

An attempt has been made to make the exercises appealing and of particular interest to business students. Besides some simple single-statement problems, the author has introduced business-oriented problems at the end of each chapter, and the students are encouraged to flowchart the solution first, before programming it. The appendixes are designed to give the students a quick reference on (a) flowcharting symbols, (b) the structure of FORTRAN statements used, (c) a guide to the flowcharts included in the book, (d) the use of the IBM 29 Card Punch, and (e) File Processing.

It is very difficult to adequately acknowledge all of those individuals who assisted me on this project. I have shamelessly imposed on my colleagues and friends for numerous examples and cases, which I have torn apart and transformed into a proper setting for this textbook. Special thanks go to Robert Nault, my assistant, who devoted many hours in running the revised programs of this text and who reorganized and reran all programs of the solutions manual.

I am grateful for the constructive criticism and helpful suggestions of the following people who reviewed the manuscript: Dr. Richard Peddicord, University of San Francisco; Dr. Dennis Anderson, Bently College; Professor Larry Hughes, Bemidji State College; Dr. T. Morris Jones, University of North Alabama; Professor Jerry Kinard, Southeastern Louisiana University; Professor Floyd Eaves, Chattanooga State Technical Community College; Dr. Andrew Vander Molen, Eastern Michigan University; Professor Kent Foster, Winthrop College. Special acknowledgement is due to Ida Mason of California State Polytechnic University—Pomona, for her contributions to its technical accuracy and general clarity.

Lastly, I am most grateful to my husband for both his patience and constructive criticism, and for his inspiration and encouragement during the development of this edition.

ANSI FORTRAN IV and FORTRAN 77
Programming with Business Applications

Introduction to Computers

1. A Brief History of Computers

Generally speaking, the oldest known computer dates back more than thirty-five hundred years. The circular arrangement of huge stones known as Stonehenge, in England, is referred to by many scientists as the first computer. Together with the sun these stones were used to predict astronomical phenomena. The description of another old "computer" can be found in the June 1959 issue of Scientific American. It deals with a machine, believed to be a Greek computer, which was discovered off the Greek island of Antikythera. It has been estimated that this machine is slightly over two thousand years old. Another ancient computing device, the abacus, was developed and used by the Chinese. This simple device for computing was introduced into Europe during Marco Polo's time.

The first adding machine was invented by the famous French mathematician B. Pascal in 1642. This calculator was improved in 1673 by the famed German mathematician Leibnitz, who made the calculator capable of use not only for the addition operation but also for the multiplication operation.

Charles Babbage is often referred to as the father of the computer. A noted English mathematician and professor of mathematics at Cambridge University, he conceived the machine (1812) that could take and act on instructions. His first machine, the Difference Engine, was a gigantic, monster computer, that was supposed to weigh approximately two tons. It was never completed, due to the lack of tooling technology at that time. Later on Babbage developed the Analytical Engine. Financial problems however, prohibited him from finishing this work. This genius envisioned that his machine would carry out arithmetic operations, one at a time; would receive instructions and data from key-punched cards; would store data and information; and would be able to make decisions between two alternatives. The stored program concept of the Analytical Engine is very close to that of modern computers.

The Harvard Mark 1 Computer was the first computer, completed in 1944. It had all started in 1937, when H. Aikens of Harvard University began the designing of the machine that would perform a sequence of arithmetic operations automatically. Though the size of the Mark 1 was only one-tenth that of Babbage's machine, it was still a huge mechanical calculator, consisting of adding accumulators, mechanical relays, switches, buttons, wire plugs, and punched tape. Soon after its completion the ENIAC (1945) and the EDVAC (1952), both by J. P. Eckert and J. W. Maughly of the Moore School of Engineering at the University of Pennsylvania, were completed.

The binary number system, to represent data and instructions, was introduced at Princeton University by Dr. J. Von Newman (after his stay at the Moore School), and the IAS computer was completed in 1952. With the EDVAC and the IAS computer, the electronic stage of the computer was entered, leaving the electromechanical stage behind.

Developments in computing have occurred in both the hardware and the software. Hardware developments are reflected in major changes of the equipment itself and have taken place in four steps or generations. First generation computers (1946–59) used vacuum tubes and were rather slow. Second generation machines (1959–65) used transistors and were smaller and faster. Third generation computers (1965–70) are characterized by integrated circuits and time-sharing capabilities. The transition to the third generation equipment meant a major change to the computer industry. Though these machines exhibited sensational increases in speed, the price of many computers dropped. This reduction in price perhaps explains why approximately 65 percent of the computers in operation today were installed in the sixties. Fourth generation computers (1970–) are the microtechnology devices being introduced today. Minicomputers and many other expected developments, such as: satellite transmission, microcomputers, laser and fluidic computers, and others, will characterize this generation.

Software developments are reflected in the various developments in computer programs and procedures, which are necessary for the operation of the computing systems. The first generation computers used a machine-oriented language. This language soon appeared to be unpractical, since each computer had its own program—one that could not be used by other systems. Symbolic assembly language was introduced during the second generation computers. Even though this language was easier to write, lack of conformity in the symbols used by the various programmers hindered the development of the symbolic assembly language. Finally, compilers and high-level languages were introduced. High-level languages have the advantage of being independent of the computer in use, and are easier to write than the previously mentioned languages. The FORTRAN programming language is one of the first of the high-level languages developed by IBM, and was published in 1957. During its life it underwent many changes. The most commonly used version is called FORTRAN IV. It is this standard FORTRAN IV, and the most current version, FORTRAN 77, that are considered in this text.

There are two major types of computers: the analog computer and the digital computer. The analog computer deals with continuous quantities, whereas the digital computer works with discrete quantities. In the early 1600s the first widely used analog computer, called the slide rule, was developed. In 1872 Lord Kelvin built his large-scale analog computer to be able to predict the changes in tides in the English harbors. Analog computers are not as widely used as digital computers and cannot be programmed in FORTRAN.

2. Programming Languages

There are two types of programming languages. These are machine oriented and problem oriented languages that were developed to enhance communications between the computer and its user.

The most basic and direct language is machine language, where statements are written in binary lists (0's and 1's). Before language translators existed, all programming was done in machine language or object code. Because machine language is a function of specific computer hardware, and because it requires a great deal of time to write in machine language, machine language code is not used by the common applications programmer. Various language translators have been developed to fill this need. Assembler would be one example.

Assembler is a sophisticated language that uses symbolic words called mnemonics (which can be acronyms or abbreviations) to communicate with the system. Even though it is the most efficient way to run a program, from the machine's point of view, it is not the most efficient language in which to write from a programmer's point of view. Application programmers prefer to write in a language that closely resembles their own. Hence, problem oriented languages were developed.

The following is a brief discussion of some of these problem oriented languages: FORTRAN, COBOL, RPG, PL/I, BASIC, ALGOL, GPSS and SIMSCRIPT.

The FORTRAN programming language was developed by IBM and published in 1957. FORTRAN (FORmula TRANslator) was originally designed to resemble mathematical formulas and, over the years, has undergone many changes. The most commonly used version is FORTRAN IV, whose standards were published in 1966 by the American National Standards Institute. As a result of these standards, there is little variation among systems using this language. The most recent development in this language was reported in the October, 1978 issue of the ACM (Association for Computing Machinery) journal. Here, a new standard FORTRAN was introduced as "American National Standard Programming Language FORTRAN, X3.9—1978," commonly referred to as FORTRAN 77. This new standard includes features that have proven to be very useful in the past, and new features that make programs easier to transport. None of the features of FORTRAN 77 are in conflict with the 1966 FORTRAN. This text discusses FORTRAN IV and introduces some of the new features of FORTRAN 77. Because of the many changes FORTRAN underwent over the years, the language is no longer limited to mathematics and formulas, but can now successfully and efficiently handle alphabetical sentences. Therefore, FORTRAN is being used in mathematics, education, business, industry, etc.

In 1960, a new language, COBOL (COmmon Business Oriented Language), was introduced. Unlike the FORTRAN language, COBOL approximates English with instructions written in sentences and paragraphs. Because it was originally designed for business data processing, it is widely used as a business language. This language requires many more instructions and is more difficult to learn than the FORTRAN language.

RPG (Report Program Generator) and its advanced version RPG II, as developed in 1969, was especially designed to ease business report printing. Once the programmer specifies the input and output information, and what calculations are needed, then the RPG II translator generates the solution procedure. This language is quite limited and is frequently used on small systems, but rarely on medium- and large-sized systems.

In 1966, IBM developed a new programming language that combines the business capabilities of COBOL with the numerical advantages of FORTRAN. The language was named PL/I (Programming Language I) and was supposed to be accepted by all computer manufacturers. To date, however, only a few manufacturers have developed PL/I compilers. Therefore, PL/I is not used as frequently as either FORTRAN or COBOL.

In 1964, BASIC (Beginner's All-purpose Symbolic Instruction Code) was developed at Dartmouth College under the supervision of Professor John G. Kemeny and Thomas E. Kurtz. This language gained in popularity during the fourth generation of computers with the introduction of minicomputers and time-sharing. It was designed for the beginning programmer. It is an algebraic language like FORTRAN, but is much more limited. It is now the primary language of the personal or minicomputer.

While FORTRAN was being develped in the United States, ALGOL (ALgebraic Oriented Language) was developed in Europe. Though ALGOL is similar to FORTRAN, it has not been accepted as widely as FORTRAN.

Two other problem oriented languages worth mentioning are GPSS and SIMISCRIPT. SIMISCRIPT was designed to facilitate the simulation of large and complex systems, and to minimize time spent designing, programming, and testing simulation models. It is a free-form, English-like language, developed by the RAND corporation. The GPSS (General Purpose Simulation System) programming language was developed in the early 1960's. It was especially designed for systems simulation, and it is easier to learn and to use than SIMISCRIPT.

New computer languages are continuously being designed, while existing ones are refined to answer an ever widening need for new applications and ease of programming.

3. Computer Time-Sharing

Time-Sharing Systems: Background Briefs

Time sharing is a system whereby two or more users may have access to the same computer and receive what appears to be simultaneous responses. Although the machine is, in fact, dividing its time among them, each user feels in complete control. Access by those who are some distance from the central computer may be gained via terminal and telephone lines. The first operational computer time-sharing system was introduced at the Massachusetts Institute of Technology only about ten years ago. Called the Compatible Time-Sharing System (CTSS), it was developed for an IBM 709 computing system in 1961. Other time-sharing systems were developed during succeeding years and were installed by many other end-users, computer manufacturers, and commercial time-sharing vendors. Some early systems are:

CTSS: developed by Bolt, Beranek, and Newman for the Digital Equipment Corporation's PDP-1 computer.
JOSS: (Johnniac Open Shop System)—developed by RAND Corporation in 1963.
CAL: (Conversational Algebraic Language)—developed by the University of California in Berkeley in 1963.
MAC: (Multiple Access Computer)—the beginning of large time-sharing systems (160 terminals at MIT and other institutions of higher learning) in 1963.
BASIC: (Beginner's All-Purpose Symbolic Instruction Code)—developed at Dartmouth College between 1964 and 66.

Many time-sharing systems were developed by major computer manufacturers, such as Burroughs, Control Data Corporation, Digital Equipment Corporation, General Electric, Hewlett-Packard, IBM, RCA, Scientific Data Systems, and UNIVAC.

In 1970, over 100 million dollars was spent for computer time-sharing, which now has become the fastest growing section of the computer industry. Examples of those who use time-sharing systems include colleges and universities, scientists, engineers, manufacturers, managers, executives, bankers, and many others.

Terminals, such as teletypes, displays, and plotters, are found in many offices and even some private homes. They have numerous applications in business—investment analysis, transportation, rate of return, project evaluation and review, financial analysis, merge analysis, inventory control, purchasing, forecasting, budgeting, production analysis, even payroll processing—and for many other objectives. Time-sharing has also enjoyed great acceptance in educational institutions, public and health service organizations, and many other sectors of our society.

Time-sharing may have special appeal for smaller corporations where the initial investment is often of major concern; however, the primary users are still larger corporations, where the turnaround time is the major factor.

Time-Sharing Languages
Several conversational time-sharing programming languages have been developed. These include:

BASIC: Beginner's All-purpose Symbolic Instruction Code, a rather simple language that has been implemented by almost all major computer manufacturers.
CAL: Conversational Algebraic Language, developed at the University of California in Berkeley, is less popular. It is available on the Scientific Data 940.
LISP: a LISt-Processing programming language that is available on many systems.

Variations of the FORTRAN programmming language have been developed specifically for time-sharing use. Some of these are QUIKTRAN, XTRAN, and CDC FORTRAN EXTENDED.

Remote Job Entry vs. Interactive Processing
In a remote job entry environment, programs and data are normally submitted using punched cards that are collected at some central point (not necessarily near the computer) and entered into the batch processing stream. All the user need see is a card reader and a printer.

In an interactive processing environment, programs, and data are entered directly into the central computer via an on-line terminal.

While this text is primarily a punched card (batch) entry system, instructors may provide the additional information necessary for on-line (interactive) processing. The FORTRAN is the same. The only difference is in how the students access the computer.

4. How Does the Computer Work?

A computer can be visualized as a black box device that performs computations automatically, accurately, and at high speed, given a set of instructions. The set of instructions combining reading, writing, arithmetic (addition, subtraction, multiplication, division, exponentiation), and data listing are aimed at the solution of some problem, and are written in a language the computer can understand or translate. These instructions are in general referred to as the program.

There are five basic components in a computer system:

1. the INPUT unit
2. the STORAGE unit
3. the ARITHMETIC/LOGIC unit
4. the CONTROL unit
5. the OUTPUT unit

together form the central processing unit (CPU). These 3 components are often physically housed in the same unit and are therefore referred to as the CPU.

These components are shown in the following figure.

The INPUT unit places the program and the data in storage. The OUTPUT unit gives the results which are in MEMORY. This is accomplished through the command of the CONTROL unit. As soon as a computer program is in memory, or in main storage, the control unit takes the first instruction, analyzes it, and makes sure that the instruction is executed properly. Depending upon the nature of the instruction, the arithmetic/logic unit, the input unit, or the output unit is commanded to perform certain duties. Or the control unit brings data from the storage to the arithmetic/logic unit, or from the arithmetic/logic unit to central storage. As soon as the first instruction is properly executed, the control unit retrieves the second instruction out of central storage, and so forth, until a HALT instruction is reached or an invalid instruction (i.e., garbage, misplaced data) is encountered, or there are none left, or an instruction becomes impossible. Note that the MAIN STORAGE unit is the heart of the system since it bridges all other units of the system. Also, it is not physically possible to separate the arithmetic/logic unit from the control unit.

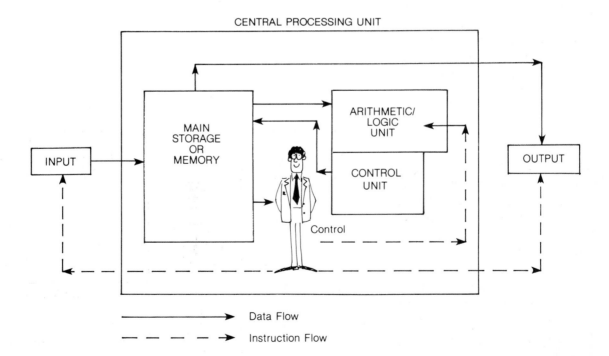

CENTRAL PROCESSING UNIT

INPUT

MAIN STORAGE OR MEMORY

ARITHMETIC/ LOGIC UNIT

CONTROL UNIT

Control

OUTPUT

——————→ Data Flow

— — — — → Instruction Flow

The five basic components therefore form a computer system.

To illustrate how the central processing unit works let us assume that the following instruction needs to be executed:

$$A = A + B$$
$$\text{where } A = 2$$
$$B = 3$$

The above is a valid Fortran instruction and means: get the value that is stored under the variable name A and add to it the value that is stored under the variable name B. The result must be stored under the variable name A. The following six cartoons illustrate in fourteen steps the process of execution, under the assumption that all instructions are ready in the main storage.

Step 1

The FORTRAN instruction:

LET A = A + B (assuming that A is equal to 2 and B is equal to 3)

is broken down into instructions and operands. The instructions are predefined machine operations such as GET, ADD, and PUT, whereas the operands usually refer to the storage locations containing the data to be operated on. The translated FORTRAN statement may be placed in storage as shown. The first five locations contained the following: get the contents of location 4, add to it the contents of location 5, put the result back in location 4, tell the control data unit where the next instruction is, data, data, . . .

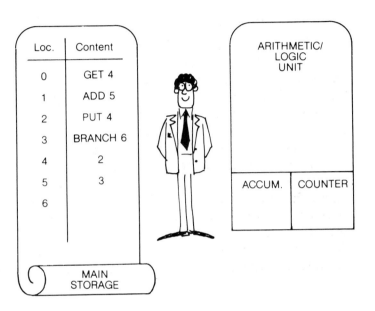

Step 2

Note that in our "mythical" computer we are able to store an instruction and an operand in each storage location. In reality the instructions in main storage are stored in binary code. For the sake of illustration, let us imagine that each location can store a string of seven ones or zeroes. Furthermore, if that location happens to contain an instruction with its operand, the instruction is represented by the first three digits (or bits), and the operand by the last four. Assuming that the manufacturer has defined the GET instruction to be

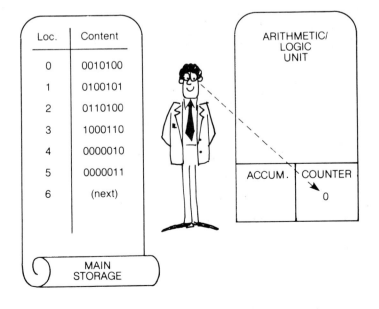

001, ADD instruction to be 010, PUT to be 011, and BRANCH to be 100, the contents of location 0 through 5 is as shown in the second cartoon. Note that 000 has never been defined by the manufacturer and is, therefore, an invalid instruction. This should not cause a problem since the BRANCH instruction in location 3 makes sure that the control unit does not try to interpret that data as an instruction.

Step 3

The instruction in location zero (0) is analyzed by the control unit. The control unit must copy the contents of location four (4) on his workbench, called the accumulator.

Step 4

The data item "2" is placed in the accumulator.

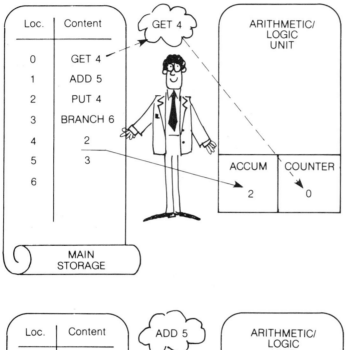

Step 5

As soon as the control unit has analyzed the above instruction, the counter value moves to "1" (one).

Step 6

The control unit analyzes the instruction in location one (1). He must add the content of location five (5) to whatever he has stored in the accumulator.

Step 7

The addition is performed in the arithmetic unit.

Step 8

The result of the addition is stored in the accumulator.

Step 9

Meanwhile, the counter value moved to "2" (two).

Step 10

The control unit analyzes the instruction in location two (2). He must put the contents of the accumulator in location four (4).

Step 11

The control unit puts five (5) in location four (4).

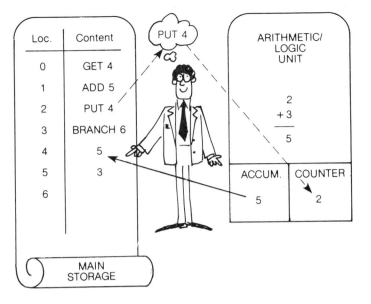

Step 12

Meanwhile, the counter value moved to "3" (three).

Step 13

The control unit analyzes the instruction in location three (3). He must branch to location six (6).

Step 14

He continues with the next operation.

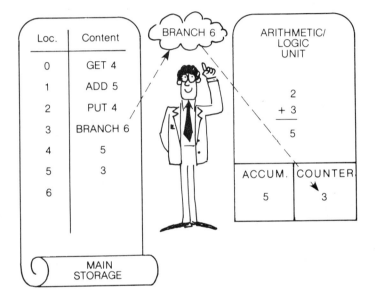

In conclusion, the previous six cartoons illustrated the following interesting characteristics of computers and computing:

1. Data and instructions are stored in binary code.
2. The instructions to be executed must be stored in a logical sequence.
3. All necessary data must be stored in specific locations and in accordance with the instructions.
4. During the execution of the instructions, neither instructions nor data are wiped out. Data values can be replaced by other values (Step 10).
5. The arithmetic/logic unit executes all arithmetic and logical steps.

Problem No. 1

The function of a computing system is described in this introduction with the aid of the skeleton diagram below. Identify the functions which correspond to each of the boxes in the diagram and describe each very briefly.

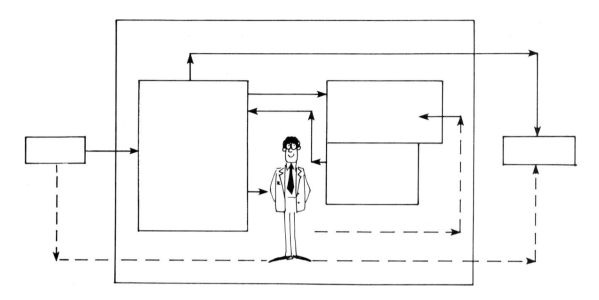

Problem No. 2

Answer each of the following review questions.

1. The most dramatic advances in processing information have occurred in _____.
    a) 3,000 BC
    b) the sixteenth century
    c) the last quarter century
    d) the nineteenth century

2. True or False:
   The significant hardware development in the third generation of computers is the use of transistors.

3. True or False:
   The digital computer, rather than the analog computer, is used for business data processing.

4. _____ is often referred to as the father of the computer.
    a) B. Pascal
    b) Leibnitz
    c) C. Babbage
    d) H. Aikens
    e) J. Von Newman

5. The binary number system for representing data and instructions was introduced by ___.
   a) C. Babbage
   b) H. Aikens
   c) J. Von Newman
   d) J. P. Eckert

6. How does time-sharing work?

7. What do the following abbreviations stand for?

CAL	BASIC	LISP	FORTRAN	COBOL
RPG	PL/I	ALGOL	GPSS	

8. Differentiate between a "machine oriented" and a "problem oriented" language.

9. What is an "Assembler"?

10. Name four problem oriented languages and briefly discuss their orientation.

2 Introduction to FORTRAN Programming

FORTRAN is an advanced high level programming language which closely resembles the ordinary language of mathematics. Each FORTRAN statement must be broken down and translated into a series of instructions in a low level machine language which can be understood and/or executed by the specific computer in use. FORTRAN coding is closely related to the program flowchart and is easier to learn than machine language.

The original FORTRAN program written by the programmer is called the "Source Program." The machine program which consists of the machine-coded instructions and which is actually used by the computer is called the "Object Program." The conversion of source programs written in FORTRAN to machine language is carried out by a special program called a "Compiler." Besides translating the programming language into machine language, the compiler also makes storage assignments, assembles and compiles the instructions into an object program in the most efficient manner, checks programming errors, and prints out error messages and diagnoses. Compilers do not check logic or spelling errors.

After the compiler has created the object module (or program) from the source program statements, the linkage editor then combines the object module with other library or user-written subprograms to form a load module. The load module is then ready to process or execute. If the program calls for reading in data, then data will now be read and processed by the load module.

Due to the general acceptance of the FORTRAN language, FORTRAN compilers are available for most of the computers manufactured in the United States. Each compiler is programmed for a specific machine and must take the actual characteristics of the machine into consideration. However, a FORTRAN program is independent from most of the computers in use. Therefore, the FORTRAN programmer needs no special comprehensive knowledge on the computer except for a general knowledge of computer operating principles and the types of input and output devices available.

1. Processing a FORTRAN IV Job

The five basic steps in executing a FORTRAN job are:

Step 1: Load the FORTRAN compiler into the computer memory. The compiler is a program designed to translate source statements into object code.

Step 2: Read the source program as data, and process it to create the object program (or object module). Usually, this object-module is written on a high-speed storage such as magnetic tape or disk.

Step 3: Link-edit to form a load module. Now, the linkage editor combines the object module with other library or user-written subprograms to form this load module.

Step 4: Execute the load module using data if any.

Step 5: Print all results.

These steps are shown schematically in the following figure.

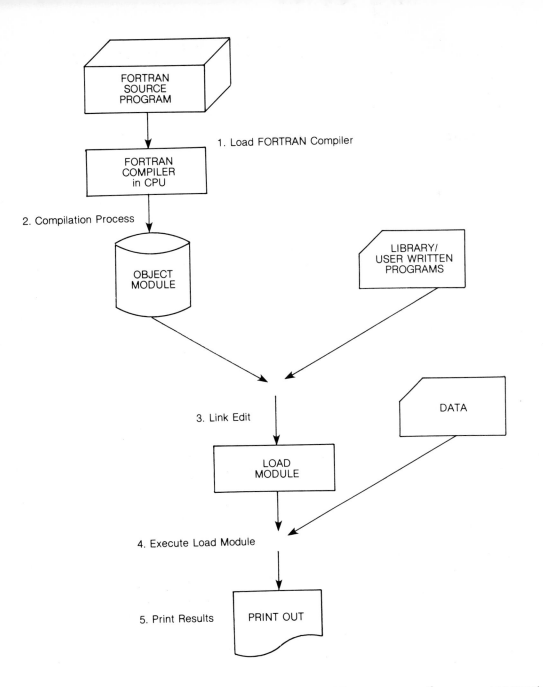

Each person who wishes to run a FORTRAN program on the computer must be able to place the FORTRAN compiler in front of his FORTRAN source program which it is supposed to compile. The only exception, of course, would be in those on-line environments where the compiler would be stored on some external storage device such as a magnetic disk. When a small computer is in use to process the FORTRAN programs, the programmer is expected to operate the computer directly. Larger and more expensive computers are normally looked after by full-time computer operators. In this case, an operating system (monitor system, or executive system) is normally used to help the computer operator reduce wasted computer time in preparing for the different jobs to be run.

To insure proper compiler loading and good "bookkeeping," the programmer must provide special control statements for the operating system. In a batch processing system, punched cards are placed in front of the FORTRAN source program. In a time-sharing system, entries would be keyed in from the terminal.

There are no standard control cards, since they are independent of the FORTRAN language; they are, instead, dependent upon the specification of the local installation. In general, these control cards or commands specify: the programmer's or user's ID number for accounting purposes, the estimated running time, the maximum number of output pages, etc. (card #1 below); systems command to load the FORTRAN compiler and FORTRAN commands to create and run the object program (cards #2, 3, and 23 below); and a FORTRAN command to release the FORTRAN compiler and to return control to the operating system (last card [#26] of the figure below).

```
/* END OF JOB                                                          26
99.00
MILLER C.V. 123.4510.
//GO.SYSIN DD *                                                       23
/* END OF JOB
       END
       STOP
5      FORMAT(///,5X,3A4,20X,F6.2,21X,F5.2,23X,F6.2,18X,F12.2)
       WRITE(6,5)N1,N2,N3,QUANT,RATEU,DISCRT,AMDUE
1T',19X,'AMOUT DUE')
4      FORMAT(//////,9X,'NAME',23X,'QUANTITY',19X,'RATE/UNIT',19X,'DISCOUN
       WRITE(6,4)
3      FORMAT(1H1,10X,'PROBLEM V/2')
       WRITE(6,3)
       AMDUE=GROSS-TOTDIS
       TOTDIS=FACT*DISCRT
       FACT=IFACT
       IFACT=GROSS/100.
       GROSS=RATEU*QUANT
2      FORMAT(F5.2)
       READ(5,2)RATEU
1      FORMAT(3A4,F6.2,F5.2)
       READ(5,1)N1,N2,N3,QUANT,DISCRT
//GO.SYSIN DD *                                                        3
//        EXEC     FORTRAN                                             2
//LNESAWU  JOB  (408002,02M,020,000),'WU,NESA           ',CLASS=K      1
```

The FORTRAN program is the source program and is written and prepared in machine readable form (punched cards, paper tape, etc.). This source program is an ordered list of executable and nonexecutable statements. Whereas the executable statements are closely related to the original algorithm or solution procedure, the nonexecutable statements describe the inputs, outputs, and other elements of the program. The source program is the data for the compiler, which transforms it into an object program. Any error (referred to as syntax error) that the compiler detects in the source program during compilation is described in the form of a written message. If no syntactical, or grammatical errors are found during compilation, then the object program is loaded into the computer, linkage is performed and then the program is executed. The debugging process continues during execution of the program; therefore, more error messages can be generated (see Appendix D). Beware of a diagnostic-free program; a diagnostic-free program may produce undesired answers, the consequence of a faulty translation of the solution procedure into the FORTRAN language.

2. The Source Statements

The FORTRAN source program is an ordered list of statements or "sentences." As already mentioned, there are two classes of statements, the executable statements and the nonexecutable statements. The executable statements are performed in a logical order—the order in which they appear in the program. The executable statements are the Input/Output statements, the Assignment statements, and the Control statements. The nonexecutable statements are the specifications and the End statement. The syntax of these five different types is explained and discussed in the following chapters. The Input/Output statements direct the computer in transmitting information between the computer's memory and the Input/Output unit.

Arithmetic and logical computations are directed by Assignment statements. The order in which statements are executed is controlled by the Control statements. The nonexecutable specification statements are descriptive in nature. Through specification statements the compiler is informed of the nature and the arrangement of Input/Output data, the types of Variables used, and the allocation of storage. Subprograms are defined, called for, and used through subprogram statements.

3. FORTRAN Coding

Consider the following FORTRAN program which is in FORTRAN coding form, and in which each line represents an 80-column keypunch card.

Note that there are 5 different fields:

Column 1. Comment field (C)

Columns 1 through 5. Statement label field

Column 6. Continue field

Columns 7 through 72. FORTRAN statement field

Columns 73 through 80. Identification field

Because FORTRAN is a formula-oriented language, it usually describes the general problem solution very well. However, it is often handy for the programmer to be able to inject notes and general comments into the program to improve its readability. These comments are made possible by the use of comment cards. A comment card has to be properly identified by a "C" in the first column. Some FORTRAN dialects require a blank space immediately following the "C." The sole purpose of comment cards is to serve as an aid for the program writer or reader in keeping track of the program parts, especially when the program is very lengthy. During the compilation of the FORTRAN program, the comment cards are ignored

IBM

FORTRAN Coding Form

M 050**
U.S.A.

PROGRAM: INTEREST CALCULATION
PROGRAMMER: NESA WU
DATE: JANUARY 12, 1980

PUNCHING INSTRUCTIONS — GRAPHIC / PUNCH

IDENTIFICATION SEQUENCE (73–80)

```
Card
(Line)
Number   C   STATEMENT   FORTRAN STATEMENT
         O   NUMBER
         M
         M
#1       C              INTEREST CALCULATION
#2       C              RATE=THE YEARLY INTEREST RATE
#3       C              CAP=THE INVESTED CAPITAL
#4       C              N=THE NUMBER OF YEARS CAP IS INVESTED
#5                      RATE=0.045
#6                      CAP=1275.00
#7                      N=17
#8                      EARN = CAP*(1.00+RATE)**N-CAP
#9                      WRITE(6,1)EARN,CAP,N
#10          1          FORMAT('1',///,5X,F7.2,2X,
#11                     'IS THE INTEREST OF AN INVESTMENT OF $',
#12          2          F8.2,2X,'OVER',2X,I2,'YEARS')
#13                     STOP
#14                     END
```

and therefore do not affect the operation of the program. In the preceding program the first 4 cards (lines) are comment cards. They serve the purpose of identifying the program name (card #1) and of indentifying the names used in the program (cards #2, #3, and #4).

In order to be able to refer to an instruction, one must number the referenced instruction. Statement labels (numbers) are placed in the first thru fifth column.

All statement labels in FORTRAN are numeric. Normally the maximum size is four digits (9999) or five digits (32767 or 99999), depending on the internal hardware of the computer in use at the location. Each statement must be uniquely labeled, i.e., a given statement label may be used to label only one statement in that program. All translators accept, but do not require, right justified statement labels; this means that statement labels have their units position in column 5 and blank spaces to the left of the statement label. The 10th card, in the preceding program is labeled "1" in column 5.

Instructions that are too long to fit on one card can be continued on the next card(s). A card (or statement) can be continued by having any character, other than a blank or zero, in column 6. Some compilers do not allow more than one continuation card. However, most compilers allow for 4, 9, or even 19 continuations. The 11th and 12th cards are continuations of the 10th card, and are therefore marked with 1 and 2 in column 6. Continuation cards must be blank in columns 1 through 5.

Columns 7 through 72 contain the FORTRAN statements, one statement per card with possible continuation cards. In general, blank spaces within FORTRAN statements are allowed, since they are ignored during compilation. Later, in the development of the FORTRAN statements, the restrictions to this general rule will be outlined. With the exception of one statement, all FORTRAN statements start with a key word, which indicates the function that the statement performs. The following FORTRAN key words are a sampling of those discussed in the various chapters:

Key words	Function
none	Assignment
REAL	Real type declaration
INTEGER	Integer type declaration
READ	Input
WRITE	Output
FORMAT	Format for Input and for Output
CALL EXIT	Terminating Execution
STOP	Terminating Execution
END	End of the program
GOTO	Unconditional and Conditional Transfer
IF	Conditional Transfers
DO	Looping
CONTINUE	Continuation of Execution
DIMENSION	Dimensioning Arrays
FUNCTION	Function Subprogram
CALL	Transfer to Subroutine
SUBROUTINE	Subroutine Subprogram
and others	

The final eight columns on the card make up the identification field. The programmer can enter any information in these columns, since they are ignored during the processing of the FORTRAN job. Experienced programmers put card numbers in columns 72–80, so that they can easily put the deck of cards back together in sequence, in case it is accidentally dropped.

Problem No. 1

Consider the following review questions, and give short answers.

1. True or False:
   The machine-coded instructions which are actually used by the computer are called the source program.

2. True or False:
   Comment cards do not affect the operation of the program.

3. True or False:
   All FORTRAN statements must be labeled.

4. Distinguish between the following pairs:
   a) OBJECT program versus SOURCE program
   b) COMPILER versus SOURCE program
   c) LOW level programming language versus HIGH level programming language.
   d) COMPILATION versus EXECUTION

5. A program that is supplied by a computer manufacturer that translates SOURCE programs into OBJECT programs is known as _____ .
   a) Program generator
   b) Subroutine
   c) Compiler
   d) None of the above

6. In general, a higher level language compared with a lower level language

   _____ .
   a) is easier to learn
   b) has coding that is more closely related to the program flowchart
   c) requires fewer lines of code
   d) all of the above
   e) none of the above

7. Which of the following tasks is not performed by a language translator program (compiler)?
   a) Conversion from a high level to a low level language program
   b) Checking for incorrectly formed expression
   c) Checking for keypunch errors in data cards
   d) Checking for invalid keywords
   e) Checking for invalid variable names

8. FORTRAN is considered to be a _____ level language; whereas the computer itself is only capable of directly understanding instructions in a _____ level language.
   a) High, Low
   b) High, High
   c) Low, High
   d) Low, Low
   e) None of the above

Problem No. 2

Read and practice the instructions in Appendix E to become acquainted with the keypunch machine. Learn your system's commands, so that you can prepare the example on page 18 for computer execution. Keypunch all system's commands and the program on page 18. Assemble the keypunched cards in correct order and submit your deck of cards to the computer operator for execution. If you do everything correctly, you will get the following as output: 1419.56 IS THE INTEREST OF AN INVESTMENT OF $1275.00 OVER 17 YEARS Your instructor may make some minor modifications to this program, so that it will run on your system.

Problem No. 3

Consider the following computer program and data that must be keypunched as shown:

Computer Program:

```
      INTEGER FIRST,SECOND,TOTAL
      READ(5,100) FIRST,SECOND
100   FORMAT(2I3)
      TOTAL = FIRST+SECOND
      WRITE(6,200) FIRST,SECOND,TOTAL
200   FORMAT(5X,'FIRST VALUE   =',I4,//,
     1        5X,'SECOND VALUE  =',I4,//,
     2        5X,'TOTAL VALUE   =',I4)
      STOP
      END
```

Data Card:

```
173425
```

a) Keypunch all system's commands that are necessary to run this program. Assemble program, data, and system's commands in the proper order, and submit your deck of cards to the computer operator for execution. (Note: Your instructor may want to make some minor changes in the preceding computer program to make it compatible with your system).

b) Look at your output. Can you describe what the above program has accomplished?

c) Replace the above data card with the following one:

New Data Card:

```
1 7   4 2
```

Rerun your program with this new data card and observe your result. Did you expect to obtain that result?

d) Again, replace the data card with the following one:

New Data Card:

```
 1 7   4 2
```

Rerun your program with this new data card and observe your result. How did your answer change?

e) Can you guess why you obtained these different answers under (a), (c) and (d)? If you cannot, do not worry because it will be explained later in the text.

f) You may wish to experiment with other data cards (one at a time). Good Luck.

Flowcharting

There is nothing magical about the way a computer works. Basically, it is a dumb machine that will do exactly what you tell it to do by the use of instructions. If you communicate the instructions correctly, then you may expect to receive correct results. Communicating the instructions correctly implies that the logic of the instructions must be complete and correctly translated by the use of an appropriate computer language that is acceptable by the computing system. Let us now briefly examine the process involved in creating a workable computer program.

Before one can actually write a computer program it is necessary to learn, or be able to solve problems in a very systematic and detailed way. This systematic approach to problem solving is reflected in the following six steps:

1. Define the problem and specify what questions need to be answered
2. Assemble and label data and/or information
3. Express all necessary relationships between variables by use of mathematical or logical relations
4. Develop the proper algorithm or procedure to solve the problem. Here, we merely organize the mathematical and logical relations in the correct sequence
5. Output the answers to the questions and check for correct results.

Several tools can be used to enforce this systematic approach. Two of these are *pseudocodes* and *flowcharts*. The development of pseudocodes was a natural response to the needs of structured programming. Pseudocode is written in a formal language that represents the logical structures of structured programming. At this point, it is rather premature to discuss the many facets of structured programming. However, as we proceed through the development of Fortran programming, structured programming will be presented and used in this text.

Flowcharting tends to illustrate a process graphically. A flowchart is made up of a set of symbols, the shapes of which indicate the nature of the operations being described, supplemented by connecting lines and arrows that show the "flow of control" between the various symbols.

Each standard flowcharting symbol can be classified as belonging to one of the following eight groups:

1. Processing group
2. Decision group
3. Input/Output group
4. Connectors and Terminal group
5. Linkage group
6. Predefined process group
7. Preparation group
8. Comment group

Appendix A summarizes the different symbol(s) in each group and their usage.

There are two basic kinds of flowcharts: the systems flowchart and the program flowchart. The systems flowchart is general and broad. It emphasizes data flow among machines and does not emphasize how the data has to be converted to obtain desired outputs. This type of flowchart is not discussed in this chapter.

The program flowchart, in contrast to the systems flowchart, is very detailed. It indicates the logical sequence of events for transforming the input to the desired output. There are two types of program flowcharts: modular and detailed. Both types will be discussed here. The reader will immediately notice that the modular flowchart can be read and understood with no prior knowledge of mathematics or the Fortran language. In practice programmers will start with a modular flowchart while they are still determining what programming language to use. When their general modular flowchart is completed, and after they have chosen the appropriate programming language, the programmer will proceed to a more detailed flowchart. Now the programmer will be guided by the modular flowchart and will use mathematics and even the programming language in the detailed flowchart.

The symbols used for program flowcharting are shown on page 25.

1. Use of Symbols for Program Flowcharting

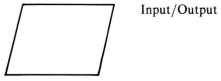
Input/Output Symbol

This symbol represents any Input/Output function. Through this symbol, information can be made available to the computer (example: read in payroll data) or processed information can be made available by the computer by printing it on an output medium (example: print out payroll checks).

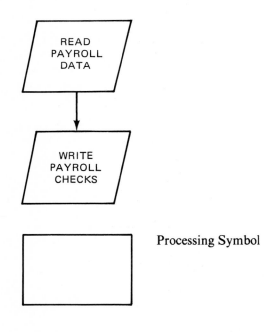

Processing Symbol

This symbol is used to represent any processing, defined operation(s) which cause change in form, value, or location of information. Arithmetic instructions and instructions for data movement are placed in these blocks.

PROCESS. Any processing function; defined operation(s) causing change in form, value or location of information.

DECISION. A decision or switching-type operation that determines which of a number of alternative paths to follow.

INPUT/OUTPUT. General I/O function; information available for processing (input), or recording of processed information (output).

TERMINAL, INTERRUPT. A terminal point in a flowchart—start, stop, halt, delay or interrupt; may show exit from a closed subroutine.

CONNECTOR. Exit to, or entry from, another part of the chart.

PAGE CONNECTOR

ARROWHEADS and FLOWLINES. In linking symbols, these show operations sequence and dataflow direction.

PREDEFINED PROCESS. One or more named operations or program steps specified in a subroutine or another set of flowcharts.

PREPARATION. Instruction modification to change program—set a switch, modify an index register, initialize a routine.

COMMENT. Additional descriptive clarification, comment. (Dotted line extends to symbols as appropriate.)

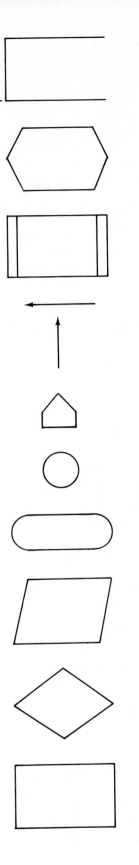

In the payroll example the PAYROLL DATA must be processed to obtain the output PAYROLL CHECKS. This transformation requires three steps:

(1) Compute Wages
(2) Compute Federal Withholding Tax
(3) Compute the Net Income

Assuming these general transformations, the modular flowchart can be redrawn as follows:

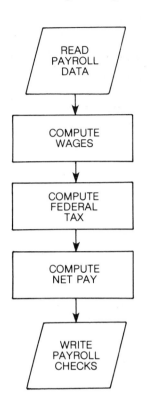

A more detailed flowchart may show the exact mathematical computation as follows:

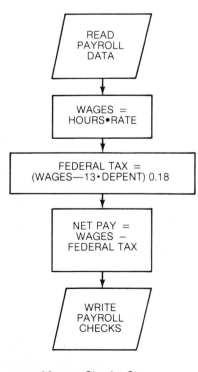

Note that a very general formula is used to calculate the federal tax, based on wages (WAGES) and number of dependents (DEPENT).

Although there is a one-to-one correspondence between the modular and the detailed flowcharts in this example, there could actually be a one-to-many relationship—i.e., one modular block may represent many detailed blocks.

Since more than one operation can appear in the process block the previous flowchart can be reduced as follows.

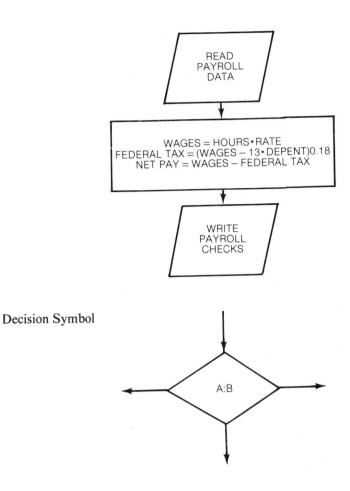

Decision Symbol

As is the case with the Input/Output and the Processing symbol, the diamond-shaped decision symbol has one entrance line. However, since the decision symbol results in a number of alternatives to be followed, there are at least two exit paths or branches. In the case of more than three exit paths, the exits are often represented as shown.

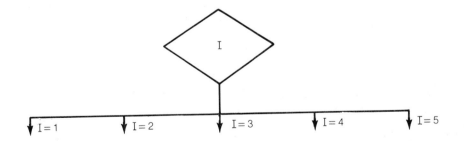

Notice that it is assumed that I can take on five different values and that for each value of I, a different path has to be chosen.

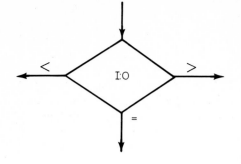

Comparisons made with the decision symbol in a detailed program flowchart are often shown with a colon (:). For example: Compare I with 0 (zero). As compared to zero, I may be equal (=) to zero, or I may be larger (>) than zero, or I may be smaller (<) than zero. So, for these three possible cases, three different paths are appropriate. Later, it will be shown how decisions might be written differently in a decision block.

In the detailed program flowchart of the PAYROLL EXAMPLE, the calculation of the FEDERAL TAX

FEDERAL TAX = (WAGES—13 · DEPENT) 0.18

may become negative if there are many dependents and if the weekly WAGES are very small. In that case the FEDERAL TAX should be equal to zero, rather than negative. Therefore, to avoid subtracting a negative income tax from the wages, it might be wise to investigate whether the calculated FEDERAL TAX is negative, zero, or positive before calculating the NET PAY, as follows:

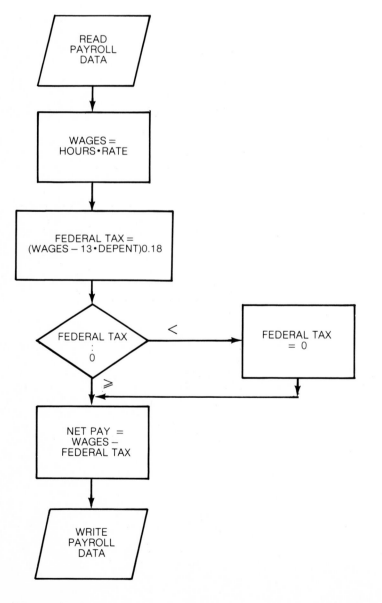

Connectors and Terminal Group

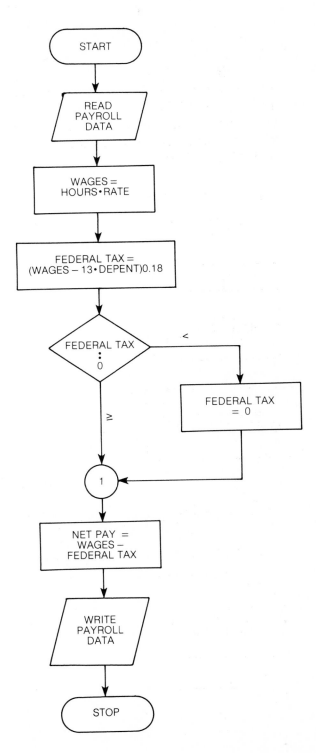

The Terminal symbol and the Starting symbol represent the ending and the starting of a flowchart respectively. Connectors are used where a single flowline is broken because of page limitation or where several flowlines pin together. With this in mind, we can complete the Payroll Flowchart as follows:

The other program flowchart symbols will be explained later when used.

PREDEFINED PROCESS   PREPARATION

"A picture is worth a thousand words" is certainly true when flowchart symbols are connected in an orderly and correct fashion. The flow direction, as shown in the payroll example, is indicated by an unbroken line between successive flowchart blocks. Arrowheads favor the readability of the flowchart direction path. The arrowheads are not always necessary, but in case of doubt, they should be used as follows:

LEFT TO RIGHT   RIGHT TO LEFT   TOP TO BOTTOM   BOTTOM TO TOP

It is not necessary to use arrowheads in a "left-to-right" flow and in a "top-to-bottom" flow.

Through flowcharting, essential facts of any problem can be communicated to those who have the ability to find the solutions to the problem. Later it will become clear that flowcharting is extremely helpful in efficient coding. Flowcharts also aid in the debugging of programs. When errors occur in programming in an initial test run, the flowchart can be used to detect and remove these mistakes.

2. Example 1. Computing the Tuition for One Student

A college controller wishes to establish a flowchart for computing the tuition one student owes. The following procedure is used to calculate the tuition.

If a student is enrolled for less than 10 credit hours, he then pays $80.00 for each credit hour he takes.

A tuition of $800.00 is charged if he enrolls for 10 or more credits.

The controller has a set of cards, one for each subject the student takes. Each card contains the student's name and number, the subject number, and the number of subject credit hours.

The general steps followed by the controller are:

1. Read credit information, one at a time, until end of cards (file) is reached
2. Accumulate all credits
3. Calculate appropriate fee
4. Write out student's bill

These steps are reflected in the following modular flowchart:

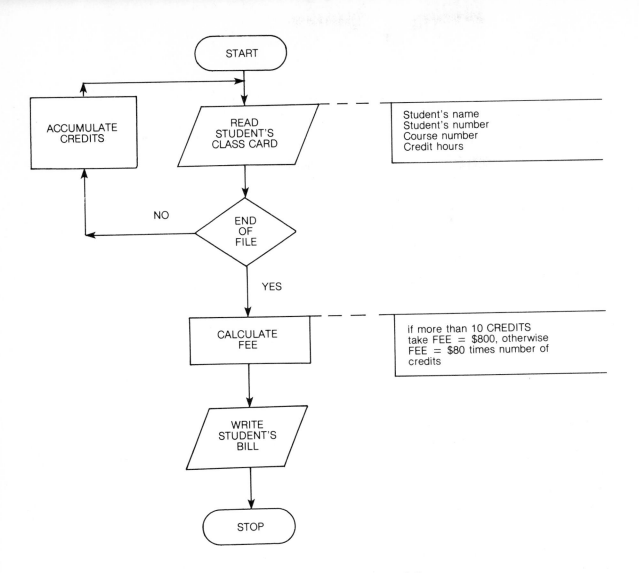

A more detailed description of this computation is as follows:

1. Before reading the credit information from the cards, the controller clears a "counter" for calculating the number of credit hours the student takes by assigning "zero" to that counter.
2. Now the controller is ready to read the student's credit information.
3. After reading the number of credits, he will add that number to the counter.
4. The controller will continue reading in credit hours, adding them to the counter until there are no more cards left.
5. When all credits are read and added by the controller, he is ready to check whether the total number of credits is less than 10 or not. If less than 10 credits are taken, then the controller multiplies the total number of credits by 80 to calculate the student's tuition. However, if the total number of credits taken by the student exceeds or equals 10, a maximum fee of $800 is charged.
6. Finally the student's name and number is printed, together with the fee he owes the university.

These 6 basic steps are represented in the following detailed flowchart.

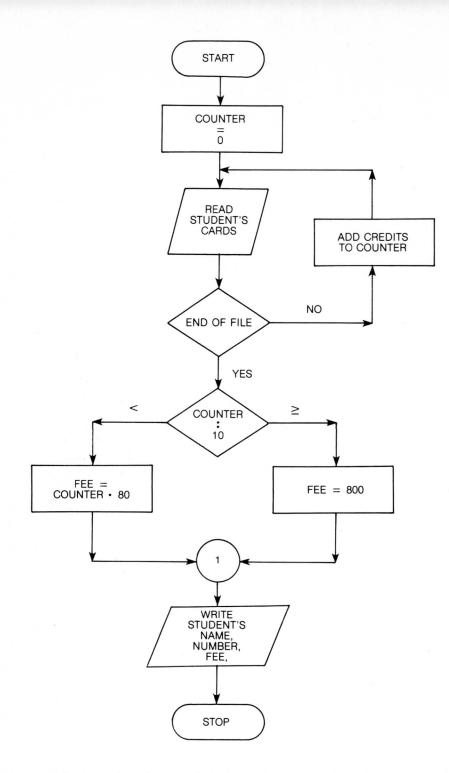

Assume that the set of cards that the controller has on the student are 80-column cards on which the information is keypunched. Any person, even a competent keypuncher, can make errors. For example, he or she may forget to keypunch the number of credit hours or may keypunch the wrong number of credit hours. It is wise to build into a flowchart the opportunity for checking such contingencies, if possible. If no credit hours are indicated, or if the number of credit hours is too large (for example, if it exceeds the maximum number of assigned credit hours [5]), then the flowchart check can take care of this error, as follows.

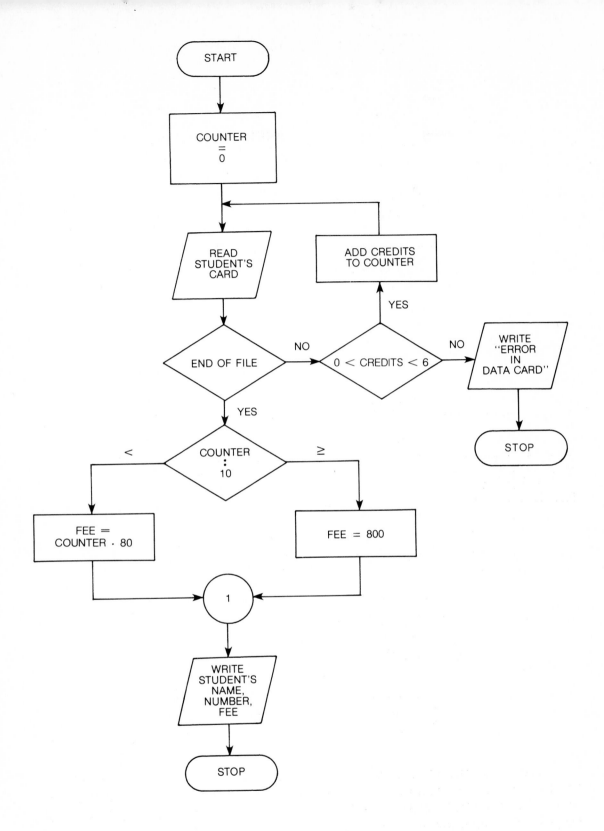

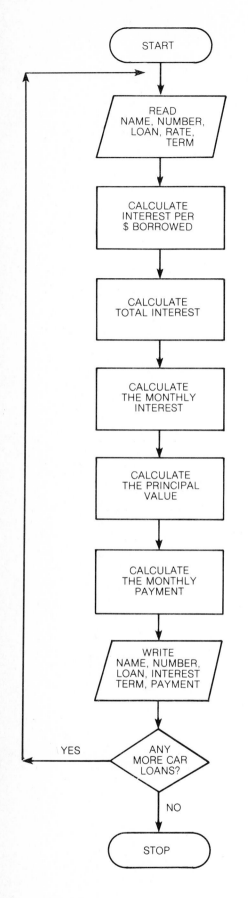

3. Example 2. Monthly Payments for a Car Loan

The monthly payments of a car loan equal the sum of the principal value of the loan and the monthly interest. If the loan is for financing a new car, the monthly interest is based on the total amount borrowed and therefore does not change from month to month.

The data used as input to calculate the monthly payment of the loan are

1. the customer's name,
2. the number of the loan,
3. the amount of the loan,
4. the interest rate,
5. the term of the loan.

The interest rate is the yearly interest for a loan of $100. The term of the loan defines the number of equal monthly payments to be made to pay off the loan. It is assumed that any number of monthly payments can be made to pay off the loan.

The procedure used to calculate the monthly payment of the loan is as follows:

1. Read in customer's name, loan number, amount borrowed, interest rate, and term of the loan.
2. Calculate the interest for $1, borrowed during one year.
3. Calculate the total interest to be paid on the loan.
4. Calculate the monthly interest.
5. Calculate the principal value of the loan.
6. Add 4 and 5 for the monthly payment.
7. Write the customer's name, loan number, amount borrowed, unit interest, term of the loan, and the monthly payment.

This procedure is executed for several loans and is represented in the flowchart.

4. Example 3. Homeowner's Real Estate Tax

A flowchart is constructed for the purpose of computing the homeowner's real estate tax for a specified period. The valuation can fall in one of the following six classes:

CLASS 1. If the valuation is equal to or greater than $50,000, the tax will be 10% of the valuation.

CLASS 2. If the valuation is equal to or greater than $40,000, but less than $50,000, the tax will be 8% of the valuation.

CLASS 3. If the valuation is equal to or greater than $30,000, but less than $40,000, the tax will be 6% of the valuation.

CLASS 4. If the valuation is equal to or greater than $20,000, but less than $30,000, the tax will be 4% of the valuation.

CLASS 5. If the valuation is equal to or greater than $10,000, but less than $20,000, the tax will be 2% of the valuation.

CLASS 6. If the valuation is greater than $00.00, but less than $10,000, the tax will be 1% of the valuation.

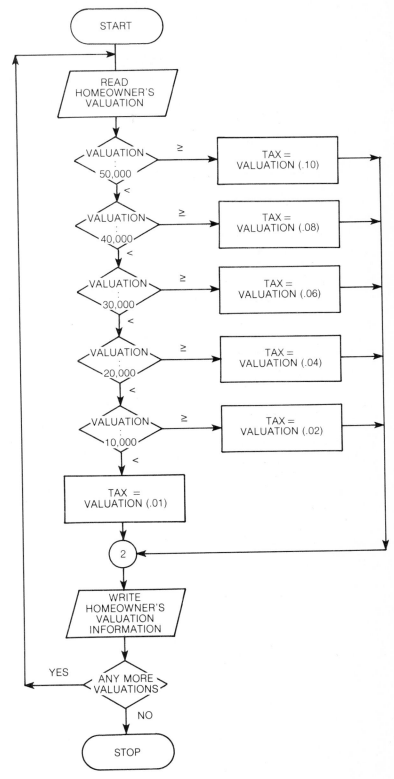

A set of cards is available on each homeowner in the community. Each of these cards contains the homeowner's name, address, and valuation. The steps taken to compute the tax are as follows:

1. Read in 1 homeowner's valuation information.
2. Check the valuation value against the previous six valuation classes in order to calculate the appropriate tax.
3. Calculate the real estate tax.
4. Print out all appropriate information: homeowner's name, valuation, tax %, and real estate tax.

The above procedure can be applied to any similar tax calculation procedure, and as many cards can be used as there are homeowners. The valuation classes and the tax base may have to be changed.

5. Checking the Logical Flow

A programmer uses flowcharting to establish the logical solution procedure for the problem he is about to code. Flowcharting facilitates the coding and the code will follow the flowcharting steps exactly. It is imperative for the flowcharting to establish the correct logical solution procedure for the problem; for if the flowchart is incorrect, the coded program will also be incorrect.

By the use of some test data, the programmer is able to check the flowchart to determine whether it generates the correct anticipated results. If the anticipated results are obtained by manipulating the test data through the flowchart, there is then good reason to believe that the flowchart is correct. One method for testing the flowchart is discussed here.

This method is illustrated by the use of the following flowchart, which is supposed to represent the solution flow of the following problem.

Employees at several divisions of Ford Motor Company took a test. The following data has been prepared:

Data Card	Content of Data Card
First Card	1. Control value giving the number of employees who took the exam (N)
	2. One of the several division numbers (D)
Remaining Cards	1. Employee's number (S)
	2. Number of division in which he works (D1)
	3. Score on exam (P)

This data has to be processed in order to compute and output the average score obtained by the employees whose division number appears on the first data card. The following steps are represented in the flowchart:

1. Read the number of people taking the exam (N) and the division number of interest (D).
2. Initialize the following counters to zero:
   —Counter T, for totaling the scores obtained by employees of division D;
   —Counter K, for the total number of people belonging to division D, and who took the exam;
   —Counter J, for counting the number of people considered in this process.
3. Read the identification number (S), division number (D1), and score (P) of one of the employees who took the exam.

4. If the employee belongs to division D (D = D1), then update counter T and K.
5. If all employees have not been considered (J < N) go to Step 3, otherwise go to Step 6.
6. After all employees have been considered, calculate the average score.
7. Write out the division number of interest (D), the total number of employees in division D who took the exam (K), and their average obtained on the exam (A).

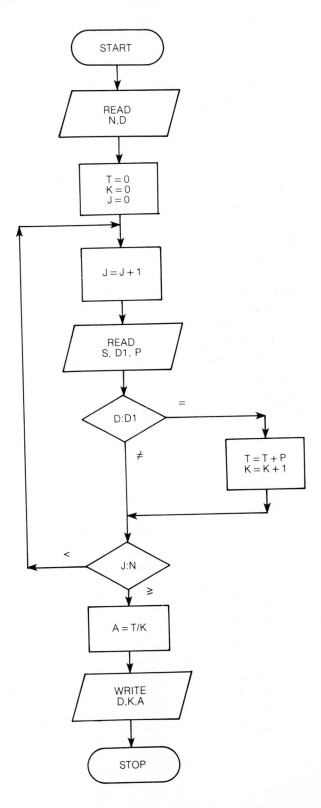

Table 3.1: Checking the Logical Flow

Flow		1st Trip	2nd Trip	3rd Trip	4th Trip	5th Trip
Read	N	5	—	—	—	—
	D	143	—	—	—	—
Initialize	T	0	—	—	—	—
	K	0	—	—	—	—
	J	0	—	—	—	—
Main Procedure $J = J + 1$		$1=0+1$	$2=1+1$	$3=2+1$	$4=3+1$	$5=4+1$
Read	S	47	58	111	143	90
	D1	118	143	148	143	163
	P	525	612	490	597	720
$T = T + P$		—	$612=0+612$	—	$1209=612+597$	—
$K = K + 1$		—	$1=0+1$	—	$2=0+1$	—
$A = T/K$		—	—	—	—	$604.5=\dfrac{1209}{2}$
Write	D	—	—	—	—	143
	K	—	—	—	—	2
	A	—	—	—	—	604.5

Note: A '—' indicates no change or that the instruction was by-passed or not executed.

Consider now the following test data and figure out the average, without going through the flowchart.

Data Card	Data
1	5,143
2	47,118,525
3	58,143,612
4	111,148,490
5	143,143,597
6	90,163,720

According to the above data, division #143 is the division of interest. Only two people out of the five who took the exam belong to that division (data cards #3 and #5). The average score for division #143 is therefore $(612 + 597)/2 = 604.5$.

The flowchart can now be checked for error by processing the above test data through the flowchart in the form of a procedure. Consider the above data and record in a grid, as shown in Table 3.1, all the changes which occur in the variable names for each trip through the logic.

The final results therefore are: $D = 143$
$$K = 2$$
$$A = 604.5$$

These results coincide with the previously calculated ones, so there is good reason to believe that the flowchart is correct.

Problem No. 1

Draw a flowchart for computing the weekly pay for several employees. The data that should be read in for each employee are:

1. The employee's name.
2. The employee's base pay rate.
3. The employee's number of hours worked.

   The flowchart should compute for each employee:

1. The employee's regular gross pay.
2. The employee's overtime gross pay (assume that the overtime pay equals 1½ the base pay). The overtime pay is paid for the number of hours the employee has worked over 40 hours.
3. The employee's total gross pay.

   Write out the following information for each employee.

1. The employee's name and base pay rate.
2. The total number of hours worked.
3. The regular gross pay.
4. The overtime gross pay.
5. The employee's total gross pay.

Problem No. 2

Draw a flowchart to evaluate capital budgeting proposals. A firm will accept a proposal that has a positive Net Present Value. The Net Present Value is equal to the present value of future cash inflows, resulting from the proposal, minus the initial cash outlay for the proposal.

   NPV = Present Value of future cash inflows—Original cash outlay

   The present value of future cash inflows is computed by multiplying the future yearly inflow by a previously calculated discount factor. (The discount factor is a function of the required rate of return and the number of years of cash inflows. Assume that the discount factor is obtained from existing tables.)

   The input data consists of the initial cash outlay, the yearly cash inflows, and the obtained discount factor.

   Generate a listing of the accepted proposals only.

Problem No. 3

Consider the following flowchart and answer (a), (b), (c). What are the values of:

FICA:
PAY:
CUMIN:

after the following data is put through the flowchart?

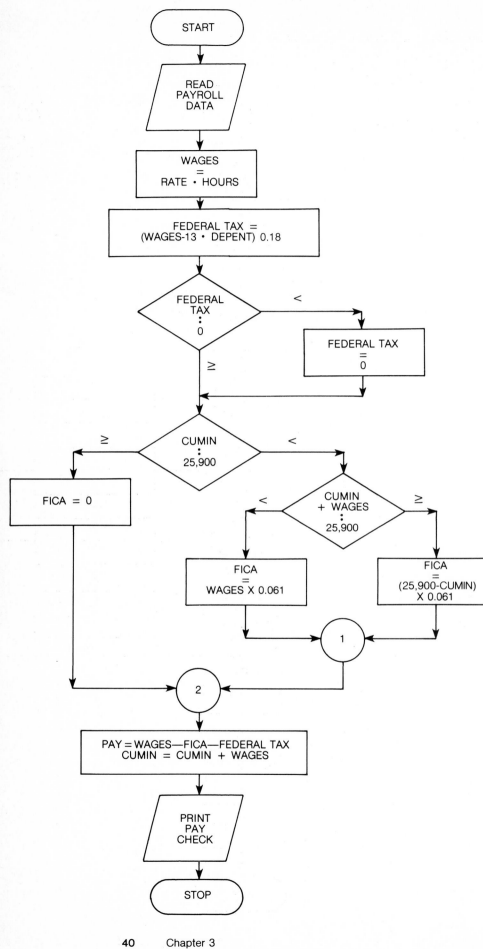

a) Name: Johnson
   SS#:   76754321
   HOURS: 40
   RATE: 15
   CUMIN: 26,000
   DEPENT: 2

b) Name: Pauls
   SS#:   23467431
   HOURS: 40
   RATE: 6
   CUMIN: 7,500
   DEPENT: 2

c) Name: Smith
   SS#:   76345216
   HOURS: 35
   RATE: 8
   CUMIN: 25,800
   DEPENT: 0

Problem No. 4

Consider the following flowchart and data, then answer the questions.

Question 1: At the time that I goes from 6 (six) to 7 (seven) what are the values of:

J _____ K _____ L _____ M _____?

Question 2: What values are printed for:

J _____ K _____ L _____ M _____?

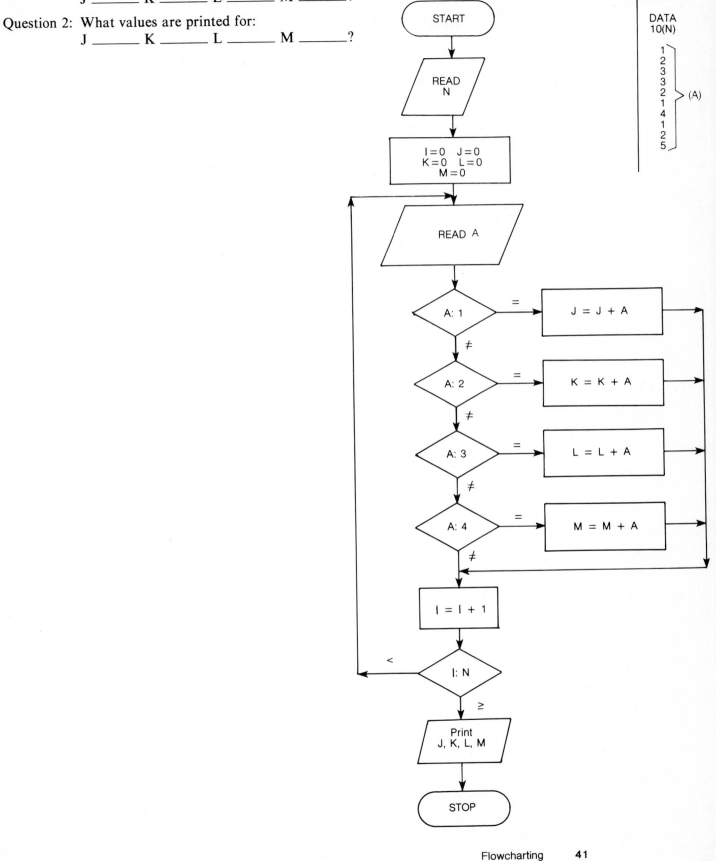

Problem No. 5

You are to prepare a flowchart to accomplish the following:

1. Read in three items of information at a time: the wholesale price, the number of units being ordered, and the percent markup.
2. Your flowchart is to compute the final total price to the customer.
3. You must print out that total price.
4. Repeat the process until a zero wholesale price is encountered.

   In writing your flowchart use the following names:

   WHOLES: for wholesale price

   UNITS: for number of units being ordered

   PMARK: for percent markup

   PRICE: for total price

Problem No. 6

Construct a flowchart that will input ten sets of three numbers (N1, N2, N3). For each set of three numbers output the three numbers and the value of K, where K equals 0 (zero) if the three numbers are unique and K equals 1 (one) otherwise. Check your flowchart for errors by processing the following data through the flowchart in the form of a procedure:

N1	N2	N3
17	18	18
17	14	15
17	19	17
17	0	0
0	17	17
4	5	9
12	12	11
5	3	4
12	12	12
11	22	33

Problem No. 7

The ABC Computer Center compiles statistics each day on the usage of its system. At the end of each work day a card is punched with the following information:

1. The number of batch job runs during that day.
2. The number of teletype sign-ons during that day.
3. The total downtime (in minutes) during that day.

   For the month of April you are given thirty cards with that data (one for each work day).

   Give the flowchart that will input this data and calculate and print the following:

1. Total number of batch job runs during the month.
2. Total number of teletype sign-ons during the month.
3. Number of days on which there were more teletype sign-ons than batch jobs.

4. Average number of teletype sign-ons on days that had no more than thirty minutes of downtime.
5. The day on which the most batch jobs were run (a number between 1 and 30, inclusive; you may assume that there are no ties).

Problem No. 8

A deck of cards has two numbers, A and B, on each card. The last card has two zeros on it. If the average of the A's is larger than the average of the B's, print "LARGER." If not, print "NOT LARGER." Draw the flowchart.

4 The Arithmetic Assignment Statements

Arithmetic operations are communicated to the computer by the use of an arithmetic assignment statement. The arithmetic assignment statement is a complete FORTRAN statement that consists of a variable name to the left of the equal sign, an equal sign, and an arithmetic expression to the right of the equal sign:

Variable name = Arithmetic expression

Nothing else besides the variable name can be to the left of the equal sign. The arithmetic expression consists of variable names, constants, and operators. It can consist of a single variable, i.e. A = B, where the portion B on the right hand side of the equal sign is the arithmetic expression. It can also consist of a single constant: A = 1 or a combination of variables and constants connected by operators: A = B + 1. Table 4.1 shows sample arithmetic assignment statements.

Table 4.1 Sample Arithmetic Assignment Statements

Variable Name	=	*Arithmetic Expression*
DIVID	=	CAP*0.045
WAGE	=	RATE*HOURS
AVG	=	SUM/QUANT
A	=	B
PERCENT	=	10

Because an arithmetic assignment statement is a defined operation that causes a change in form, value, and/or location, the processing symbol is used to represent it in a flowchart:

```
+-------------------------+
|                         |
|      VARIABLE NAME      |
|            =            |
|   ARITHMETIC EXPRESSION |
|                         |
+-------------------------+
```

In this chapter, we will discuss the syntax of the arithmetic assignment statement and include a brief discussion of the use of variable names and the structure of arithmetic expressions. Because it is essential that you understand how FORTRAN expressions are executed, a detailed explanation of arithmetic rules are presented and illustrated with appropriate examples. Finally, a set of examples closes this chapter to reinforce the material.

1. Variable Name

A FORTRAN variable is a name or symbolic representation of a quantity that is stored within the computer's main storage or memory. The symbolic or variable names consist of one to six letters or digits, the first character of which must be a letter. So, if one wishes to make up a name in FORTRAN, one must use only letters and digits, no more than six in total, and the first character must be a letter.

The following variable names are too long:

INTEREST, CAPITAL, DIVIDEND, AVERAGE, QUANTITY

In order to improve the readability of a FORTRAN IV program, meaningful variable names should be constructed and used, such as:

INTRST for interest

CAP for capital

DIV for dividend

AVG for average

QUANT for quantity

RATE for wage rate

HOURS for number of hours worked

DEPENT for number of dependents

The FORTRAN language distinguishes between "real variables" and "integer variables." A real-variable name begins with a letter A thru H and/or O thru Z. Any variable name that starts with a letter I thru N (I, J, K, L, M, N) is considered to be an integer, unless otherwise declared. Note that it is fairly easy to remember what an integer variable name starts with by remembering the first two letters of the word INteger.

The reason for discriminating between these two variables is that integer constants (constants without decimal points) are associated with integer variables, whereas real constants (constants with decimal points) are associated with real variables.

It is possible to declare explicitly a variable name like "INTRST" to be a real-variable name by the use of a "type declaration" statement:

REAL INTRST

Likewise, it is possible to declare a variable name "QUANT" to be an integer variable name by the use of the following "type declaration" statement:

INTEGER QUANT

It is quite correct to REAL or INTEGER more than one variable. For example in the following INTEGER statement, both variable names "BOXES" and "CODES" are declared to be integer variables:

INTEGER BOXES, CODES

Any made up name (INTRST, CAP, WAGE) is often called a "symbolic name," while "INTEGER" and "REAL" are part of the FORTRAN language, and, therefore should not be used as a symbolic name. As indicated in the above examples, the symbolic name INTRST is declared to to be a real variable by the word REAL followed by the symbolic name INTRST; whereas, the symbolic name QUANT is declared to be an integer variable by the word INTEGER followed by the symbolic name QUANT.

Any type declaration statement, such as INTEGER and REAL, must appear at the beginning of the program, to precede any executable statement.

2. Arithmetic Expression

An arithmetic expression is an orderly arrangement of constants and/or variables joined by operators.

Examples of arithmetic expressions follow:

CAP*.045	[1]
RATE*HOURS	[2]
SUM/QUANT	[3]
B	[4]
10	[5]
(WAGES−13.0*DEPENT)*.18	[6]
NUMBER+1	[7]

Note that a single constant or variable can be an expression as in [4] or [5].

Constants

There are two types of constants—integer and real. An integer constant is either a consecutive string of one or more digits, or it is a decimal number without a decimal point. The maximum length of the string depends on the computer and the compiler in use. The maximum length, for example, on the IBM System/360 is $2^{31}-1$ (equivalent to 2147483647). On the IBM 1620, an integer constant cannot exceed 4 digits. Any integer constant can be preceded by a plus (+) or minus (−) sign. In previous examples, expressions [5] and [7] are the only arithmetic expressions which contain an integer constant: 10 in [5] and 1 in [7].

Other examples of integer constants:

$$0, -81, +73314, -2147483647$$

Integer constants are often referred to as fixed-point constants.

A real constant is a number with a decimal point. The maximum number of allowable digits in a real constant also depends on the computer and the compiler in use.

On the IBM System/360, the magnitude of a regular real constant ranges from 0 or 16^{-65} (approximately 10^{-78}) through 16^{63} (approximately 10^{75}) with a precision of 7.2 decimal digit unless the DOUBLE PRECISION or REAL * 8 statements are used, which more than doubles the precision of the constant (17 digits). DOUBLE PRECISION and REAL * 8 statements are discussed in a later chapter. Examples of real constants are:

$$13.0, 9.0, 0.0, +5.8, 999.99$$

Variable Names

Variable names, as discussed previously, are either declared to be integer, or start with the letters I, J, K, L, M, or N and can only take on integer constants. Similarly real constants are associated with variable names declared to be real.

Operators

Names and constants are connected in an arithmetic expression by operators. The arithmetic operators are:

addition (+)

subtraction (−)

multiplication (*)

division (/)

exponentiation (**)

Examples of arithmetic expressions are:

RATE*HOURS → multiply the value stored for RATE by the value stored for HOURS.

CAP*.045 → multiply the value stored for CAP by 4.5%.

CAP*(1.+.045)**10 → multiply the value stored for CAP by $(1+.045)^{10}$ to calculate the accumulated savings.

GROSS−FEDTAX → take whatever value is found in the storage location called FEDTAX and subtract it from the value found in the place called GROSS.

(WAGES−13.0*DEPENT)*.18 → multiply 18% by the difference between the value stored for WAGES and 13 times the value stored for DEPENT.

WAGES*.02 → go to the place called WAGES and multiply whatever value is stored therein by .02.

SUM/XN → divide the value stored for SUM by the value stored for XN.

3. Arithmetic Rules

For simplicity, many of the following rules are illustrated with constants and single-character variable names.

Rule 1—Hierarchy of Operations

FORTRAN IV operations are performed in a specific order or hierarchy, summarized as follows:

1. Expressions are evaluated from left to right
2. Expressions in parentheses will be performed before other operations, with the innermost set being performed first
3. All exponentiations are performed first
4. All multiplications and division are performed next
5. Finally, all additions and subtractions are performed

The above hierarchy is used to define which of two consecutive operations[1] is performed first. If the hierarchy of the first operator is higher than, or equal to that of the second, then the first operation is performed. Otherwise, the comparison continues with the second and third operations, etc.

---

[1]There are several interpretations to the rule of the hierarchy; all lead to the same result.

Examples:

    2.0*3.0+4.0**2/2.0   [1]

In example [1], the operations are performed in the following order:

first   2.0*3.0 with a result equal to 6.0 [6.0+4.0**2/2.0]

second   4.0**2 with a result equal to 16.0 [6.0+16.0/2.0]

third   16.0/2.0 with a result equal to 8.0 [6.0+8.0]

fourth   6.0+8.0 with a final result of 14.0

    5.0+2.0/5.0*25.0**0.5   [2]

In example [2] the operations are performed in the following order:

first   2.0/5.0 with a result equal to .40 [5.0+.4*25.0**.5]

second   25.0**.5 with a result equal to 5.0 [5.0+.4*5.0]

third   .4*5.0 with a result equal to 2.0 [5.0+2.0]

fourth   5.0+2.0 with a result equal to 7.0

    6.0/2.0*5.0−2.0**3.0   [3]

In example [3] the operations are performed in the following order:

first   6.0/2.0 with a result equal to 3.0 [3.0*5.0−2.0**3.0]

second   3.0*5.0 with a result equal to 15.0 [15.0−2.0**3.0]

third   2.0**3.0 with a result equal to 8.0 [15.0−8.0]

fourth   15.0−8.0 with a result equal to 7.0

As mentioned in the summary of the rule of hierarchy, parentheses may be used to indicate the desired order of operations. When there are nested parentheses, the calculations proceed from the inner to the outer parentheses. Necessary parentheses should never be left out, but each left parenthesis should have a matching right parenthesis.

The following algebraic expression $\frac{A+B}{C+D}$ can be written in FORTRAN IV correctly as follows: (A+B)/(C+D)

In order to avoid errors, a good rule of thumb is to always include parentheses before writing the FORTRAN statement. For example:

$$Y=\frac{A+B}{C-D}=\frac{(A+B)}{(C-D)}$$

The FORTRAN expression then becomes Y=(A+B)/(C−D)

Examples:

    2.0*(3.0+4.0**2/2.0)   [4]

In example [4], the operations are performed in the following order:

first   4.0**2 with a result equal to 16.0 [2.0*(3.0+16.0/2.0)]

second   16.0/2.0 with a result equal to 8.0 [2.0*(3.0+8.0)]

third   3.0+8.0 with a result equal to 11.0 [2.0*11.0]

fourth   2.0*11.0 with a result equal to 22.0

$5.0 + 2.0 / (5.0 * 25.0 ** 0.5)$ [5]

In example [5], the operations are performed in the following order:

first $25.0 ** 0.5$ with a result equal to 5.0 $[5.0 + 2.0/(5.0 * 5.0)]$

second $5.0 * 5.0$ with a result equal to 25.0 $[5.0 + 2.0/25.0]$

third $2.0/25.0$ with a result equal to .08 $[5.0 + .08]$

fourth $5.0 + .08$ with a result equal to 5.08

$16.0/(2.0 * 5.0) - 2.0 ** 3.0$ [6]

In example [6], the operations are performed in the following order:

first $2.0 * 5.0$ with a result equal to 10.0 $[6.0/10.0 - 2.0 ** 3.0]$

second $6.0/10.0$ with a result equal to .6 $[.6 - 2.0 ** 3.0]$

third $2.0 ** 3.0$ with a result equal to 8.0 $[.6 - 8.0]$

fourth $.6 - 8.0$ with a result equal to -7.4

Rule 2—The Mode of the Expression

Most FORTRAN IV compilers expect the variables and constants in an expression to be in the same mode: either in integer or real mode. The following expressions violate the above rule.

INCOME − FEDTAX   [7]
SAVING + INTRST   [8]

An expression is in real mode if it consists entirely of real constants and/or real variable names which are linked with operators. The above expressions [7] and [8] can be made real expressions by declaring the integer variables to be real, as follows:

REAL   INCOME   [7]
INCOME − FEDTAX

REAL   INTRST   [8]
SAVING + INTRST

An expression is in integer mode if it consists entirely of integer constants and/or integer variable names which are linked with operators

Examples:

6/(2*5) − 2**3   [9]
5+4/3−2   [10]
I − J   [11]

Integer arithmetic is used to evaluate integer expressions. As all integer arithmetic operations produce integer results, the integer division will always truncate the result of the division, leaving only the integer part of the quotient.

In example [9], the integer arithmetic operations are performed as follows:

first $2*5$ with an integer result equal to 10 $[6/10 - 2**3]$

second $6/10$ with an integer result equal to 0 $[0 - 2**3]$

third $2**3$ with an integer result equal to 8 $[0 - 8]$

fourth $0 - 8$ with an integer result equal to -8

In example [10], the integer arithmetic operations are performed as follows:

first   4/3 with an integer result of 1 [5+1−2]

second   5+1 with an integer result of 6 [6−2]

third   6−2 with an integer result of 4

Whenever you have the choice between integer or real arithmetic, it is wise to construct real expressions to avoid truncation of results.

Some systems allow you to mix modes in expressions. An expression is in mixed mode if there are real and integer constants and/or variable names in the expression. Mixed mode arithmetic will be used as illustrated.

Examples:

16/(2*5)−2.**3   [12]

In example [12], the operations are performed in the following way:

first   2*5 with an integer result equal to 10 [16/10−2.**3.]

second   16/10 with an integer result equal to 1 [1−2.**3.]

third   2.0**3 with a real result equal to 8. [1−8.]

fourth   conversion of integer 1 to real 1. [1.−8.]

fifth   1.−8. with real result −7.

However, compare this result with the value obtained in example [6].

9.+11.1(2+(4/3))   [13]

In example [13] the operations are performed in the following way:

first   4/3 with an integer equal to 1 [9.+11.1/(2+1)]

second   2+1 with an integer result equal to 3 [9.+11.1/3]

third   conversion of integer 3 to real 3. [9.+11.1/3]

fourth   11.1/3, with a real result equal to 3.7 [9.+3.7]

fifth   9.+3.7 with a real result equal to 12.7

The good observer probably noticed that mixed-mode arithmetic is like Russian Roulette. It is recommended not to use mixed-mode arithmetic since the results it produces could surprise you.

In this book the general rule of "not mixing modes in expression" will be used.

A real quantity can be raised to an integer or real power. This is not considered mixing modes.

Examples:

A**3 or A**3.0   [14]
A**(3/2) or A**(3./2.)   [15]

However, note that A**(3/2) yields a result different from A**(3./2.) as a 3/2 equals 1 and 3./2. equals 1.5.

A negative real quantity can never be raised to a real quantity. For example, the following arithmetic expression is not allowed in FORTRAN.

(−14.55)**5.5   [16]

Also, an integer quantity can never be raised to a real quantity. Therefore, the following is erroneous:

15**0.5   [17]

Rule 3—Organization of Operators, Constants, and/or Symbolic Names

Two arithmetic operators can never be next to each other.

For example, the correct way to indicate that A is to be multiplied by minus B is as follows:

$$A*(-B) \qquad [18]$$

Two constants and/or symbolic names may never appear next to each other. The conventional way of indicating the multiplication between A and B in algebra is AB. In FORTRAN, the multiplication has to be indicated explicitly as follows:

$$A*B \qquad [19]$$

Rule 4—Exponentiation

Very few systems allow for the following expression A**B**C. This expression will then be executed from right to left. It is wise, however, to use parentheses: A**(B**C) or (A**B)**C, whichever is appropriate:

$$A**(B**C) \neq (A**B)**C$$

Example:

$$2**(3**2) = 512$$
$$(2**3)**2 = 64$$

Rule 5—The Assignment Rule

When the real result of an expression has to be assigned to an integer variable name, then the real result is truncated, leaving only the integer part of the real result.

Example:

$$I = 9. + 11.1/3. \qquad [20]$$

The real expression of statement [20] yields 12.7 which has to be assigned to the integer symbolic name I. The value of I therefore equals 12.

When the integer result of an expression has to be assigned to a real variable name, then the integer result is converted to a real constant.

Example:

$$A = 6/(2*5) - 2**3 \qquad [21]$$

The integer expression of statement [21] yields −8, which has to be assigned to the real symbolic name A. The value of A therefore equals −8.0.

By now, you may have noticed that there are two ways of truncating numbers; one is by using integer arithmetic:

$$Y = 3/2 \qquad [22]$$

or by storing a real number at an integer location:

$$I = 3.0/2.0 \qquad [23]$$

The result in both cases would be the same and would equal 1.

4. Examples of Arithmetic Assignment Statements

The One-Year-Investment

In calculating the investment of a capital sum at the end of one year, the following formula can be used:

SAVINGS=CAPITAL(1+INTEREST RATE)

If we chose the following variable names in FORTRAN:

SAVE for SAVINGS

CAP for CAPITAL

RATE for INTEREST RATE

Then the appropriate FORTRAN IV statement is:

SAVE=CAP*(1.0+RATE)

Note the need for the multiplication (*) sign. The above statement is valid in a FORTRAN program, if the variable names CAP and RATE are previously defined within the same FORTRAN program:

CAP=1000.0

RATE=.05

SAVE=CAP*(1.0+RATE)

The Compound Interest Problem

The one-year investment problem can easily be extended to compute the compound interest after N years, by the use of the following algebraic expressions:

$$SAVINGS=CAPITAL(1+RATE)^{YEARS}$$
$$INTEREST=SAVINGS-CAPITAL$$

A complete set of FORTRAN statements are:

REAL INTRST

CAP=1000.0

RATE=.05

N=12

SAVE=CAP*(1.0+RATE)**N

INTRST=SAVE-CAP

The Economical Borrowing Amount

The following algebraic expression is the EOQ (Economic Order Quantity) interpretation to the economic borrowing amount problem:

$$EBA=\sqrt{\frac{2 \cdot FC \cdot CASH}{COST}}$$

where FC is the incremental fixed cost of obtaining money on a loan basis.

CASH is the total amount of cash to be used in next time period.

COST is the cost of keeping $1 on hand.

The above expression can be rewritten as follows:

$$EBA=\left(\frac{2 \cdot FC \cdot CASH}{COST}\right)^{.5}$$

Recall that the square root of a value is the same as raising the value to the one half power

Therefore, a suitable FORTRAN statement is:

EBA=((2.0*FC*CASH)/COST)**.5

Again FC, CASH, and COST must have been defined in previous statements.

Later on, when we discuss library functions, we will see that there exists, square root function that can be used to accomplish the same thing as the above arithmetic assignment statement.

The Root Problem

In computing the roots of

$$AX^2+BX+C=0$$

the discriminant must be calculated as follows:

$$D=B^2-4AC$$

Under the assumption that the discriminant is positive, the two roots for the above algebraic statement can be calculated as follows:

$$X1=\frac{-B+\sqrt{D}}{2A} \quad \text{or} \quad X1=\frac{-B+D^{.5}}{2A}$$

$$X2=\frac{-B-\sqrt{D}}{2A} \quad \text{or} \quad X2=\frac{-B-D^{.5}}{2A}$$

Under the assumption that A, B, and C are known to FORTRAN, the three FORTRAN statements accomplish the task of root finding:

D=B**2−4.0*A*C
X1=(−B+D**.5)/(2.0*A)
X2=(−B−D**.5)/(2.0*A)

The Digit Problem

Consider an integer constant assigned to an integer variable I. Design the correct expression that assigns to the variable K the 2nd digit from the right. This can be accomplished by the use of the following integer arithmetic:

K=(I−I/100*100)/10

If I equals, for example, 2735, then (I−I/100*100)/10 equals 3, which is the 2nd digit from the right:

first	I/100 with an integer result of 27 [(I−27*100)/10]
second	27*100 with an integer result of 2700 [(I−2700)/10]
third	I−2700 with an integer result of 35 [35/10]
fourth	35/10 with an integer result of 3

5. FORTRAN 77 Character-Constants and Assignments

The introduction of character-constants and manipulation of character-constants as introduced by FORTRAN 77 standards is a significant change in standard FORTRAN. A character string is a string of characters enclosed by apostrophes.

Examples of character constants are:

'BALL', 'SILK', '$VALUE'   (1)
'JOHNSON'S HOUSE'   (2)

Any character that the processor can store can be used in the string of characters to form a character-constant, such as letters of the alphabet, punctuation, and special characters like the $ sign. Greek or other characters might not be acceptable. Double apostrophes are used to represent the single apostrophe character in a character-constant as shown in example (2).

The length of a character-constant is defined by a specification statement, called CHARACTER specification statement. Examples of CHARACTER specification statements are:

CHARACTER *4 ITEM   (3)
CHARACTER *15 LABEL, HEAD   (4)

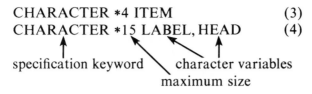

specification keyword   character variables
                    maximum size

According to the CHARACTER specification statement (3), the character variable ITEM has a length of 4 characters and, therefore, no more than 4 characters can be assigned to that variable. If one attempts to assign less than 4 characters, then blank characters are added on the right to fill up the string. However, if one attempts more than 4 characters, then the string of characters are truncated on the right before assignment takes place. These rules are illustrated in the following examples:

ITEM = 'BALL'   (5)
ITEM = 'SOP'   (6)
ITEM = 'SCOPE'   (7)

In example (5) all characters in the string BALL are stored under the character variable ITEM, whereas in example (6) all characters in the string SOP, followed by a blank character, are stored under the character variable ITEM. Finally in example (7), only the first four characters of the string SCOPE will be stored under the character variable ITEM.

Reconsider now our previous CHARACTER specification examples. CHARACTER specification example (4) assigns a length of 15 characters to both character variables LABEL and HEAD. If the size of a character variable is not given, then it has a default size of one character. Note, however, that all character variables must be specified as such in a CHARACTER specification statement regardless of whether its default size is acceptable or not. Character specifications of variables of different size can be placed in one specification statement. The following examples combine examples (3) and (4).

CHARACTER *15 LABEL,ITEM*4,HEAD   (8)

or

CHARACTER *4 LABEL*15,ITEM,HEAD*15 (9)

FORTRAN 77 allows for two basic character string operations. They are: linking or concatenation of strings and replacement of specific characters within the string of characters. These operations are illustrated in the following examples:

Example (10):

CHARACTER *2 FIRST
CHARACTER *6 NAME
FIRST = 'K'
NAME = FIRST//'MART'

In example (10), the first CHARACTER specification statement specifies FIRST to be a character variable of length 2, and the second CHARACTER specification statement specifies NAME to be a character variable of length 6. The first assignment statement assigns the character string K, followed by a blank, to the character variable FIRST. The 2 strokes in the last assignment statement is the concatenation operator that chains the character string of K, followed by blank, to the character string MART. This new string, K MART, is then assigned to the character variable NAME.

Example (11):

    CHARACTER *4 ITEM,THING
    CHARACTER *15 LABEL
    .
    .
    .
    ITEM=LABEL(8:11)
    THING(3:3)='A'

In the first assignment statement of example (11) a substring of the string variable LABEL is assigned to the string variable ITEM. The substring is identified by specifying the beginning character position (8) and the ending character position (11). In the second and last assignment statement of example (11), the third character (3:3) of THING is being replaced by the single character A.

Exercises

Problem No. 1

Indicate whether the following symbolic names are Real (R), Integer (I), or Illegal (X).

MUTUAL	CAPITAL	OK
LIFE	BALANCE	QUANT
INSURANCE	GOODS	AMOUNT
MARKET	LOSS	CUSTOMER
VALUE	DEBT	F.I.F.O.
DEPEND	AVERAGE	L.I.F.O.
TAX	WAGES	MARKET
INCOME	TOLL	SHARES
PRICE	QUEUE	DEBET
DIVIDENT	O.R	CREDIT
A—14	CHICAGO	P42
BOSTON	1X	A2.1
DOL—$	X25Y	XYZ3

Problem No. 2
Identify the following as integer constants, integer variables, real constants, real variables, or illegal.

1975	XYZ2	HOHOHO
JIMMI	−B	ALPHA
PARENTS	3,750*	−832.
1347F	$3750	−832
17E1	12/L	+734.
C+B	A/B	E+2
H30	FAR	

Problem No. 3
Write a single FORTRAN IV expression for each of the following:

a) $x+y^3$

b) $(x+y)^3$

c) x^4

d) $a+\dfrac{b}{c}$

e) $\dfrac{a+b}{c+d}$

f) $a[x+b(x+c)]$

g) $x+y^3+z(a+b)$

h) $\dfrac{a+b}{c}$

i) $a+\dfrac{b}{c+d}$

j) $\dfrac{(a+b+c)^d}{x-y-z}$

Problem No. 4
Indicate the errors, if any, in the following arithmetic assignment statements.

a) L=(B+C)**2

b) E2=K**A

c) I=((A+D)/F+E)**(J+K/2)

d) −V=A*B+C

e) y=(4+K)*INTEGER(A)

f) D=E4.

g) X+34*A**3/4.+B

Problem No. 5
Answer each of the following multiple choice questions.

1. If K=2 and I=3, what is the value of the following expression: K*I/K*I
   a) 1
   b) 3
   c) 6
   d) 9
   e) none of the above

2. If X=2.0, Y=3.0 and Z=4.0, what is the value of the following expression:
   3.0*X**Y/Z+Z
   a) 7
   b) 8
   c) 10
   d) 58
   e) none of the above

3. If I=2, J=3, and K=4, what is the value of the following expression: K+I**J/K
   a) 4
   b) 5
   c) 6
   d) 8
   e) none of the above

4. If I=2, J=3, and K=4, what is the value of the following expression: 3*I*I*K/J+J
   a) 9
   b) 12
   c) 18
   d) 19
   e) 48
   f) none of the above

5. If I=2, J=3, and K=4, what is the value of the following expression: 3*(I**K/J)+J
   a) 9
   b) 12
   c) 18
   d) 19
   e) 48
   f) none of the above

6. If I=2, J=3, K=1, what is the value of the following expression: J/I/K*J/K
   a) 0
   b) 1
   c) 2
   d) 3
   e) 4.5
   f) none of the above

7. If A=2.5, B=4.6, C=2.0 and I=2, what is the value of N if N=A**I+B/C
   a) 8
   b) 8.55
   c) 9
   d) cannot be determined, invalid statement
   e) can be determined, but none of the above

8. If I=4, J=2, K=3, what is the value of M, where M=J+I**(J/I)*I/K
   a) 2
   b) 3
   c) 4
   d) 9
   e) none of the above

Problem No. 6
Find the value for X or I after each of the following expressions is executed, and indicate the order of operations.

I=25/3**3+7/10*(2*(7−3))
X=4/5*(4**2−6)
X=5.0+2.0/5.0*25.0**0.5
I=7/8**2+10/2**3
I=5/2*2**2

X=5.0+5.0/5.0**2
X=10.0−3.0/5.0*25.00**0.5
I=5.0+9.0**0.5/2.0
X=5/6*3/4
I=(6/2*5/6)+2**3

Problem No. 7

Consider the integer value INT with four decimal digits. Write four arithmetic assignment statements to assign to I1 the 4th decimal digit; to assign to I2 and 3rd decimal digit; to assign to I3 the 2nd decimal digit; and to assign to I4 the 1st decimal digit.

Example: 7453: I1=3; I2=5; I3=4; I4=7

Problem No. 8 (FORTRAN 77)

Consider the dealer's address (ADDRES), consisting of:

1. his name (maximum 12 characters) NAME
2. street address (maximum 15 characters) STREET
3. town (maximum 12 characters) TOWN
4. state (maximum 2 characters) STATE
5. ZIP (maximum 5 characters) ZIP

Write out all appropriate character specifications:

Assign a fictitious name to the character variable NAME

Assign a fictitious street address to the character variable STREET

Assign a fictitious town to the character variable TOWN

Assign a fictitious state to the character variable STATE

Assign a fictitious zip to the character variable ZIP

Now string the whole address and assign it to the character variable ADDRES.

Assume that the dealer moved within the same city to a new street. Adjust the character string assigned to ADDRES to reflect this change. (Dream up a new street address to accomplish this.)

Input/Output Statements

A thorough understanding of INPUT/OUTPUT and their FORMAT statements is necessary before moving on to the art of FORTRAN programming. Special attention must be paid to the syntax of FORMAT statements, since it has been estimated that at least 60% of the errors in students' programs are found in FORMAT statements. Most of these errors are caused by oversight rather than a lack of understanding. To avoid such errors, it is necessary to develop your material in a very systematic way. You are encouraged to study each example carefully.

The FORTRAN IV INPUT/OUTPUT statements are the READ and the WRITE statements. The general INPUT/OUTPUT symbol is used to represent a READ or WRITE operation in a flowchart.

1. Input/Output Statements

The READ statement is used to read input data from an input medium into the memory of the computer. A typical example of a READ statement is as follows:

    READ(5,68) CAP, YEARS, RATE

This example tells the system to read from data card(s), as indicated by the device or unit number 5 and the FORMAT statement number 68, the first real constant to be stored in the location named CAP, the second real constant to be stored in the location named YEARS, and the third real constant to be stored in the location named RATE.

The general form of the READ statement is thus:

    READ(i,n₁,END=n₂)<list>

where: i: symbolic unit number of an input device

  n_1:   the statement label of the format statement which applies to the particular input record to be used

  END=n_2: (is optional) implies that control has to be transferred to the statement that is labeled n_2 if no more input is available.

  <list>:   ordered set of one or more variable names

The symbolic unit number, reflecting the input medium, depends upon the specific computer system. The symbolic unit number of an input device can either be an appropriate integer constant, or an integer variable that is previously initialized in the program. If integer variables are used to represent the input device, the READ statement becomes device independent. That is, the device may be changed with a minimum of effort.

The WRITE statement is used to write results stored in the memory of the computer on an output medium.

A typical example of a WRITE statement is as follows:

WRITE(6,69)CAP,YEARS,RATE

In general, the above statement means that the current real values stored under the variable names CAP,YEARS,RATE will be printed on paper in accordance with the format statement that is labeled #69. The general form of the WRITE statement is thus:

WRITE(i,n)<list>

where: i: symbolic unit number of an output device (typically 6 for printer)
       n: the statement label of the format statement which applies to the particular output record to be used.
       <list>: ordered set of variable names (optional)

Just as for the READ statement, the symbolic unit number, reflecting the output medium, depends on the computer system and can be either an appropriate constant or a previously defined integer variable. The <list> in the WRITE statement is only used when one wants to write values stored in the memory of the computer under particular variable names, not when titles or column headings are written (unless one has some variable data that can be written within these titles or column headings) as will be discussed later in this chapter.

2. FORMAT

Neither a READ nor a WRITE statement can be executed without an appropriate FORMAT statement. The general form of a FORMAT statement is:

n FORMAT($S_1,S_2,S_3,....,S_n$)

where: n: is the statement label that is referenced by an associated I/O statement.
       S_i: are the FORMAT specifications.

The FORMAT specifications indicate how data must be read and printed. Unlike the READ and WRITE statements, the FORMAT statements are nonexecutable statements and can appear almost anywhere in a FORTRAN program. However, it is good programming practice to put all the format statements either after the respective READ or WRITE statements, or in the beginning of the program, or at the end of the program, before the END statement.

3. READ/FORMAT Specifications

As mentioned before, the READ statement is used to read in data from data cards, or from other data records to be stored under the variable names indicated in the list of the READ statement. Many FORTRAN programs may require more than one data record. These data records are not located within the FORTRAN program but follow it. The following figure shows a typical organization of a program deck if data cards are used as records. Each time a READ statement is executed, at least one DATA CARD will be read from the set of DATA cards. All eighty columns can be used in preparing data for the FORTRAN program. Data records on cards are used for all illustrations shown in this section.

Organization of Program Deck

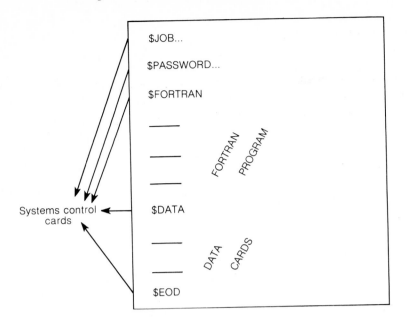

1. The Integer Specification nIw

If the integer nIw is used for a READ statement, then the computer reads n integer values out of n fields of a data card. Each field is w columns wide. These integer values are stored under the respective integer variables of the READ list. "n" is optional and is not used when only one integer value is to be read.

Example [1]

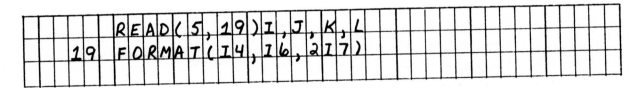

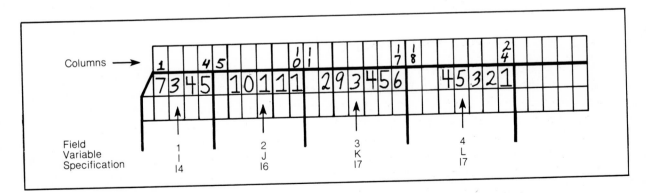

When executing the READ statement the computer reads:

out of the first field of four (4) columns the integer value 7345, to be stored in the location named I;

out of the second field of six (6) columns the integer value 10110, to be stored in the location named J;

out of the third field of seven (7) columns the integer value 293456, to be stored in the location named K;

out of the fourth field of seven (7) columns the integer value 45321, to be stored in the location named L.

Note that blanks are read in or interpreted as zeros.

2. The Real Specification nFw.d

If the real specification nFw.d is used for a READ statement, then the computer reads n real values out of n fields of a data card. Each field is w columns wide, and the digits in the last d columns of the field are considered to be the numbers behind the decimal point, unless it is punched, and then it is implicitly stored when punched. In other words, when the decimal point is actually punched on the data card, the decimal position on the data card will override the one in the format statement. The real values that are thus read are stored under the respective real variables of the READ list.

Example [2]

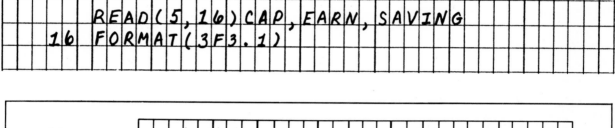

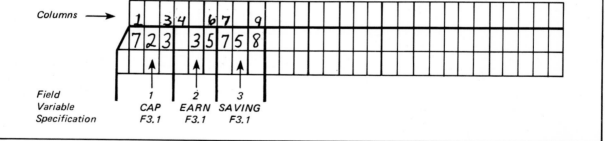

When executing the READ statement the computer reads:

out of the first field of three (3) columns the real value 72.3, to be stored in the location named CAP;

out of the second field of three (3) columns the real value 3.5, to be stored in the location named EARN;

out of the third field of three (3) columns the real value 75.8, to be stored in the location named SAVING.

3. The Alphanumeric Specification nAw

If the alphanumeric specification nAw is used for a READ statement, then the computer reads n strings of alphanumeric data out of n fields of a data card. Each field is w columns wide. These alphanumeric strings are stored under the respective variable names of the READ list. Some compilers require that A formats be used with integer variables, otherwise real or integer variables can be used. What is actually stored internally depends on the number of characters that can be held in the particular storage location of the machine, which may range from 2 to 10. Let us call this number "v". If w < v, w characters are read and the remaining rightmost characters are replaced by blanks. If w > v, v characters will be taken into storage and the last characters are skipped (with some compilers, if w > v, the rightmost v characters will be taken). This book uses four characters for v.

These rules are now illustrated by three case samples as shown in the following example:

Example [3]

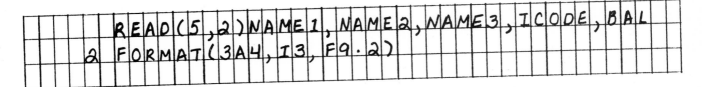

Case #1: if three characters, ABC, are read in using an A3, then the ABC characters will be stored left justified, leaving one blank character to their right.

Case #2: is very straight forward; all four characters ABCD are stored using an A4 specification.

Case #3: since there is only space to store 4 characters, the first four characters ABCD are stored and the fifth character is lost.

Consider now the following example:

Example [4]

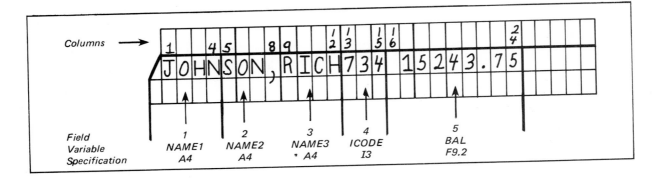

When executing the READ statement the computer reads:

out of the first field of four (4) columns the alphanumeric string JOHN, to be stored in the location named NAME1;

out of the second field of four (4) columns the alphanumeric string SON,, to be stored in the location named NAME2;

out of the third field of four (4) columns the alphanumeric string RICH, to be stored in the location named NAME3;

out of the fourth field of three (3) columns the integer value 734, to be stored in the location named ICODE;

out of the fifth field of nine (9) columns the real value 15243.75, to be stored in the location named BAL.

Note that in order to store all twelve (12) alphabetic characters of the name—JOHNSON,RICH—it was necessary to create three (3) variable names, each storing (4) characters.

4. The Skip Specification nX

If nX is specified for a READ statement, then the computer skips n columns on the card that is read into the computer, whether anything is keypunched in these columns or not.

Example [5]

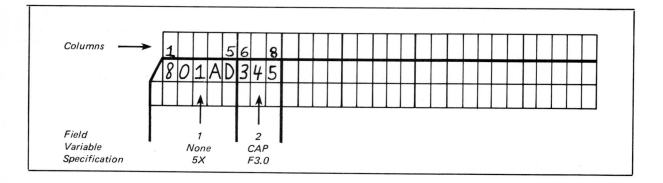

When executing the READ statement, the computer:

skips the first field of five (5) columns (5X),

reads out of the second field of three (3) columns the real value 345.0, to be stored in the location named CAP.

5. The Slash Specification

As illustrated in the above examples, a data card is fed and read each time a READ statement is encountered. A new data card can also be fed when a slash (/) is encountered in the FORMAT code.

So, if a / is specified for a READ statement, then the computer feeds a new card as shown in Example [6]

Example [6]

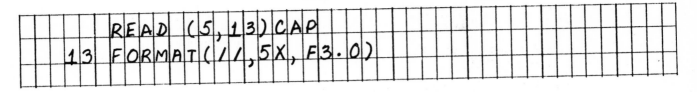

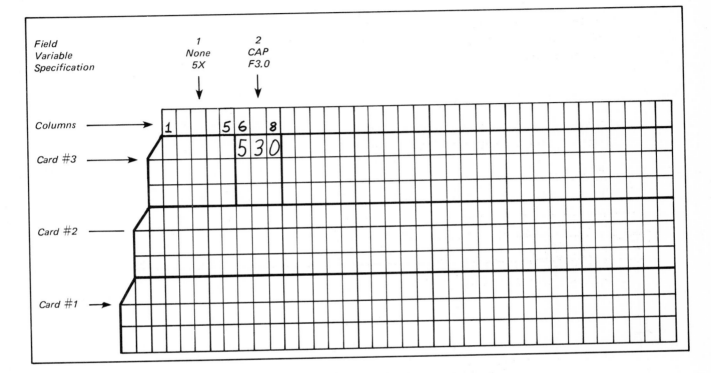

In Example [6] the READ statement feeds a new card (card #1) and, together with the specifications in the FORMAT statement, result in the following:

> two more cards are fed, bringing us to card #3 (//);
>
> the first field of five (5) columns on the third card is skipped (5X);
>
> from the third card out of the second field of three (3) columns, the real value 530.0 is read and stored in the location named CAP.

Note that the comma between the "2nd slash" and "5" in the FORMAT statement is optional.

4. WRITE/FORMAT Specifications

As indicated previously, the WRITE statement is used to print internally stored values, via the high speed printer, onto paper. The fanfolded output pages are 15 inches wide by 11 inches deep. A maximum line length of 132 characters and a maximum page depth of 60 lines are common. The FORMAT statement associated with the WRITE statement provides the specifications needed for printing. All previously discussed specifications can be used—the integer specification (nIw), the real specification (nFw.d), the alphanumeric specification (nAw), the skip specification (nX) the slash specifications (/)—in addition to others as explained in this section. The actual output never contains the first character of an output line as specified in the specification of the FORMAT statement. In other words, the first space on each line is used for the carriage control. The carriage control can also be taken care of by the use of special carriage control characters or by overspecifying the first line specification of the FORMAT statement, as illustrated in the following sections.

In general, an output image is formed when a WRITE statement is encountered or when a slash (/) is encountered in the FORMAT specifications. The existing image is printed when a slash is encountered in the FORMAT codes or when the right most parenthesis is reached in the FORMAT statement. This implies that, each time a slash is encountered in the FORMAT statement, the existing image is printed and a new image is formed. This will be illustrated in the following examples.

1. The Horizontal Spacing Specification nX

If nX is specified for a WRITE statement, then the printer skips n spaces on the printing line.

Example [7]

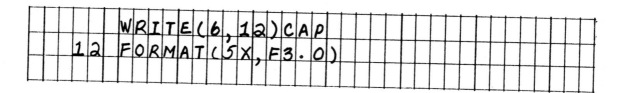

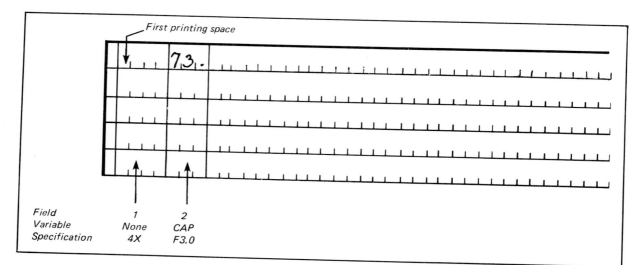

When executing the WRITE statement the printer:

   moves to the next printing line (one of the 5X's (1X) is used for the carriage control);

   skips a field of four horizontal printing spaces (4X);

   and prints in the next field of three (3) spaces the real value that is stored under the variable name CAP:73.

2. The Integer Specification nIw

If the integer specification nIw is used for a WRITE statement, then the printer prints in n fields the n integer values which are stored under the respective integer variables of the WRITE list. Each printing field is w spaces wide.

Example [8]

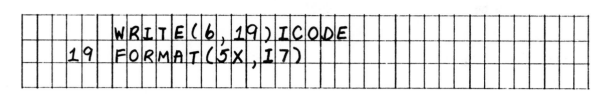

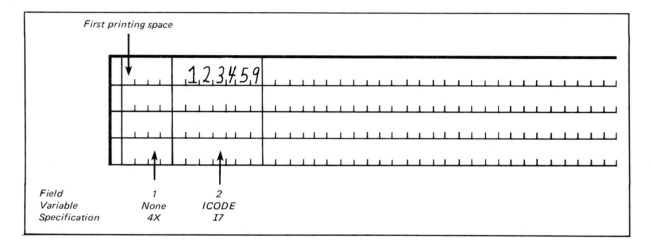

Field	1	2
Variable	None	ICODE
Specification	4X	I7

If 123459 is stored under the variable name ICODE, then when executing the WRITE statement the printer

moves to the next printing line (1X for carriage control);

skips a field of four (4) horizontal printing spaces (4X);

and prints right justified, in the next field of seven (7) spaces the integer value that is stored under the variable name ICODE: 123459.

The integer specification must be wide enough to print the entire integer value. If the value is negative, then an extra space must be provided to print the minus (−) sign.

It is safe to overspecify the field width. If the field is overspecified, then the integer value is right justified.

3. The Real Specification nFw.d

If the real specification nFw.d is used for a WRITE statement, then the printer prints in n fields the n real values which are stored under the respective real variables of the WRITE list. Each printing field is w spaces wide and d digits behind the decimal point are printed.

Example [9]

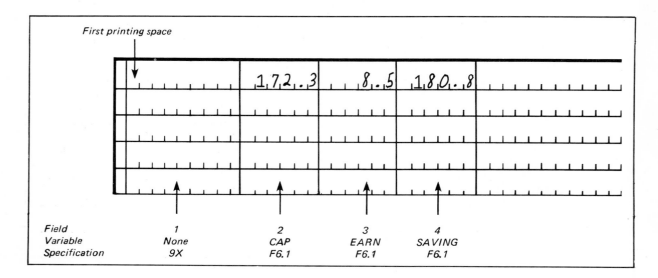

Field	1	2	3	4
Variable	None	CAP	EARN	SAVING
Specification	9X	F6.1	F6.1	F6.1

When executing the WRITE statement the printer:

> moves to the next printing line (1X for carriage control);
>
> skips a field of nine (9) horizontal printing spaces (9X);
>
> prints right justified in the next field of six (6) spaces the real value that is stored under the variable name CAP with one (1) digit behind the decimal point;
>
> prints right justified in the next field of six (6) spaces the real value that is stored under the variable name EARN with one (1) digit behind the decimal point;
>
> and prints right justified in the next field of six (6) spaces the real value that is stored under the variable name SAVING with one (1) digit behind the decimal point.

Again, extreme care should be taken when defining real specifications, so that ample space is provided. Remember that the decimal point and the minus (−) sign, if any, each take up one printing space. Most computers do not issue error messages or warnings if the specification is too small. Instead, asterisks are printed on the output medium.

4. The Vertical Spacing Specification /

If the slash ("/") is placed at the beginning or end of the FORMAT specifications, the printer places one blank output record (skips one printing line) between the output records. If the slashes are put in the middle of the FORMAT statement, the first slash causes a return to the carriage control position, and any additional slash causes a blank line to be printed before returning to the carriage control position. However, even though the slash is used for printing blank records or the skipping of lines of output, it is not used for carriage control per se. A character control character, other than the slash, must be used for each new line of output. If a special carriage control character is not used, then the first character of the first specification will be used as carriage control. It is good programming practice to use special characters for carriage control despite the fact that, for various reasons, this was not always done in the following examples.

Consider the following examples:

Example [10]

```
      WRITE(6,14)CAP
   14 FORMAT(//,6X,F3.0)
```

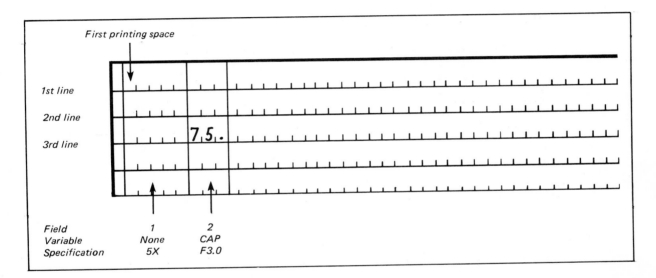

When executing the WRITE statement the printer:

    prints the image of two blank lines (skip two lines)(//);

    skips on the third line a field of five (5) horizontal printing spaces (5X, 1X is for carriage control);

    and prints in the next field of three (3) spaces the real value that is stored under the variable name CAP:75.

Example [11]

```
      I = 745
      J = 623
      WRITE(6,15) I,J
   15 FORMAT(1X,I3,/,1X,I3)
```

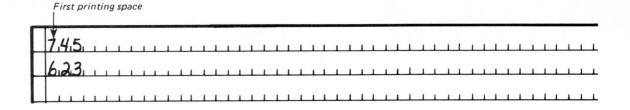

First printing space

When executing the WRITE statement the printer:

prints in the first field of three spaces the integer constant that is stored under the variable name I (1X is for carriage control);

returns to the carriage control position (/);

prints on the second line, in the first field of three spaces, the integer constant that is stored under the variable name J (1X is for carriage control).

5. The Alphanumeric Specification nAw

If the alphanumeric specification nAw is used for a WRITE statement, then the printer prints in n fields the n alphanumeric strings which are stored under the respective variables of the WRITE list. Each printing field is w spaces wide.

If w > v, w − v blanks will appear on the output, followed by a string of alphanumeric v characters. If w < v, then the leftmost w characters from storage will be printed.

(On some systems, if w > v, a string of v alphanumeric characters followed by w − v blanks will appear on the output; if w < v, then the right most w characters from storage will be printed):

Example [12]

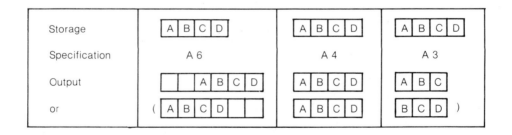

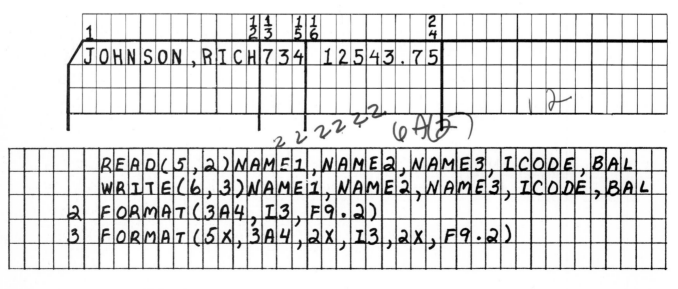

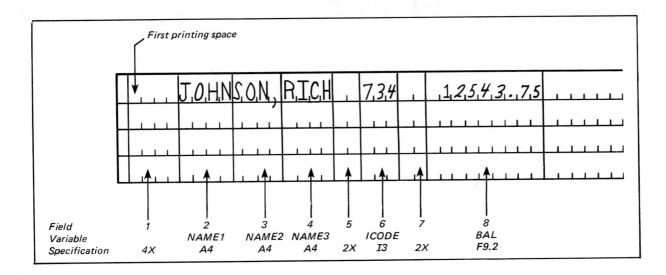

Field	1	2	3	4	5	6	7	8
Variable		NAME1	NAME2	NAME3		ICODE		BAL
Specification	4X	A4	A4	A4	2X	I3	2X	F9.2

When after the READ statement the WRITE statement is executed the printer:

  moves to the next printing line (1X for carriage control);

  skips a field of four (4) horizontal printing spaces (4X);

  prints right adjusted in the next field of four (4) spaces the alphanumeric characters which are stored under the variable name NAME1;

  prints right adjusted in the next field of four (4) spaces the alphanumeric characters which are stored under the varible name NAME2;

  prints right adjusted in the next field of four (4) spaces the alphanumeric characters which are stored under the variable name NAME3;

  skips a field of two (2) horizontal printing spaces (2X);

  and prints right adjusted in the next field of nine (9) spaces the real value that is stored under the variable name BAL. Two digits are printed behind the decimal point.

Since FORTRAN 77 allows for character constants to be assigned in assignment statements, you can verify that the following statements in example [13] result in the same output as given by example [12].

Example [13]

```
      CHARACTER *12 NAME
      NAME = 'JOHNSON,RICH'
      ICODE = 734
      BAL = 12543.75
      WRITE(6,14) NAME,ICODE,BAL
   14 FORMAT(5X,A12,I3,F9.2)
```

6. The Hollerith Specification wH

With the previous specifications we were able to input or output values and alphanumeric strings. In many cases it may be desirable to print a heading (example: heading for a problem, heading on a table, etc.).

If the wH specification is used for a WRITE statement, then the printer prints all w characters that follow the H of the specification as illustrated in the following example.

Example [14]

```
      WRITE(6,21)
21    FORMAT(6X,15HFORTRAN PROBLEM)
```

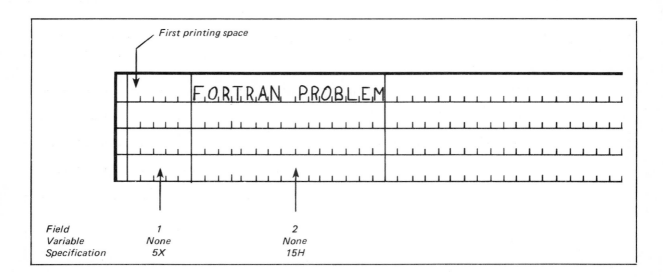

Field	1	2
Variable	None	None
Specification	5X	15H

When executing the WRITE statement the printer:

moves to the next printing line (1X for carriage control);

skips a field of five (5) horizontal printing spaces (5X);

prints the heading FORTRAN PROBLEM in the next field of fifteen (15) spaces.

Most FORTRAN compilers accept apostrophes as well as the wH specification. If apostrophes are used, the previous example is as follows:

```
      WRITE(6,21)
21    FORMAT(6X,'FORTRAN PROBLEM')
```

Standard FORTRAN permits one to read information from a card to be stored in the Hollerith, so that it can be printed via a WRITE statement on the output sheet. Both READ and WRITE statement must then refer to the same FORMAT statement as illustrated in the following example.

Example [15]

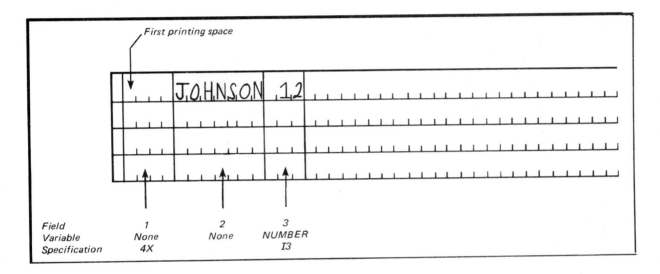

Field	1	2	3
Variable	None	None	NUMBER
Specification	4X		I3

After the READ statement, the WRITE statement is executed and the printer:

  moves to the next printing line (1X for carriage control);

  skips a field of four (4) horizontal printing spaces (4X);

  prints the name JOHNSON in the next field of seven (7) spaces;

  prints in a field of three (3) spaces the integer value that is stored under the variable name NUMBER.

7. Special Carriage Controls

The following Hollerith specifications are special carriage controls when they are specified as the first specification in the list of a FORMAT statement. They control the vertical spacing as follows:

  1H^b: single spacing (b stands for blank)

  1HO: double space

  1H1: next page

  1H2: ½ a page

  1H3: ⅓ of a page

  1H+: no spacing

Special carriage control characters can also be placed in quotes as follows:

' ' instead of 1H[b]

'0' instead of 1HO

'1' instead of 1H1

'2' instead of 1H2

'3' instead of 1H3

'+' instead of 1H+

Not all systems allow for the above carriage controls. Carriage controls can be used by themselves in a format statement:

```
        WRITE(6,30)
    30  FORMAT( '1')
```

The two statements above can be used to cause a skip to a new page outside of a program loop (as discussed later on).

Example [16]

```
      CAP = 172.34
      EARN = 8.5
      SAVING = CAP + EARN
      WRITE(6,41) CAP, EARN, SAVING
  41  FORMAT(1H1,///,6X,'NAME', 11X,'CAPITAL',2X
     *      'INTEREST',2X,'SAVINGS',//,6X,
     *      'JOHNSON,RICH',3X,F7.2,2X,F8.2,2X,F7.2)
```

First printing space   New page

1st line

2nd line

3rd line

4th line   NAME   CAPITAL   INTEREST   SAVINGS

5th line

6th line   JOHNSON,RICH   172.34   8.50   180.84

7th line

When the WRITE statement in example 16 is executed, the printer:

  moves to the next page (carriage control 1H1);

  skips three (3) lines (///)

  skips on the fourth line five (5) horizontal spaces (5X, 1X is for carriage control)

  prints the heading NAME in the next field of four (4) spaces;

  skips a field of eleven (11) horizontal spaces (11X);

  prints the heading CAPITAL in the next field of seven (7) spaces;

  skips a field of two (2) horizontal spaces (2X);

  prints the heading INTEREST in the next field of eight (8) spaces;

  skips a field of two (2) horizontal spaces (2X);

  prints the heading SAVINGS in the next field of seven (7) spaces;

  returns to the carriage control position (/);

  skips the next line (the fifth line) (/);

  skips on the sixth line five (5) spaces (5X, 1X is for carriage control)

  prints the characters JOHNSON,RICH in the next field of twelve (12) spaces;

  skips three (3) horizontal spaces (3X);

  prints in the next field of seven (7) spaces the real value stored under the variable name CAP with two digits behind the decimal point (F7.2);

  skips two (2) horizontal printing spaces;

  prints in the next field of eight (8) spaces the real value stored under the variable name EARN with two digits behind the decimal point (F8.2);

  skips two (2) horizontal printing spaces;

  and finally prints in the next field of seven (7) spaces the real value stored under the variable name SAVING with two digits behind the decimal point (F7.2).

8. The Tab Specification Tn

The tab specification can be used for horizontal spacing. Since the Tn specification indicates to skip to the nth printing position, it is especially useful to avoid counting spaces when it is known where the field begins.

Using the Tab specification, the FORMAT specifications of example [16] can be rewritten as follows:

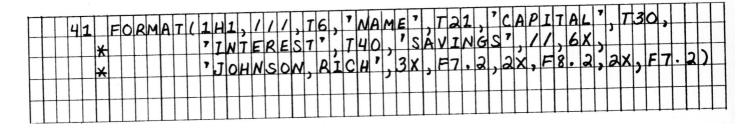

5. FORMAT Rules

Rule 1—Implied Decimal Points

It is not necessary to keypunch the decimal point on the input data. The format specification dictates where the decimal point has to be put when the data is read in and stored in memory.

Example [17]

INPUT	74321	2492
SPECIFICATION	F5.2	F4.0
VALUE ASSIGNED	743.21	2492.

Rule 2—Punched Decimal Points

If a decimal point is punched in an input data field, and if the position of the decimal point is different from that indicated in the format specification, the decimal point as punched takes priority over the position indicated in the format specification.

Example [18]

INPUT	72.54	755.1	6.1525
SPECIFICATION	F5.3	F5.2	F6.2
VALUE ASSIGNED	72.54	755.1	6.1525

Rule 3—Repetition Factor

An unsigned integer constant preceding a FORMAT specification indicates the number of times a specification has to be repeated.

Example [19]

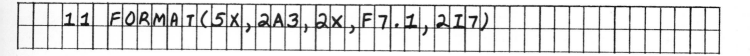

The following FORMAT is equivalent to the preceding one.

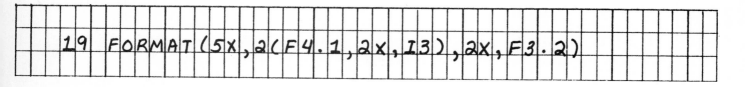

Rule 4—Repetition of a Set of Specifications

Consecutive specifications can be repeated by placing parentheses around the group of specifications to be repeated. An unsigned integer constant preceding the parenthesis indicates the number of times the group of specifications has to be repeated.

Example [20]

19 FORMAT(5X,2(F4.1,2X,I3),2X,F3.2)

The following FORMAT is equivalent to the preceding one.

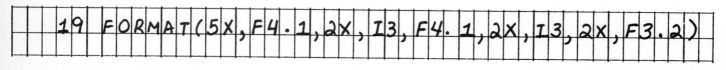

Rule 5—Extra Specifications

The FORMAT statement may contain more specifications than list items in the I/O statement. At the execution of the INPUT/OUTPUT statement the extra specifications are ignored.

Rule 6—Format Rescanning

The INPUT/OUTPUT list may contain more list items than specifications in the FORMAT statement. If there are more items in the INPUT/OUTPUT list than there are specifications in the FORMAT statement, the system will return to the rightmost left parenthesis in the FORMAT statement and repeat the specifications from that point on as many times as necessary. Whenever the rightmost parenthesis of a FORMAT statement is encountered and when there are more items in the list, the rightmost parenthesis causes the system to reset for a new record (card) or line (printing paper).

Example [21]

```
      READ(5,60)CAP, EARN, SAVING
60    FORMAT(F3.1)
```

The values to be stored under CAP, EARN, and SAVING are read from three different cards.

6. FORTRAN 77 Additional INPUT/OUTPUT

We will discuss here, briefly, through analogy with FORTRAN 66 standard, some new standard features as added by FORTRAN 77. Recall that the general READ/WRITE statement is as follows:

READ(UNIT,FMT)   <list>

or:

WRITE(UNIT,FMT)   <list>

where: READ/WRITE: are the keywords
UNIT: stands for the input/output unit number
FMT: stands for the number of the Format statement that will be used
list: stands for a list of variable names

FORTRAN 77 allows for reversing the "UNIT,FMT" order in a READ or WRITE statement. If we desire to do so, we must use the keywords UNIT and FMT as shown in example [22].

Example [22]

READ(5,57)VALUE1,VALUE2

or (1977 standard)

READ(FMT=57,UNIT=5)VALUE1,VALUE2

FORTRAN 77 allows for list directed Input and Output by the use of an asterisk (*). Here an asterisk (*) is used instead of a format statement number as shown in examples [23] and [24].

Example [23]

READ(5,*)VALUE1,VALUE2

When using the above READ statement, it is not necessary to place the input data in certain specific columns. Rather, we must separate the data by either a comma, blank, or a slash.

Example [24]

    WRITE(6,*)VALUE1,VALUE2

Rather than the programmer defining the output format in example [24], the system will do it.

Other FORTRAN 77 acceptable standards are shown in Example [25].

Example [25]

            WRITE(6,*)'TOTAL=',VALUE1+VALUE2
    or

            WRITE(6,17)'TOTAL=',VALUE1+VALUE2
        17 FORMAT(A,F12.2)
    or

            WRITE(6,'(A,F12.2)')'TOTAL=',VALUE1+VALUE2
    or

            CHARACTER*9 SPEC
            SPEC='(A,F12.2)'
            WRITE(6,SPEC)'TOTAL=',VALUE1+VALUE2
    or

            CHARACTER *9 SPEC
            SPEC='(A,F12.2)'
            WRITE(FMT=SPEC,UNIT=6)'TOTAL=',VALUE1+VALUE2
    or (1966 standard FORTRAN)
            SUM=VALUE1+VALUE2
            WRITE(6,17)SUM
        17 FORMAT(1X,'TOTAL=',F12.2)

7. Summary of Format Specifications

Table 5.1   Format Specifications

SPECIFICATION	MEANING	
	Input	*Output*
1. nX	skip n columns on card	skip n spaces on printing line
2. /	feed a new card	return to carriage control
3. nIw	read n integer values, each out of w columns	write n integer values, each occupying w spaces
4. nFw.d	read n real floating-point values, each out of w columns of which the last d columns are the digits behind the decimal point	print n real floating-point values, each occupying w spaces and having d places behind the decimal point
5. nAw	read n alphanumeric strings, each out of w columns	write n alphanumeric strings, each occupying w spaces
6. wH	replace all w characters behind the H specification with the w characters read from the w columns of an input card	write all w characters which are behind the H specification on the output medium
7. 1st Specification:		
1H0		double space
1H1		go to the next printing page
1H2		skip ½ a page
1H3		skip ⅓ of a page
1H+		no vertical spacing
1H^b		single vertical spacing
8. Tn	tab to the nth column	tab to the nth printing space

Exercises

Problem No. 1

Consider the following Review Questions and give short answers

1. State the purpose of each of the elements in the following FORTRAN READ statement:

   20 READ(5,11)TIME,SECOND,MINS,HRS

   a) 20:
   b) 5:
   c) 11:
   d) TIME,SECOND,MINS,HRS:

2. What is wrong with the following READ statement?

   33 READ(5,33)A,B,C

3. Why do we use FORMAT statements? Comment on their use for both input and output operations.
4. Describe the carriage control of the printer. Include a discussion of how it is accomplished and give a listing of acceptable control characters.
5. Fill in the following table for the indicated format specifications:

Format Specification	Purpose	Sample Example
/		
X		
I		
F		
E		
H		
A		

6. Contrast the H and the A specifications.
7. Given the same numeric quantity to be processed, input and output FORMAT specifications are apt to differ from one another. Why? Give an example.
8. What happens when an attempt is made to write a data item having more places to the left of the decimal than the FORMAT specification allows?

Problem No. 2

Consider the following statements:

       READ (5,1) INTRST, CAP, NUMBER
     1 FORMAT (I2,2X,F5.2,I3)

and suppose that the READ is executed. What values are stored for INTRST, CAP, and NUMBER if each line in the following illustration represents a different data card which is read in by above READ statement.

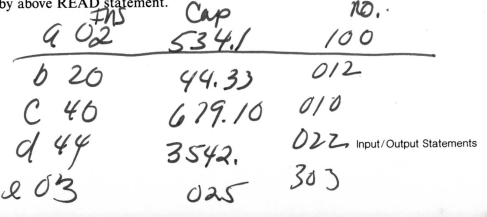

	INTRST	Cap	NO.
a	02	534.1	100
b	20	44.33	012
c	40	679.10	010
d	44	3542.	022
e	03	025	30

card columns	1	2	3	4	5	6	7	8	9	10	11	12
a)		2		4	5	3	4	•	1	1	0	0
b)	2				4	4	•	3	3		1	2
c)	4		1	5	6	7	9	1	0		1	
d)	4	4			3	5	4	2	•		2	2
e)		3					0	2	5	3		3

Problem No. 3

Consider the following data card:

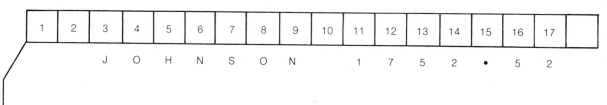

and the following statements:

    READ(5,1)CAP
    WRITE(6,1)CAP
    1 FORMAT(2X,'BLABLAB',F8.3)

Johnson 1752.53

What does the printout look like when the above statements are executed?

Problem No. 4

Consider the following data card:

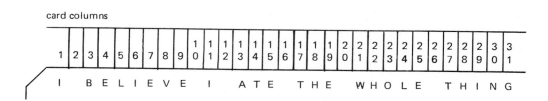

and the following READ statements and indicate the values that will be stored for A,B,C,D,E, etc.

a) READ(5,1)A,B,C,D,E,F
    1 FORMAT(6A4)
b) READ(5,2)A,B,C,D,E,F
    2 FORMAT(A1,A7,A5,A3,A5,A5)
c) READ(5,3)A,B,C,D,E,F
    3 FORMAT(3A4)

Problem No. 5

What are the minium specifications to write the following stored data?

a) 17.2   F4.1

b) ABCDE

c) 1252   I4

d) 1234.25E—04

Problem No. 6

How many data cards must be prepared to read each set of statements?

a) READ(5,1)A,B,C,D
    1 FORMAT(/,2F4.1)

b) READ(5,2)I,J,K,L
    2 FORMAT(2I2,2(I3,I4))

c) READ(5,3)A,B,I,J,C,D,K,L
    3 FORMAT(2(2F5.2,2I3,//))

Problem No. 7

Write a WRITE and a FORMAT statement to accomplish the following:

a. Five lines down from the top of a new page, print the heading, TABLE OF PARAMETERS, centered on the page, then skip 2 full lines.

b. On the fifth printing line of a new page, print the heading, HERE IS CHARLIE BROWN, centered on the page, then move the printer to the eighth printing line.

Problem No. 8

Consider the following data card:

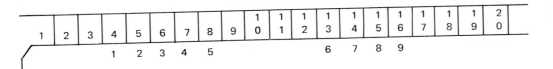

and write the appropriate statements to:

a) read A and B from the above card as 12.34 and 67.89 respectively

b) read A and B from the above card as 0. and 6789. respectively

c) read A as the constant 123.45 and B as the characters 6789

6 Some Elementary Business Programs

Now we are ready to use the assignment statements and input/output statements to write some elementary business programs. In developing these programs, special attention is focused on good overall documentation. This includes: 1. flowcharting of the solutions procedure; 2. definition of all variable names used in the program, and 3. the use of appropriate comment statements throughout the FORTRAN program.

Besides good documentation, the programmer must pay attention to some fundamental rules that enhance good programming practices. Some of these are listed below and others will be mentioned as new material is developed in this text. Here they are:

Rule 1:
Use a reasonable amount of comment statements to either identify and explain the program, or to identify and explain the meaning of important program variable names. When the program is large it is preferable to identify these on a separate sheet of paper.

Rule 2:
Use comment statements to identify routines and flows within the program.

Rule 3:
Spell out important variable names to the fullest extent possible. Use the INTEGER/REAL type declaration statement rather than changing the first letter of the variable name to accommodate the mode.

Rule 4:
Attempt to keep statement numbers in ascending order. Initially, when constructing the first program, try to use multiples of 10,50,100,etc. and if at all possible, avoid using digits 1 through 9 in the units position. If this rule is followed, it will be easier later on to add statements to a program without having to adjust already existing statement numbers.

It is preferable to right-justify statement numbers in their five-column field so that it is easier to locate statements.

Rule 5:
Place all the FORMAT statements either after the corresponding READ or WRITE statements, or in the beginning of the program, or at the end of the program before the END statement. This makes it easier to locate any FORMAT statement quickly.

Rule 6:
Indent all continuation statements by approximately five spaces.

Rule 7:

If more than one line of output is shown in a FORMAT statement, it is preferable to indent each separate line and start the specifications for each new output line on a separate continuation card. Also, a line of output in a FORMAT statement should end on a slash and all new lines should be aligned under the previous line's carriage control character—that is, the carriage control characters for all lines should be aligned. . . . (rules to be continued in following chapters).

Note that above rules only aid in making the program more readable. We still need to construct the right logic and translate it using the correct FORTRAN syntax before correct results are generated.

The above type of documentation and rules are used throughout the examples of this chapter and the book. Though the examples in this chapter are rather simple, and all identical in structure, the students are encouraged to run some of them on their computing system after changing the input/output specifications. Because each FORTRAN program must contain at least one halt statement and only one END statement, these two types of statements are discussed first.

1. Halt Statements

Any program must have at least one explicit terminating statement. The terminating statements in use are

CALL EXIT
STOP
PAUSE or PAUSE n

The execution of the object program is terminated by the use of a STOP statement or a CALL EXIT statement. The STOP or CALL EXIT statement is used for the logical end of a program; that is, the end of the algorithm used to solve the particular problem. Even though a program can contain several STOP or CALL EXIT statements, using more than one is discouraged since it may undermine the structure of the program.

If a temporary halt is necessary when processing the object program, a PAUSE statement can be used. This statement halts the computer during execution of the object program, and the manual depressing of a start key can cause the computer to resume the execution of the program with the next executable FORTRAN statement. When a "PAUSE n" is encountered, the "n" constant is printed on the typewriter when the PAUSE statement is executed. In general, the PAUSE statement gives the operator a chance to analyze intermediate results, to change tapes if necessary, to debug the program, and to do other desirable things.

Pause statements should only be used with the permission of your instructor. On machines with a single job stream a great deal of computer time will be wasted while the operator tries to find out why the machine halted.

The END statement is used to show the physical end of a program. It is a nonexecutable statement and is used to signal the FORTRAN compiler that the physical end of the source program deck has been reached. The form of the END statement is as follows:

END

Unlike the STOP statement, the END statement can be used only once in each FORTRAN program.

2. Simple Business Examples

The One-Year-Investment Example

Consider the investment of $17345.(CAP) for a one-year period at an interest of .055 per dollar investment.

At the end of one year, the generated savings (SAVING) equals CAP(1+RATE).

The investment, the unit interest rate, and the generated savings are finally outputed.

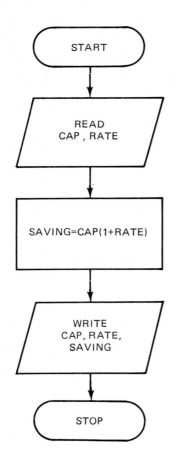

A short note is in order regarding the mapping or positioning of output on a page, as it is wise to use some means of organizing the same. One may use printer spacing charts, graph paper, coding sheets, or any hard drawn facsimile to determine just where given characters will be printed on the page.

```
C  ***  CALCULATION OF ONE-YEAR-INVESTMENT
C  ***  FOLLOWING VARIABLE NAMES ARE USED:
C  ***  CAP: CAPITAL INVESTED
C  ***  RATE: YEARLY INTEREST RATE
C  ***  SAVING: GENERATED SAVINGS
       READ(5,100) CAP, RATE
100    FORMAT(F6.0, F5.3)
       SAVING = CAP*(1.0 + RATE)
       WRITE(6,200) CAP, RATE, SAVING
200    FORMAT(1H1,///,5X,'ONE-YEAR-INVESTMENT',//,
      *       5X,'CAPITAL',F9.2,/,
      *       5X,'RATE',F6.3,/,
      *       5X,'SAVINGS',F9.2)
       STOP
       END
```

According to the FORMAT specifications associated with the READ statement, the following data card must be prepared.

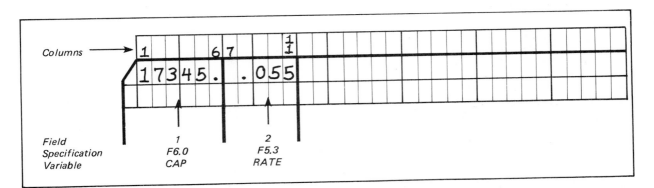

The generated output for the above program looks like this:

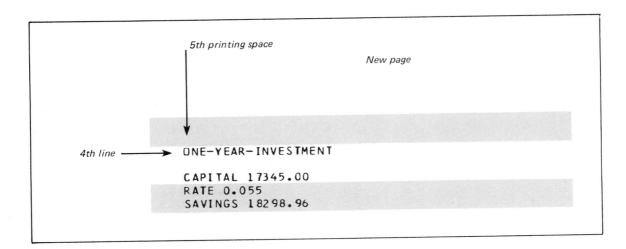

The Compound-Interest-Investment Example

Consider the investment of $17345. (CAP) for ten years (N); at an interest of .055 per dollar investment (RATE)

If the investment is kept for 1 year, the savings are

$CAP(1+RATE)$

If the investment is kept for 2 years, the savings are

$CAP(1+RATE)(1+RATE)=CAP(1+RATE)^2$

If the investment is kept for N years, the savings are

$CAP(1+RATE)^N$

The accumulated savings (SAVING) is printed out, together with the initial investment (CAP), the number of years the investment is made (N), and the interest-rate-per-dollar investment.

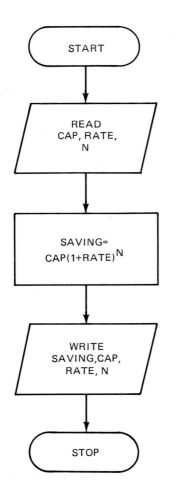

```
C   *** CALCULATION OF COMPOUNDED INVESTMENT
C   *** FOLLOWING VARIABLE NAMES ARE USED:
C   *** CAP: CAPITAL INVESTED
C   *** RATE: YEARLY INTEREST RATE
C   *** N: NUMBER OF YEARS INVESTMENT IS MADE
C   *** SAVING: GENERATED SAVINGS
      READ(5,100) CAP, RATE, N
100   FORMAT(F6.0,F5.3,I3)
      SAVING = CAP*(1.0 + RATE)**N
      WRITE(6,200) SAVING, CAP, RATE, N
200   FORMAT(1H1,///,5X,'COMPOUNDED INTEREST',//,
     *          5X,'SAVINGS',F10.2,/,
     *          5X,'CAPITAL',F10.2,/,
     *          5X,'RATE',F6.3,/,
     *          5X,'YEARS',I3)
      STOP
      END
```

According to the FORMAT specifications associated with the READ statement, the following data card must be prepared.

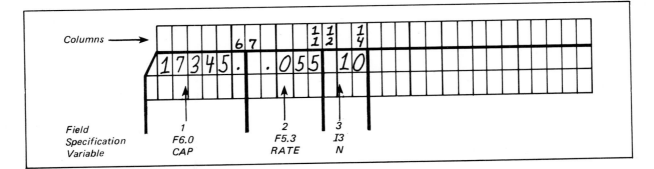

This program generates the following output:

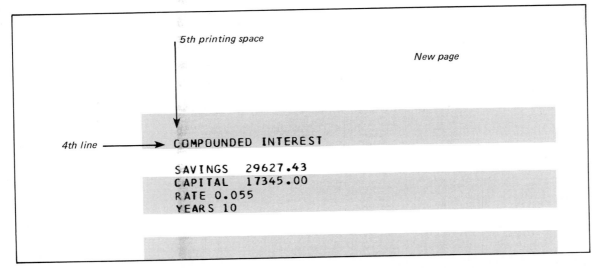

The Gross-Profit and Net-Profit Example

The Gross sales (GSALES), the cost of the goods sold (COST) and the operating expenses (OEXP) are read into the computer to calculate the gross profit (GPROFT) and the net profit (NPROFT), as follows:

GPROFT=GSALES−COST
NPROFT=GPROFT−OEXP

The calculated gross profit and the net profit are finally printed.

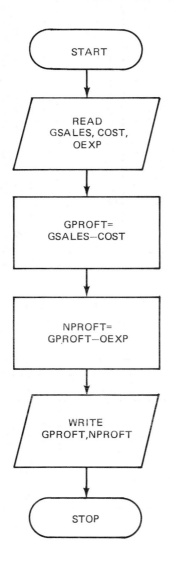

```
C   ***  CALCULATION OF GROSS AND NET PROFIT
C   ***  FOLLOWING VARIABLE NAMES ARE USED
C   ***  GSALES: $VALUE OF GROSS SALES
C   ***  COST: COST OF GOODS
C   ***  OEXP: OPERATING EXPENSES
C   ***  GPROFT: GROSS PROFIT
C   ***  NPROFT: NET PROFIT
      REAL NPROFT
      READ(5,100) GSALES, COST, OEXP
100   FORMAT(F5.0,F5.0,F4.0)
      GPROFT = GSALES - COST
      NPROFT = GPROFT - OEXP
      WRITE(6,200) GPROFT, NPROFT
200   FORMAT(1H1,///,5X,'GROSS AND NET PROFIT',//,
     *       5X,'GROSS PROFIT',F8.2,/,
     *       5X,'NET PROFIT',F8.2)
      STOP
      END
```

According to the FORMAT specifications associated with the READ statement, the following data card must be prepared.

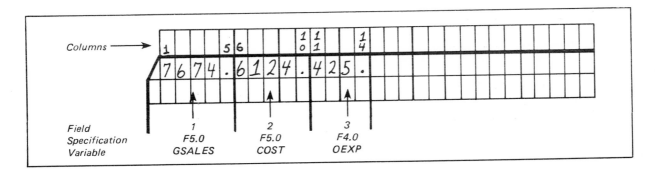

The program generates the following output:

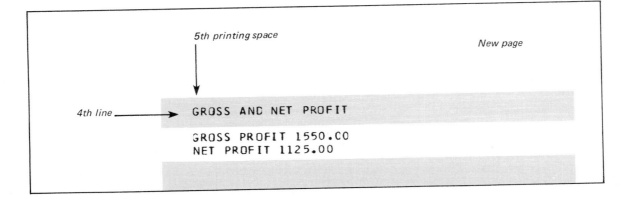

The Straight-Line-Depreciation Example

A press is purchased for $17,500 (PRMCH) and has an expected life of 12 years (YEARS). The straight-line-depreciation formula is:

PRMCH/YEARS

The name of the machine (MACH), the purchase price, and the yearly depreciation value, DEPREC, are printed.

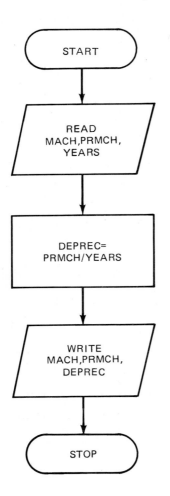

```
C *** STRAIGHT LINE DEPRECIATION
C *** FOLLOWING VARIABLE NAMES ARE USED
C *** MACH1,MACH2,MACH3: NAME OF THE MACHINE
C *** PRMCH: PURCHASE PRICE OF MACHINE
C *** YEARS: EXPECTED LIFE OF THE MACHINE
C *** DEPREC: YEARLY DEPRECIATION VALUE
      READ(5,100) MACH1, MACH2, MACH3, PRMCH, YEARS
100   FORMAT(3A4,F6.0,F4.0)
      DEPREC = PRMCH/YEARS
      WRITE(6,200) MACH1, MACH2, MACH3 ,
     *             PRMCH, DEPREC
200   FORMAT(1H1,//,5X,'STRAIGHT LINE DEPRECIATION',/,
     *       5X,'MACHINE IDENTIFICATION',2X,3A4,/,
     *       5X,'VALUE',F8.0,/,
     *       5X,'DEPRECIATION',F8.2)
      STOP
      END
```

According to the FORMAT specifications associated with the READ statement, the following data card must be prepared.

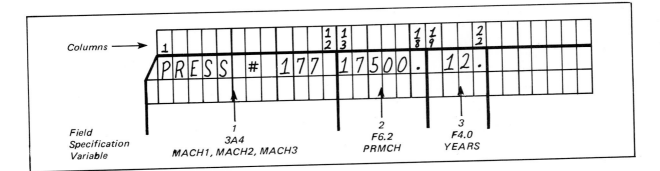

The program generates the following output:

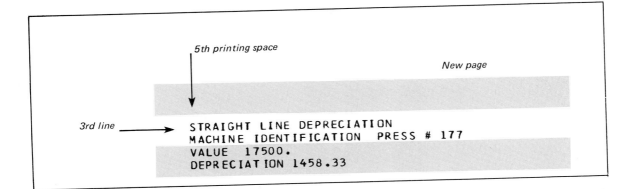

The EOQ Example

EOQ stands for the "economic order quantity," when stock replenishment is instantaneous.
The EOQ depends on:

the annual usage of the stock item: AUSAGE

the order cost of the stock item: ORDERC

the carrying cost: CARRYC

The carrying cost equals the interest rate (RATE) multiplied by the unit cost price of the stock item (UNITC).

$$EOQ = \sqrt{\frac{2 \times AUSAGE \times ORDERC}{CARRYC}}$$

The input consists of AUSAGE, ORDERC, RATE, UNITC

The printout shows the AUSAGE, ORDERC, CARRYC, and EOQ

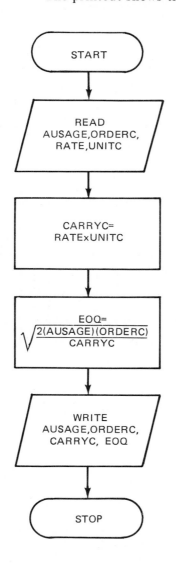

```
C   ***  THE EOQ CALCULATION
C   ***  FOLLOWING VARIABLE NAMES ARE USED
C   ***  EOQ: ECONOMIC ORDER QUANTITY
C   ***  AUSAGE: ANNUAL USAGE
C   ***  ORDERC: ORDER COST              RATE: INTEREST RATE
C   ***  CARRYC: CARRYING COST           UNITC: UNIT COST
         READ(5,100) AUSAGE, ORDERC, RATE,UNITC
100      FORMAT(F5.0,F3.0,F4.2,F5.2)
         CARRYC = RATE * UNITC
         EOQ = (2.0 * AUSAGE * ORDERC/CARRYC)**0.5
         WRITE(6,200)AUSAGE, ORDERC, CARRYC, EOQ
200      FORMAT(1H1,///,5X,'THE EOQ PROBLEM',//,
     *          5X,'ANNUAL USAGE',F8.0,/,
     *          5X,'ORDER COST',F5.0,/,
     *          5X,'CARRYING COST',F7.2,/,
     *          5X,'ORDER QUANTITY',F7.2)
         STOP
         END
```

According to the FORMAT specifications associated with the READ statement, the following data card must be prepared.

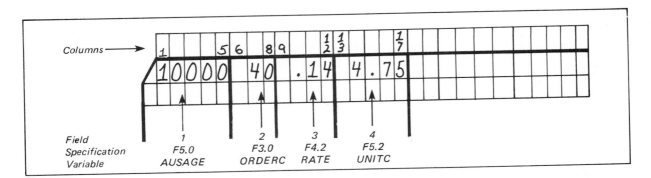

The program generates the following output:

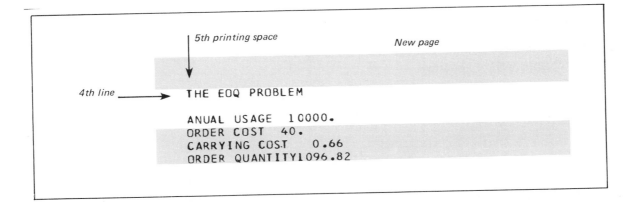

Problem No. 1

You are required to draw a flowchart and to write a program that will calculate the yearly compound *interest* (to be earned at the end of 1981) for an investment of $75 made by your parents at the end of the year of your birth. Assume that the interest rate was always constant and is 5.50% yearly.

You are required to read in one data card in which $75 is keypunched.

Besides your name and a reasonable title, you are expected to give your date of birth and the final result, which is labeled as follows: "Accumulated interest earned at the end of 1981 on the $75 invested the last day of 19—."

Problem No. 2

You are supposed to read in two cards with the following information on them:
Card #1

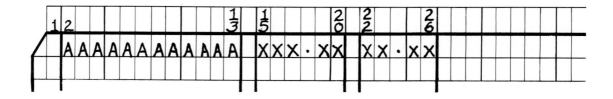

where: AAA....AA: is the customer's name (12 columns)
        XXX.XX: is the quantity ordered
        XX.XX: is the discount for each one hundred dollars of merchandise bought
                  (no discount on units or tens of dollars)

Card #2

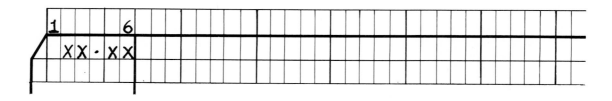

where: XX.XX: is the rate per unit goods

Calculate the amount the customer owes the company given the above information. Print out with appropriate headings:

Customer's name, quantity bought, rate/unit, discount, and the amount due.
Before writing the program, flowchart the solution procedure.

Problem No. 3

As a result of a FORTRAN program, a picture of Charlie Brown was printed as shown:

You are required to write a complete FORTRAN program that will accomplish this "piece of art" without the use of a READ statement

Note: The alphanumeric characters used in printing the picture are:

the letters X, V,O

the minus sign —

the sign for closing parenthesis)

Problem No. 4

Write a program that reads in a card containing the name of an automobile and its price. Assume a 4% sales tax. Print out, with the appropriate headings, the name, price, sales tax, and the total cost of the automobile.

Problem No. 5 Weighted Average Cost of Capital

Given the following input data:

1. total capitalization (TC)
2. amount of debt (DEBT)
3. amount of preferred stock (PS)
4. amount of net worth (NW)
5. the after-tax cost of a debt (CDEBT)
6. the after-tax cost of preferred stock (CPS)
7. the after-tax cost of net worth (CNW)

Draw a detailed flowchart and write a FORTRAN program to calculate the weighted average cost of capital (WACCAP).

The weighted average cost of capital is the sum of three weighted costs:

1. the weighted cost of the debt (WDEBT)
2. the weighted cost of the preferred stocks (WPS)
3. the weighted cost of the net worth (WNW)

These costs are calculated as follows:

1. $\text{WDEBT} = \left(\dfrac{\text{DEBT}}{\text{TC}}\right) \text{CDEBT}$

2. $\text{WPS} = \left(\dfrac{\text{PS}}{\text{TC}}\right) \text{CPS}$

3. $\text{WNW} = \left(\dfrac{\text{NW}}{\text{TC}}\right) \text{CNW}$

Problem No. 6 Economical Borrowing Amount—An EOQ Approach

Given the following input data:

1. incremental fixed cost of obtaining money on a loan basis (FC)
2. total amount of cash to be used in next time period (CASH)
3. the cost of keeping $1 on hand (COST)

draw a flowchart and write a FORTRAN program to calculate the Economical Borrowing Amount (EBA).

Use the same procedure as for the EOQ inventory model.

$$\text{EBA} = \sqrt{\dfrac{2*\text{FC}*\text{CASH}}{\text{COST}}}$$

Problem No. 7 The Original Investment Problem

Assume you receive $3000 from an investment you made 10 years ago. For income tax purposes you must know what the amount of the original investment was. All you can determine, other than the already given information, is that the interest rate on the investment was 6%.

Draw a flowchart to determine the original investment, and then write a FORTRAN program and run it on the computer.

Problem No. 8

The distance between two points on a plane with coordinates (x_1, y_1) and (x_2, y_2) is given by the formula

$$\text{distance} = \sqrt{(x_1 - x_2)^2 + (y_1 - y_2)^2}$$

You are to write a program that will read in the coordinates of two points, and then calculate and print out the distance. Keypunch the following numbers on your data card: 1.5, 2.0, 15.2, −4.8.

They represent the values of $x_1, y_1, x_2,$ and y_2 respectively.

Transfer and Decision Statements

As a rule, FORTRAN statements are executed sequentially in the order in which they are written. However, sometimes one may wish to execute statements in a different order. This can be accomplished through transfer statements. The following transfer statements are discussed below:

1. GO TO statement
2. The Arithmetic IF statement
3. The Computed GO TO statement
4. The Logical IF statement

1. GO TO Statement

The GO TO statement is the simplest and most direct transfer statement. It causes an unconditional transfer of control. The general form of the GO TO statement is:

GO TO n
where: n: is a statement label

This transfer statement provides the means of transferring control to some statement other than the next one in sequence. The statement to which control is transferred must be labeled "n" and must be an executable statement. The statement to which control is transferred may precede or follow the GO TO statement.

At this point, it is advisable to use GO TO statements frequently because you do not have a complete knowledge of FORTRAN. Later, however, when you become more acquainted with FORTRAN 77 and other FORTRAN statements, you will learn to minimize the use of GO TO statements through careful structuring of programs.

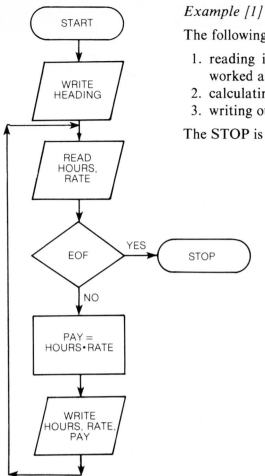

Example [1]

The following flowchart describes the flow of:

1. reading in a card that contains the number of hours (HOURS) worked and the rate (RATE) per hour,
2. calculating the weekly pay (PAY), and
3. writing out the HOURS, RATE, and PAY values.

The STOP is reached if no additional information or input data exists.

This flowchart is coded in FORTRAN as follows:

```
C   *** PAYROLL EXAMPLE
C   *** FOLLOWING VARIABLE NAMES ARE USED
C   *** HOURS: NUMBER OF HOURS WORKED
C   *** RATE: HOURLY WAGE RATE
C   *** PAY: AMOUNT PAID FOR HOURS WORKED
        WRITE(6,10)
    10  FORMAT(1H1,10X,'NAME',4X,'HRS',1X,
       1        'RT',1X,'INCOME',//)
    20  READ(5,30,END=40) HOURS,RATE
    30  FORMAT(6X,'                    ',F3.0,F4.1,F7.2)
        PAY = HOURS*RATE
        WRITE(6,30) HOURS, RATE, PAY
        GO TO 20
    40  STOP
        END
```

The READ statement in this program implies that control has to be transferred to statement #40 (STOP), as soon as no more input is available. If the above program did not contain "END=40" the program would terminate abnormally.

The "GO TO 20" statement transfers control to statement number 20, the READ statement. The GO TO statement may be placed wherever desired in a program, but some care must be taken that the STOP statement can be reached during the execution of the program.

The output for the previous program is as follows:

```
           NAME       HRS RT INCOME


      JOHNSON,LEE 42.  3.5  147.00
      THOMPSON,JIM26.  5.3  137.80
      SIMONS,KIM   45.  6.2  279.00
      CHANG,TONY   40.  7.5  300.00
```

2. The Arithmetic IF Statement

The Arithmetic IF statement is a conditional transfer statement in FORTRAN. The general form of the statement is

IF (arithmetic expression) n_1, n_2, n_3
where: n_1, n_2 and n_3 are statement labels

The arithmetic expression can be a single variable or a combination of variables with operators. When two operators are compared, i.e.:

IF(A-B)

this, then, is the same as asking whether A is less than, equal to, or greater than B.

When, in the execution of a FORTRAN program, the arithmetic IF statement is reached, the arithmetic expression is evaluated. If the result is negative, a transfer to statement labeled n_1 is made; if the result is zero, a transfer to statement labeled n_2 is made; and if the result is positive, a transfer to statement labeled n_3 is made. The three statement labels need not be distinct. As a decision has to be made to choose to transfer in one of three possible directions, the decision symbol is used in a flowchart to indicate the logic in the flow as follows:

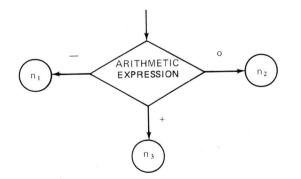

Example [2]

Consider the federal tax example (as illustrated in the third chapter) consisting of the following procedure, shown in the flowchart.

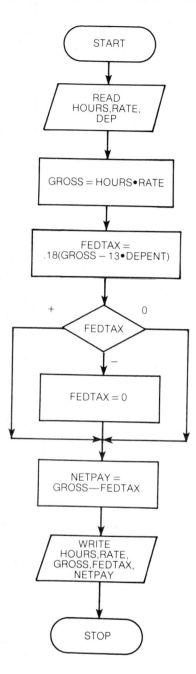

1. Read in the number of hours a person has worked (HOURS), the rate per hour (RATE), and the number of dependents (DEPENT).
2. Calculate the gross pay (GROSS).

3. Calculate the federal tax (FEDTAX) through the standard procedure: .18(GROSS−13×DEPENT).
4. Check whether the calculated FEDTAX is negative or positive.

5. If FEDTAX is negative, put it equal to zero.

6. The net pay (NETPAY) equals GROSS-FEDTAX.

7. Finally, print out all appropriate information.

```
C  ***  CALCULATION OF NETPAYMENT OF INCOME
C  ***  FOLLOWING VARIABLE NAMES ARE USED
C  ***  NETPAY: NET INCOME
C  ***  HOURS: HOURS WORKED
C  ***  RATE: HOURLY RATE
C  ***  DEP: NUMBER OF DEPENDENTS
C  ***  GROSS: GROSS INCOME
C  ***  FEDTAX: FEDERAL TAX WITHHELD
       REAL NETPAY
       READ(5,10) HOURS, RATE, DEP
   10  FORMAT(6X, F4.0, F4.1, F3.0)
       GROSS = HOURS*RATE
       FEDTAX = 0.18*(GROSS-13.0*DEP)
       IF(FEDTAX)20,30,30
   20  FEDTAX = 0.0
   30  NETPAY = GROSS-FEDTAX
       WRITE(6,40) HOURS, RATE, GROSS, FEDTAX, NETPAY
   40  FORMAT(1H1,///,5X,'NETPAY CALCULATION',//,
      1       5X,'HOURS WORKED',F4.0,/,
      2       5X,'RATE',F4.1,/,
      3       5X,'GROSS PAY',F7.2,/,
      4       5X,'FEDERAL TAX',F6.2,/,
      5       5X,'NETPAY',F7.2)
       STOP
       END
```

The following data is processed.

```
     40. 5.5  7
```

This program generates the following output:

```
NETPAY CALCULATION

HOURS WORKED 40.
RATE 5.5
GROSS PAY 220.00
FEDERAL TAX 23.22
NETPAY 196.78
```

3. The Computed GO TO Statement

The Computed GO TO statement is more flexible than the GO TO statement. The general form of the Computed GO TO statement is:

GO TO $(n_1,n_2n_3,...,n_m),i$

where: $n_1,n_2,...,n_m$ are statement labels;

i is an integer variable name that represents a value which has been defined previously.

Notice the necessary punctuation (,) after closing parenthesis in the above GO TO statement.

This statement provides us with an m-way check and one single transfer, based upon the value of the integer variable name:

if the variable name "i" equals 1, then transfer is made to n_1

if the variable name "i" equals 2, then transfer is made to n_2

if the variable name "i" equals m, then transfer is made to n_m

When a multiple check needs to be made for one single transfer, the following decision set-up can be used in a flowchart:

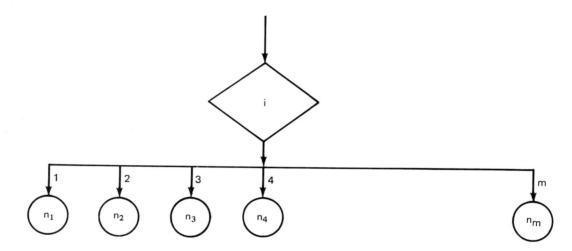

Example [3] The Salary Increase Problem

The flowchart on page 103 illustrates the updating of employees' data records for a salary increase, as follows:

If an employee has worked 1 year, his salary increase is $100.

If an employee has worked 2 years, his salary increase is $200.

If an employee has worked 3 years, his salary increase is $400.

If an employee has worked 4 years, his salary increase is $600.

If an employee has worked 5 years, his salary increase is $1000.

If an employee has worked 6 years, his salary increase is $1500.

The data card that is read in for each employee contains his name, his yearly income (PAY), and the number of years he has served the company (NUMBER). Assume that no one has served more than 6 years.

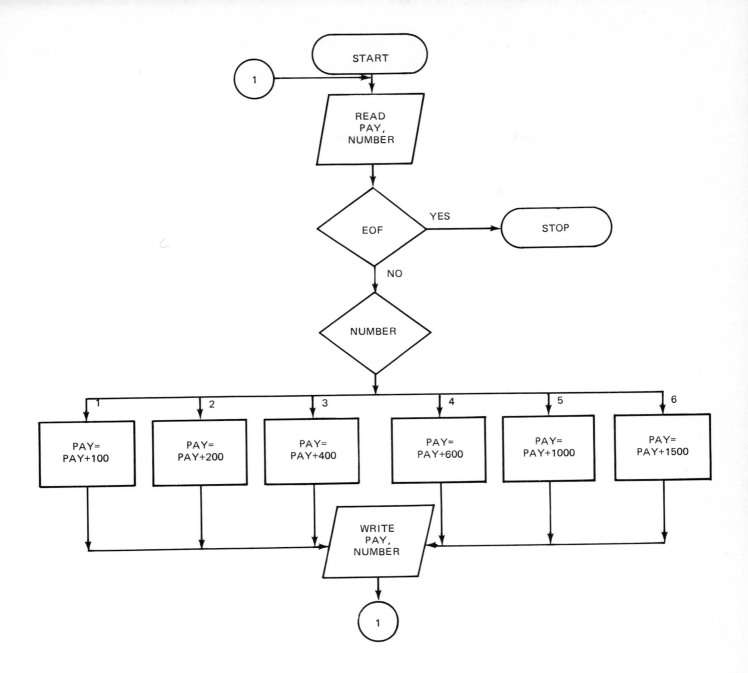

```
C  *** THE SALARY INCREASE PROBLEM
C  *** FOLLOWING VARIABLE NAMES ARE USED
C  *** PAY: SALARY PAID
C  *** NUMBER: NUMBER OF YEARS WITH THE COMPANY
       WRITE(6,10)
    10 FORMAT(1H1,//,5X,'EMPLOYEES RECORD',//,
      *           5X,'NAME',11X,'PAY',2X,'YEARS',//)
    20 READ(5,30,END=110) PAY, NUMBER
    30 FORMAT(5X,'                    ',F8.0,I3)
       GO TO (40,50,60,70,80,90), NUMBER
    40 PAY = PAY + 100.0
       GO TO 100
    50 PAY = PAY + 200.0
       GO TO 100
    60 PAY = PAY + 400.0
       GO TO 100
    70 PAY = PAY + 600.0
       GO TO 100
    80 PAY = PAY + 1000.0
       GO TO 100
    90 PAY = PAY + 1500.0
   100 WRITE(6,30)PAY, NUMBER
       GO TO 20
   110 STOP
       END
```

The following data is processed:

```
JOHNSON            15500  4
TAYLOR             12000  2
SIMONS             22000  5
DANZIG              7000  1
```

Note the use of the computed GO TO statement, containing a six-way check and a one-way transfer.

GO TO statements are used to collect the divergent paths at statement #10. The following output is obtained from the above program:

```
EMPLOYEES   RECORD

NAME            PAY   YEARS


JOHNSON      16100.   4
TAYLOR       12200.   2
SIMONS       23000.   5
DANZIG        7100.   1
```

A number of GO TO statements in the previous program can be eliminated by carefully studying the yearly increases and by restructuring the pay increase statements.

In doing so, you may agree that the following statements are equivalent to statements #40 thru #90 of the previous program.

```
90  PAY = PAY + 500
80  PAY = PAY + 400
70  PAY = PAY + 200
60  PAY = PAY + 200
50  PAY = PAY + 100
40  PAY = PAY + 100
```

Some people may refer to this arrangement as a better structure; however, in the next section a preferred structure is shown.

4. Logical IF Statement

The Logical IF statement is a decision statement that is suitable when one of two possible alternatives has to be executed.

The form of the Logical IF statement is closer to the English language than the Arithmetic IF or the Computed GO TO statement. Therefore, perhaps, the Logical IF is preferred over the Arithmetic IF statement. Its general form is:

IF(e)S
where: e is a logical expression
       S is an executable statement

This Logical IF statement is read as follows:

IF the logical expression (e) is true, then execute the executable statement (S); IF the logical expression (e) is not true, then do not execute the executable statement (S), but proceed to the next executable statement.

The statement S has certain restrictions: it cannot be another IF or a DO statement.

The logical IF can be represented in several ways in a flowchart; here are a few flowchart samples which illustrate the way logical IFs work.

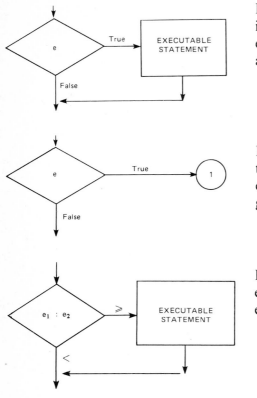

If the logical expression is true, then the executable statement is executed; if the logical expression is false, then the executable statement is not executed. In either case, the next statement executed will be the next one after the logical IF.

If the executable statement S is a GO TO statement, control will be transferred to the statement specified in the GO TO when the logical expression is true. Otherwise, the next sequential statement in the program will be executed.

If the expression e_1 is larger than or equal to the expression e_2, then the executable statement is executed; if the expression e_1 is less than the expression e_2, then the executable statement is not executed.

Logical Expressions

Just like the arithmetic expression, the logical expression generates a constant which is the result of the evaluated logical expression. Logical constants, however, take the value of .TRUE. or .FALSE. (not true). A logical expression is composed of relational expression(s). A relational expression consists of two arithmetic expressions (either both real or both integer), separated by a relational operator. The two arithmetic expressions which are linked with a relational operator must always be in the same mode. If they are not, then the statement will be executed incorrectly. The six relational operators are

FORTRAN coding	Algebraic form	Meaning
.GT.	$>$	greater than
.GE.	$\geq$	greater than or equal to
.LT.	$<$	less than
.LE.	$\leq$	less than or equal to
.EQ.	$=$	equal to
.NE.	$\neq$	not equal to

Compound logical expressions can be formed by the use of logical operators to link logical expressions. The three logical operators are:

FORTRAN coding	Meaning
.AND.	conjunction
.OR.	disjunction
.NOT.	negation

If two logical expressions, a and b, are linked with a logical operator, then the resulting logical value is as follows:

a.AND.b : is .TRUE., if both a and b are .TRUE.
a.OR.b : is .TRUE., unless both a and b are .FALSE.
.NOT.a : is .TRUE., if a is .FALSE.

If more than one operator appears in an expression, use the following list as a priority scale to evaluate these from the highest to the lowest:

Operators

.EQ., .NE., .LT., .LE., .GT., and .GE.

.NOT.

.AND.

.OR.

The following examples illustrate the use of the logical IF statement:

Example [4]

IF(FEDTAX.LT.0.0)FEDTAX=0.0

This Logical IF statement reads as follows:

If the federal tax (FEDTAX) is less than zero (0.0), then put the federal tax (FEDTAX) equal to zero (0.0), otherwise proceed with the next executable statement. This Logical IF statement can replace the following two statements in Example [2]:

    IF(FEDTAX)20,30,30
20 FEDTAX=0.0
30

Example [5] The Salary Increase Problem Reconsidered

Reconsider the salary increase problem as discussed in example [3]. Logical IF statements can now be applied to illustrate good structured programming, since they eliminate many of the GO TO statements. Using logical IF statements, the computed GO TO statement and statements #40 thru #90 are redone as follows:

```
IF(NUMBER.EQ.1) PAY = PAY + 100.0
IF(NUMBER.EQ.2) PAY = PAY + 200.0
IF(NUMBER.EQ.3) PAY = PAY + 400.0
IF(NUMBER.EQ.4) PAY = PAY + 600.0
IF(NUMBER.EQ.5) PAY = PAY +1000.0
IF(NUMBER.EQ.6) PAY = PAY +1500.0
```

This is perhaps the most structured and preferred way to program this example. In general, logical IF statements are preferred over the arithmetic IF or computed GO TO statement.

Example [6] Calculation of the Gross Pay

The following flowchart and program illustrate the computation of the gross earnings. Note that in this example overtime payment is considered.

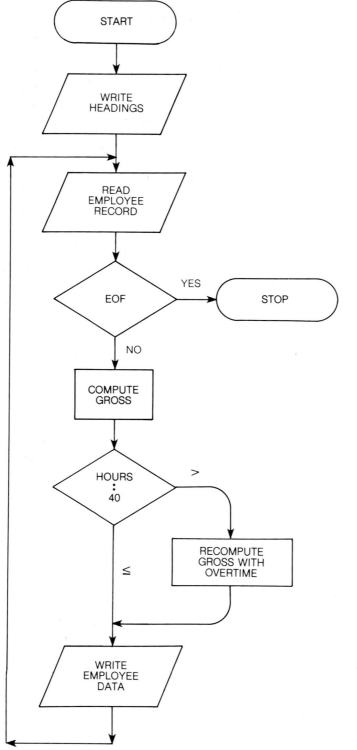

Programming Procedure:

1. Headings show employee identification number (IDNUM), pay scale (RATE), hours worked (HOURS) and gross pay (GROSS).

2. Read in identification number, hours worked and pay scale.

3. Compute the gross pay: GROSS=HOURS*PAY

4. If the employee has worked more than 40 hours, then recompute gross pay, considering overtime as follows: GROSS=(40.0+1.5* (HOURS−40.0))*RATE

5. Write out identification number, pay scale, hours worked and gross pay.

The FORTRAN program is as follows:

```
C  ***  CALCULATION OF GROSS PAY
C  ***  FOLLOWING VARIABLE NAMES ARE USED:
C  ***  IDNUM: EMPLOYEE IDENTIFICATION NUMBER
C  ***  HOURS: NUMBER OF HOURS WORKED
C  ***  RATE: PAY SCALE
C  ***  GROSS: GROSS PAY
       WRITE(6,20)
   20  FORMAT(1H1,//,2X,'IDENTIFICATION NUMBER',
      *        3X,'PAY SCALE',3X,'HOURS WORKED',
      *        3X,'GROSS PAY')
   40  READ(5,60,END=120) IDNUM, HOURS, RATE
   60  FORMAT(I5,F4.1,F5.2)
       GROSS = HOURS * RATE
       IF(HOURS.GT.40.0) GROSS =(40.0 + 1.5 *
      *              (HOURS - 40.0))* RATE
       WRITE(6,80) IDNUM, RATE, HOURS, GROSS
   80  FORMAT(10X,I5,13X,F5.2,9X,F4.1,8X,F7.2)
       GO TO 40
  120  STOP
       END
```

The figure above contains one logical IF statement. The logical expression (HOURS.GT.40.0) determines whether the employee worked more than 40 hours. If so, the employee's gross payment is recomputed. Otherwise, it remains the same as computed by the assignment statement GROSS=HOURS*RATE. According to FORMAT statement #60, the following data can be submitted with this program:

```
17324 425 12.5
 2536 36. 9.25
34375 51.10.50
```

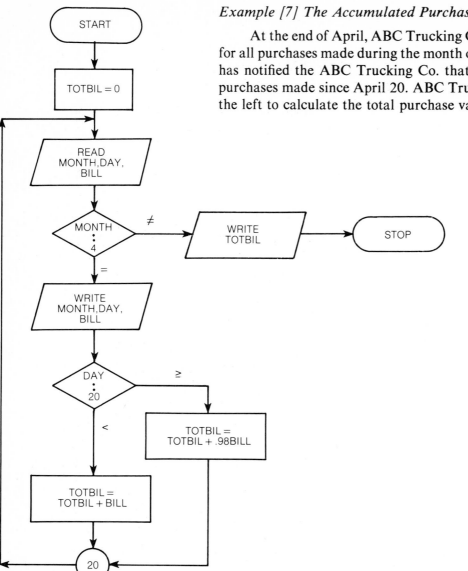

Example [7] The Accumulated Purchase Value

At the end of April, ABC Trucking Co. pays Ace Industrial Supplies for all purchases made during the month of April. Ace Industrial Supplies has notified the ABC Trucking Co. that it allows a 2% discount on all purchases made since April 20. ABC Trucking Co. uses the procedure at the left to calculate the total purchase value:

The flowchart is coded in FORTRAN as follows:

```
C   ***  THE ACCUMULATED PURCHASE VALUE
C   ***  FOLLOWING VARIABLE NAMES ARE USED
C   ***  DAY: DAY OF MONTH PURCHASE IS MADE
C   ***  BILL: AMOUNT OF INDIVIDUAL BILL
C   ***  TOTBIL: TOTAL MONTHLY BILL
         INTEGER DAY
         TOTBIL = 0
         WRITE(6,10)
   10    FORMAT(1H1,//,5X,'ABC TRUCKING CO.',//,
        *          5X,'MONTH/DATE',5X,'BILL',//)
   20    READ(5,30)MONTH, DAY, BILL
   30    FORMAT(I1,I2,F6.2)
         IF(MONTH.NE.4) GO TO 60
         WRITE(6,40) MONTH, DAY, BILL
   40    FORMAT(9X,I1,'/',I2,7X,F6.2)
C   ***  FIND OUT WHETHER A 2% IS APPLICABLE
         IF (DAY.GE.20) GO TO 50
         TOTBIL = TOTBIL + BILL
         GO TO 20
   50    TOTBIL = TOTBIL + 0.98*BILL
         GO TO 20
   60    WRITE(6,70)TOTBIL
   70    FORMAT(5X,'NET PURCHASE VALUE',F10.2)
         STOP
         END
```

The following data is processed:

```
4 7725.00
412 12.50
427120.00
415 75.00
425213.00
413145.60
420 70.50
5
```

Explanation of the FORTRAN program:

"DAY" is an integer variable name, as it is so declared in the first statement. The program contains two Logical IF statements, each followed by a GO TO statement. The first Logical IF statement checks whether the bill pertains to the month of April (MONTH.NE.4). If MONTH does not equal 4, then transfer is made to statement #60, the TOTBIL value is printed, and the program is terminated. Note that this Logical IF statement is used to provide a means for terminating the program if the last data card does not contain "4." If MONTH equals 4, then MONTH,DAY, and BILL is printed out.

The second Logical IF statement checks whether the value associated with "DAY" equals 20 or is larger than 20 (DAY.GE.20). If DAY$\geq$20, a 2% discount is given on the purchase price by transferring control to statement #50. If DAY is not $\geq$20, the next executable statement adds the purchase value (BILL) to the accumulated purchase value (TOTBIL).

The FORTRAN program generates the following output:

```
ABC  TRUCKING  CO.

MONTH/DATE        BILL


     4/ 7        725.00
     4/12         12.50
     4/27        120.00
     4/15         75.00
     4/25        213.00
     4/13        145.60
     4/20         70.50
NET  PURCHASE  VALUE     1353.53
```

Example [8] Measuring the Profitability of Investment in Assets

The ABC Company has established a minimum of 10% as the rate of return on investments. The ABC Company considers buying several pieces of equipment provided they yield at least a 10% rate of return. The following procedure is used to calculate the rate of return in order to come up with a listing of favorable investments.

1. Read in the name of the piece of equipment (this is done in Hollerith), its original cost (COST), its useful life (LIFE), the expected income it will yield during its life (INCOME).
2. Calculate the net income (NETINC)

$$NETINC = INCOME - COST$$

3. Calculate the average net income (AVGNET)

$$AVGNET = NETINC/LIFE$$

4. Calculate the average investment (AVGINV), under the assumption of straight line depreciation and no residual value.

$$AVGINV = COST/2$$

5. Find the average rate of return (RATERT)

$$RATERT = AVGNET/AVGINV$$

6. If the average rate of return is 10% or more, list the name of the equipment and other pertinent data.

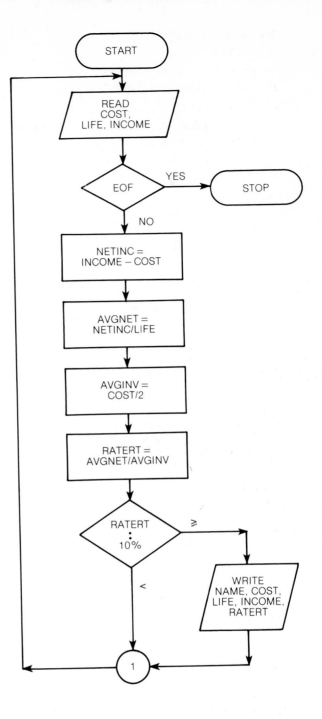

```
C   *** PROFITABILITY OF INVESTMENT IN ASSETS
C   *** COST: ORIGINAL COST OF EQUIPMENT
C   *** LIFE: USEFUL LIFE OF EQUIPMENT
C   *** INCOME: EXPECTED LIFETIME INCOME
C   *** NETINC: NET INCOME
C   *** AUGINV: AVERAGE INVESTMENT
C   *** AVGNET: AVERAGE NET INCOME
C   *** RATERT: AVERAGE RATE OF RETURN
        REAL LIFE, INCOME, NETINC
        WRITE(6,10)
   10 FORMAT(1H1,//,5X,'INVESTMENT PROFITABILITY',//,
      *      8X,'NAME',7X,'COST',4X,'LIFE',3X,'INCOME',
      *      3X,'RATE',/)
   20 READ(5,30,END=40) COST, LIFE, INCOME
   30 FORMAT(5X,'                    ',3X,F6.0,4X,F3.0,3X,
      *      F6.0,3X,F3.2)
C   *** CALCULATION OF THE AVERAGE RETURN ON INVESTMENT
        NETINC = INCOME - COST
        AVGNET = NETINC/LIFE
        AVGINV = COST/2.0
        RATERT = AVGNET/AVGINV
C   *** IS THE RATE OF RETURN 10% OR MORE?
        IF(RATERT.GE.0.10) WRITE(6,30) COST, LIFE,
      *                                INCOME, RATERT
        GO TO 20
   40 STOP
        END
```

The following data is processed:

```
      PRESS # 68    10000.    10.    30000.
      PRESS # 71    10000.     5.    15000.
      PRESS # 18    10000.     4.    11000.
```

The following printout is generated:

```
INVESTMENT PROFITABILITY

   NAME       COST    LIFE   INCOME    RATE

  PRESS # 68  10000.   10.   30000.    .40
  PRESS # 71  10000.    5.   15000.    .20
```

5. FORTRAN 77 Additional Control Statements

In order to increase the ability of the programmer to write understandable programs, FOR-TRAN 77 is provided with the IF-THEN-ELSE structure. FORTRAN 77 provides us with two types of structures; these are:

the IF-THEN structure

the IF-THEN-ELSE structure

We will analyze both of them.

The IF-THEN Structure

The IF-THEN structure allows the execution of one or more processing statements when the logical expression is true. It does not allow the execution of these processing statements when the logical expression is false. Its general structure is as follows:

```
IF(logical expression)THEN
    processing statements
END IF
```

This structure is illustrated by the following examples.
Reconsider the Payroll example [4] with the following FORTRAN statement:

```
IF(FEDTAX.LT.0.0)FEDTAX=0.0
```

Its equivalent IF-THEN structure is:

```
IF(FEDTAX.LT.0.0)THEN
    FEDTAX=0.0
END IF
```

Also, reconsider the calculation of gross pay as shown in example [6]. The FORTRAN statement:

```
IF(HOURS.GT.40.0)GROSS=(40.0+1.5*(HOURS-40.0))*RATE
```

is equivalent to the following FORTRAN 77 statement:

```
IF(HOURS.GT.40.0)THEN
    GROSS=(40.0+1.5*(HOURS-40.0))*RATE
END IF
```

The IF-THEN-ELSE Structure

The IF-THEN-ELSE structure allows for the execution of one set of processing statements when the logical expression is true and for another set of processing statements if the logical expression is false. Its general structure is as follows:

```
IF(logical expression)THEN
      processing statements
   ELSE
      processing statements
   END IF
```

To illustrate the IF-THEN-ELSE structure let us reconsider example [7], the Accumulated Purchase Value example. The following FORTRAN structure

```
   . . .
   IF(DAY.GE.20)GO TO 50
   TOTBIL=TOTBIL+BILL
   GO TO 20
50 TOTBIL=TOTBIL+0.98*BILL
   GO TO 20
   . . .
```

can be redone in FORTRAN 77 as follows:

```
   . . .
   IF(DAY.GE.20)THEN
      TOTBIL=TOTBIL+0.98*BILL
   ELSE
      TOTBIL=TOTBIL+BILL
   END IF
   GO TO 20
   . . .
```

Now we can use the IF-THEN-ELSE structure to rewrite the entire program of example [7] in a more structured way. It should be structured as follows (comment statements are left out):

```
IF level
              C  ***  STRUCTURED PROGRAM FOR EXAMPLE # 7
   0                 INTEGER DAY
   0                 TOTBIL = 0
   0                 WRITE(6,10)
   0            10   FORMAT(1H1,//,5X,'ABC TRUCKING CO.',//,
   0             *          5X,'MONTH/DATE',5X,'BILL',//)
   0            20   READ(5,30)MONTH, DAY, BILL
   0            30   FORMAT(I1,I2,F6.2)
   1                 IF(MONTH.NE.4) THEN
   1                    WRITE(6,70) TOTBIL
   1            70      FORMAT(5X,'NET PURCHASE VALUE',F10.2)
   1                    STOP
   1                 ELSE
   1                    WRITE(6,40) MONTH,DAY,BILL
   1            40      FORMAT(9X,I1,'/',I2,7X,F6.2)
   2                    IF(DAY.GE.20) THEN
   2                       TOTBIL = TOTBIL + 0.98*BILL
   2                    ELSE
   2                       TOTBIL = TOTBIL + BILL
   2                    END IF
   1                    GO TO 20
   1                 END IF
                     END
```

Note how much easier it is to read this FORTRAN 77 program as compared to the earlier presented FORTRAN program. The indentation clearly identifies the level of each block IF statements. The second level block IF statements are said to be **nested** block IF statements within the first block IF statements.

The IF-THEN-ELSE-IF Structure

When a decision must be made amongst three or more processing statements, then the IF-THEN-ELSE-IF structure can be used. Its general structure is as follows:

```
    IF(logical expression)THEN
         processing statements
      ELSE IF(logical expression)THEN
             processing statements
          ELSE IF(logical expression)THEN
                 processing statements
    END IF
    END IF
    END IF
```

Let us now illustrate the IF-THEN-ELSE-IF structure by considering the following partial flowchart:

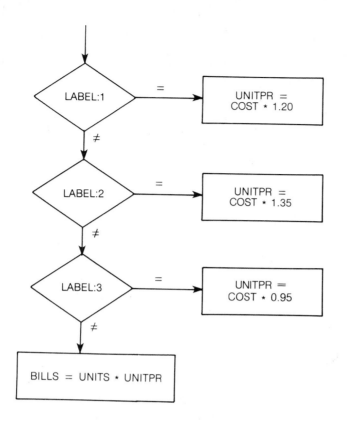

Its corresponding FORTRAN 77 statements are:

```
IF(LABEL.EQ.1)THEN
        UNITPR=COST*1.20
    ELSE IF(LABEL.EQ.2)THEN
            UNITPR=COST*1.35
        ELSE IF(LABEL.EQ.3)THEN
                UNITPR=COST*0.95
END IF
BILL=UNITS*UNITPR
```

6. Good Programming Style (continued)

We can now add to the rules as presented in chapter 6 to encourage good programming style.

Rule 8:

Avoid using the GO TO statement, since the GO TO statement is considered a manifestation of poor programming habits. FORTRAN 77 is a better vehicle to avoid GO TO statements. Therefore, if a FORTRAN 77 compiler is available, use the FORTRAN 77 control structures, rather than the FORTRAN 66 structures.

Rule 9:

Indent control structures (as shown in the FORTRAN 77 examples) in order to identify the various control levels and to make programs more readable.

Problem No. 1

Consider the following questions and give brief answers.

1. The statements used in FORTRAN that determine the sequence the statements will follow are known as:
   a) transfer statements
   b) specification statements
   c) input/output statements
   d) subprogram statements

2. If X=23., Y=4.6, A=2.6, what is the value of the following relational expression:

   X/Y+A.GT.8.0.OR.A−2.0.LE.1.0

   a) cannot be determined from information given
   b) cannot be determined
   c) true
   d) false
   e) none of the above but can be determined

   5 + 2.6

   7.6 > 8.0 or .6 less 1

3. Transfer statements in FORTRAN are used to:
   a) indicate to the compiler the next statement to be converted into machine language.
   b) control the input and output of data from the computer.
   c) tell the computer which instruction to execute next.
   d) tell the executive or monitor system which job should be executed next.
   e) none of above is true.

Problem No. 2

Draw a partial flowchart for the computation of the WAGES for the salesmen of the SELL-NOLESS COMPANY. Their commission is computed as follows:

1. If SALES is less than or equal to QUOTA, then WAGES equals BASE.
2. If SALES is greater than QUOTA, but less than or equal to CEIL, then WAGES is given by BASE plus RATE1 times the excess of SALES over QUOTA.
3. If SALES is greater than CEIL, then WAGES is given by BASE, plus RATE1 times the difference between CEIL and QUOTA, plus RATE2 times the excess of SALES over CEIL.

Problem No. 3

Draw a partial flowchart for the computation of TAX, based on the value of EARN (earnings), according to the following stipulations:

1. If earnings are less than $2,500.00, TAX equals zero (0).
2. If earnings are between $2,500.00 and 5,000.00, TAX equals 2 percent of the amount over $2,500.00.
3. If earnings are over $5,000.00, TAX equals $60.00 plus 5 percent of the amount of earnings over $5,000.00.

Problem No. 4

Indicate and correct all errors in the following statements:

a) IF(W.EQ.X)GO TO 5

b) IF(A.GE.B)FORMAT(3X,F5.2)

c) IF(K=J+M)GO TO 10

d) IF A.LT.B GO TO 15

e) IF(A.LT.B)WRITE(6,101)A

f) IF(A−35.)95,7,837

g) IF(A1−B1)32,99,15

h) IF(J−35.)3,2,1

i) IF(AJ−BJ)32,99,105

j) IF(LSD+POT−DOPE)−(KICKS))0,0,96

k) GO TO(17,14,4,3,1,77)ICODE

l) IF(TAX=.18*(GROSS−13*DEPENT))12,13,13

m) IF(NETPAY=0)GO TO 7

n) GO TO(17,13,14,18),CAP

o) IF(A.LT.B.OR.GT.C)D=E+F

p) IF(I.EQ.B)GO TO 7

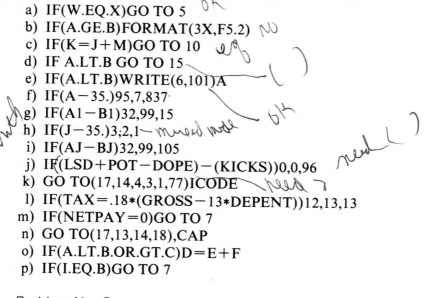

Problem No. 5

Given: J=5   L=2   B=3.0   D=6.7
         K=3   A=14.4   C=4.5

evaluate the following expressions:

a) (J.GT.K+L)

b) (.NOT.(A.GT.B*D).OR.J/L.LE.L)

c) (C−D.LT.C−B.AND.C/D.LT.C/B)

Problem No. 6

Complete the partial FORTRAN program below which reads in a single integer parameter INT and determines whether it is odd or even. Your program should transfer to statement 40 or 50 depending on the value read in for INT.

```
        READ(5,10) INT
     10 FORMAT(I5)
        / Insert     \
        | Necessary   |
        | FORTRAN     |
        \ Statements /
     40 WRITE(6,41) INT
     41 FORMAT('1','THE INTEGER',I5,'IS EVEN')
        STOP
     50 WRITE(6,51) INT
     51 FORMAT('1','THE INTEGER',I5,'IS ODD')
        STOP
        END
```

Problem No. 7

Write FORTRAN statements for the following:

a) If S=0, assign the larger of A or B to C, otherwise, set S=0.

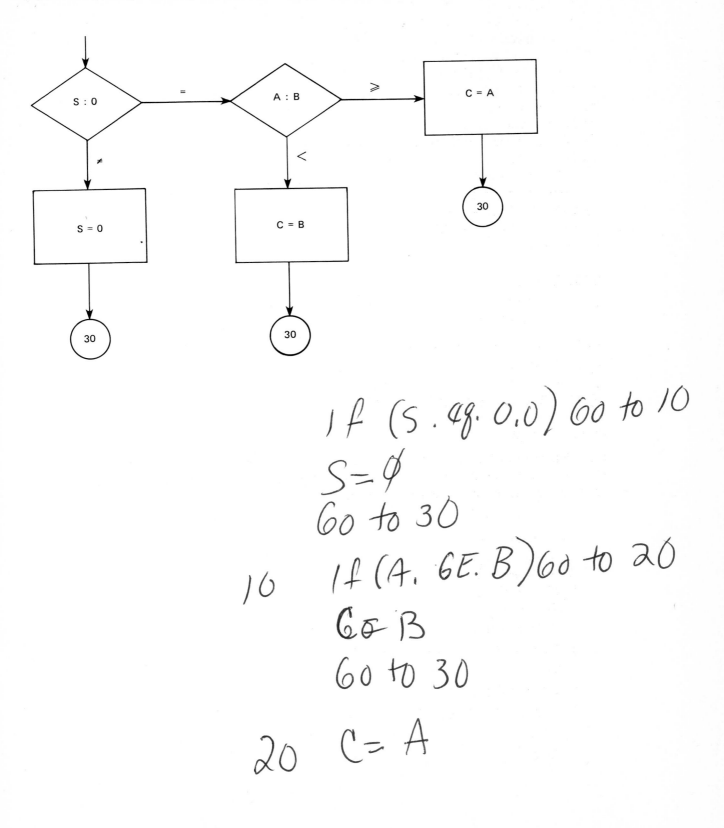

$$IF (S.EQ.0.0) \; GO \; to \; 10$$
$$S=\emptyset$$
$$GO \; to \; 30$$
$$10 \quad IF (A.GE.B) GO \; to \; 20$$
$$C=B$$
$$GO \; to \; 30$$
$$20 \quad C=A$$

b) If I lies between 1 and 8 inclusive, and if at the same time J also lies between 1 and 8 inclusive, set the contents of K equal to I+J; otherwise, proceed to statement 250.

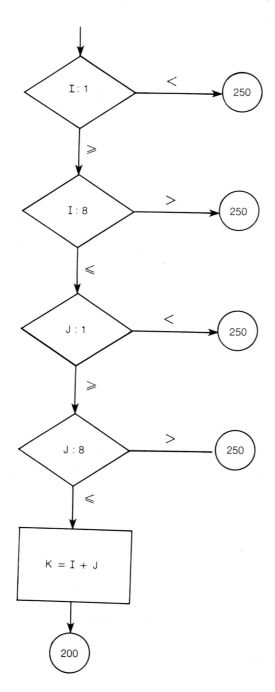

c)

If ICODE is less than or equal to 99 go to the logic for handling invalid code (statement 10);

If ICODE is between 100 and 199 go to the logic for handling straight line depreciation (statement 20);

If ICODE is between 200 and 299 set DEPR equal to zero (0);

If ICODE is 300 or greater go to the logic for handling invalid codes (statement 10).

d)

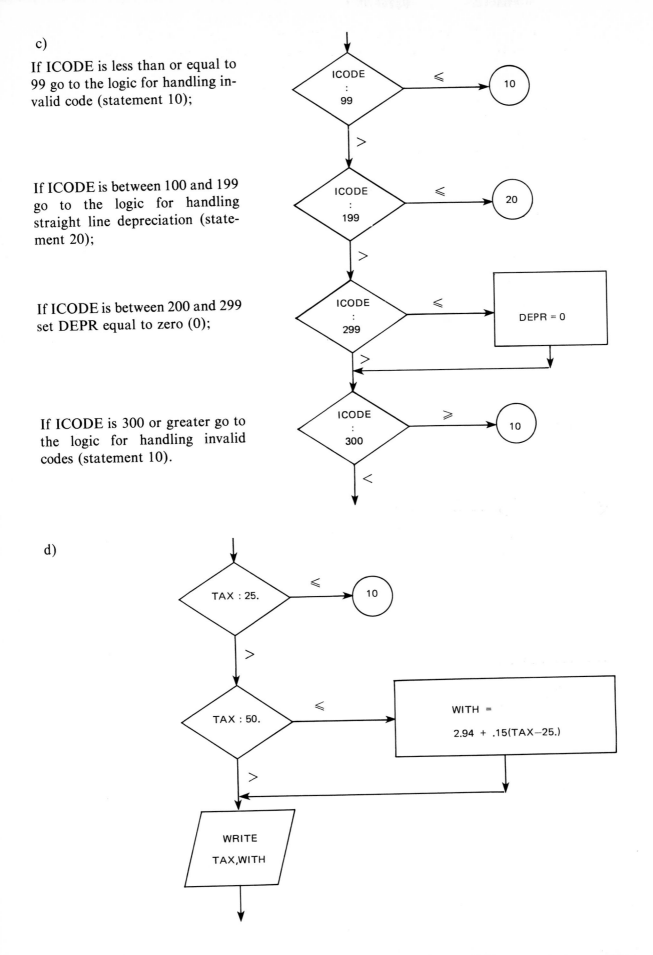

e)

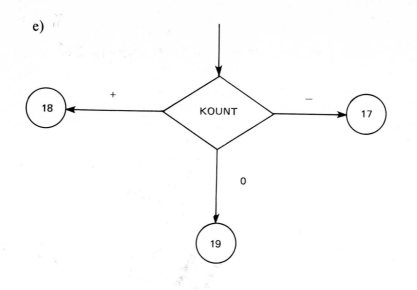

f) The Donotworry Company calculates the commission for their salesmen as follows:
   (1) The commission (COMMS) is $0, if gross (GROSS) sales are $5000 or less.
   (2) If the gross sales amount is greater than $5,000, but does not exceed $10,000, the commission is equal to 15% of the gross sales amount.
   (3) If the gross sales amount is greater than $10,000, the commission is $1,500 plus 20% of the amount by which the gross sales amount exceeds $10,000.

Problem No. 8

Run the program of example 6 with the data provided in the text.

Problem No. 9

Write a program for calculating the weekly pay for several employees, as explained in problem 1 of chapter 1.

Problem No. 10

Write a program for evaluating capital budgeting proposals, as explained in problem 2 of chapter 1.

Problem No. 11

Write a program for the flowchart in problem 3 of chapter 3 and run it with the given data.

Problem No. 12

Write a program for the flowchart in problem 4 of chapter 3 and run it with the given data.

Problem No. 13

Consider the following flowchart. Write its program and run it with the following data.

5				
1	7	2	3	0
2	7	4	5	0
0	5	3	2	4
3	9	2	7	4
1	2	3	4	5

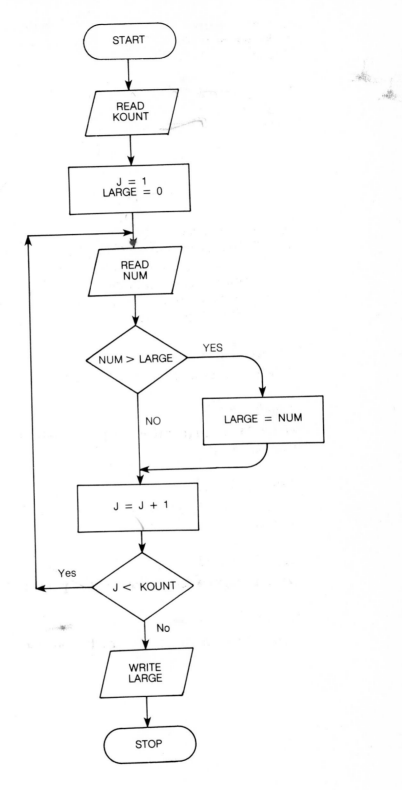

Problem No. 14

Consider the following flowchart. Write its FORTRAN program and test it with a prime and non-prime number. Your program will identify whether a number is prime or not.

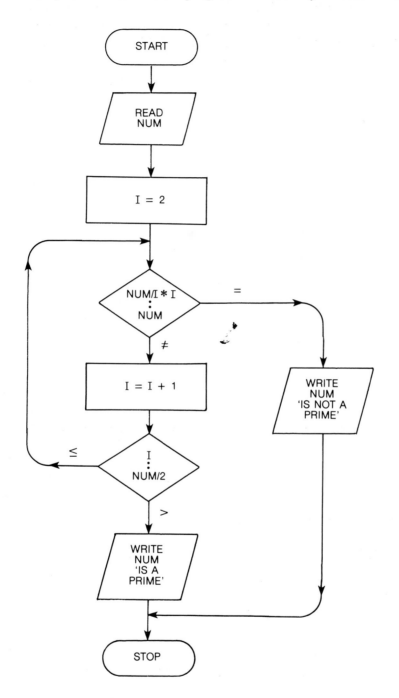

Problem No. 15

Write a complete FORTRAN program that will compute the difference in minutes between two times, both expressed in hours and minutes since midnight, such as 0145, 1130, or 2350, for 10 sets of times. You are guaranteed that the first time is earlier than the second time and that they are less than 24 hours apart. You are not guaranteed that they are in the same day: for instance, 2350 before midnight is earlier than 0200 after midnight of the same night. Each set of times is punched on a single card in the following format:

Columns	Description
60–61	Hours portion of the first time
62–63	Minutes portion of the first time
66–67	Hours portion of the second time
68–69	Minutes portion of the second time

For each set of times, print out the two times and the difference between them in minutes. Use the following data:

```
1012,  1412
1015,   200
1015,  1400
1206,  1403
 705,   603
1205,  2307
2400,  2305
1205,  0203
0505,  0403
1705,  0503
```

Problem No. 16

In the "Good Samaritan" hospital, a record of all blood donors of the village is kept on punched cards as follows:

ᵇAA...AAᵇXXᵇX

Where: AA...AA: name of donor (12 columns)

XX: age of donor

X: blood code, according to the following table:

X	TYPE
1	A
2	B
3	AB
4	O

An emergency occurs where an injured person needs to get AB blood.

You are supposed to draw a flowchart and write a program to read in donors' records and print out a listing of the names of all AB donors.

Problem No. 17

You are required to read values of x, perform certain checkings on x, and compute a value of y according to the following step function:

$$y = \begin{cases} 8.72 \text{ if } 0 < x \leqslant 10.9 \\ 16.19 \text{ if } 10.9 < x \leqslant 21.6 \\ 24.07 \text{ if } 21.6 < x \leqslant 50 \end{cases}$$

The values of x and y are then to be printed. If $x < 0$ or $x > 50$ you are to stop the processing. The last card in your data deck has a value of x greater than 50, which will terminate the processing. Draw the flowchart, write the FORTRAN program, and run it for the following x values:

14.03

37.05

9.03

15.07

51.02

Problem No. 18

We want to compute the roots of $AX^2 + BX + C = 0$; on a data card we have the values of A, B and C. If it turns out that the discriminant is negative, then we have to calculate the real and imaginary part, and label them on the output. Recall the following formulas:

$$DISCR = B^2 - 4AC \text{(discriminant)}$$

$$X1 = \frac{-B + \sqrt{DISCR}}{2A} \text{(first root if } DISCR \geq 0)$$

$$X2 = \frac{-B - \sqrt{DISCR}}{2A} \text{(second root if } DISCR \geq 0)$$

$$X1 = \frac{-B}{2A} \text{is real (if } DISCR < 0)$$

$$X2 = \frac{\sqrt{-D}}{2A} \text{ is imaginary (if } DISCR < 0)$$

Draw the flowchart, and write the FORTRAN IV program.

Problem No. 19

You are requested to read in ten sets of two numbers. Each set of two numbers represents a different bank. The first number reflects the bank's total deposits (in millions) as of January 1, 1975, and the second number represents the bank's total deposits (in millions) as of January 1, 1976. Prepare a flowchart and a FORTRAN program to output the following:

1. the average deposits as of January 1, 1975.
2. the average deposits as of January 1, 1976.
3. the range between the above two averages.
4. the average January 1, 1976, deposits of all banks that suffered a decline in total deposits during 1975.
5. the average January 1, 1976, deposits of all banks that incurred an increase in total deposits during 1975.
6. the number of banks that started off 1975 and 1976 with total deposits which exceeded $100 million.

DO Loop

In chapter 7, transfer statements were introduced as a means of developing simple loops whereby the computer was able to perform repetitive instructions. An alternate and much more effective means of looping may be accomplished through the use of the DO statement. The DO statement will instruct the computer to follow the same commands or perform the same calcuations over and over again, creating what is termed a DO loop.

1. The DO Loop

The DO statement is a control statement that allows one to set up a simple iterative loop in one statement. The general form of the DO statement is as follows:

DO n i=m_1,m_2,m_3

where:
- n: statement label which is the end of the range of the DO loop (terminal statement)
- m_1,m_2,m_3: unsigned integer constants, or nonsubscripted, unsigned integer variables (called parameters of the DO loop)
- i: is a nonsubscripted integer variable (called the index counter or DO variable)
- m_1: initial value; is ≥ 1
- m_2: test value (ending value), $m_1 \leq m_2$
- m_3: increment, $m_3 \geq 1$

The DO statement causes the repeated execution of all statements following the DO statement up to and including the statement labeled "n." The first time the statements are executed, "i" has the value m_1. Each succeeding time the statements are executed, "i" is increased by m_3. This repetition continues as long as "i" remains less than or equal to m_2. As soon as m_2 is exceeded, the cycle is completed and repetitions are halted with control passing to the next statement following "n." This next statement is then executed, and the value of "i" becomes unpredictable and no longer usable in the program. If the increment, m_3, is not specified, it is assumed to be equal to one. In this case, the general form of the DO statement is:

DO n i=m_1,m_2

The label n, marks the end of the range of the DO loop and must appear after the DO statement.

The five statements that are necessary to iterate a sequence of statements are built in the DO statement. These five statements are:

1. initialize a counter: $i = m_1$
2. execute the range or body of the DO loop
3. increment the counter: $i = i + m_3$ or $i = i + 1$
4. test the counter: if $i > m_2$ transfer control to the executable statement following statement n
5. define the ending statement in the LOOP: n

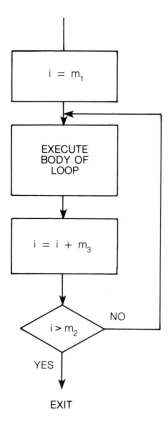

A simple formula can be used to determine the number of times a loop will be executed:

$$\text{loop count} = \text{integer part of} \left(\frac{m_2 - m_1}{m_3} + 1 \right)$$

Consider for example the following statement:

DO 10 I=3,72,6

The number of times this loop will be executed equals the integer part of $\left(\frac{72-3}{6} + 1 \right)$ or the integer part of (12.5) or 12 times.

There are two ways of representing a DO loop in a flowchart: one may use either the processing symbol, or the preparation symbol. The preparation symbol will be used throughout this textbook.

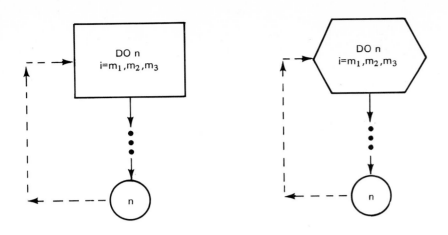

Example [1]

The following are three ways for evaluating the sum of the integers from 1 to 100.

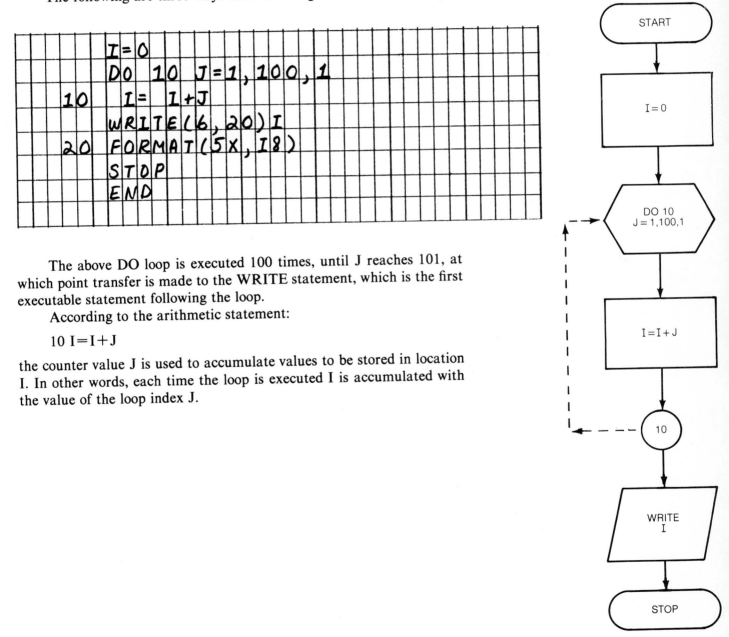

```
      I = 0
      DO 10 J = 1, 100, 1
10    I = I + J
      WRITE(6, 20) I
20    FORMAT(5X, I8)
      STOP
      END
```

The above DO loop is executed 100 times, until J reaches 101, at which point transfer is made to the **WRITE** statement, which is the first executable statement following the loop.

According to the arithmetic statement:

10 I = I + J

the counter value J is used to accumulate values to be stored in location I. In other words, each time the loop is executed I is accumulated with the value of the loop index J.

As in the previous program, this program executes the loop 100 times.

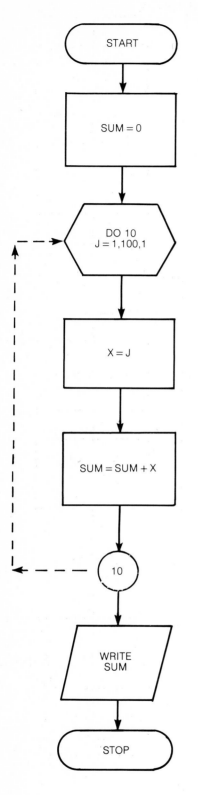

```
      SUM = 0
      DO 10 J=1,100,1
      X=J
10    SUM = SUM + X
      WRITE(6,20) SUM
20    FORMAT(5X,F9.0)
      STOP
      END
```

Here, the counter value J is assigned to a real variable X. This real variable X is then used in the real expression.

SUM+X,

whose value is assigned to the real variable SUM.

The WRITE statement, which is outside the range of the DO loop, writes out the real constant associated with the variable name SUM.

```
      SUM = 0
      X = 1
      DO 10 J=1,100,1
         SUM = SUM + X
10       X = X+1.
      WRITE(6,20)SUM
20    FORMAT(5X,F8.0)
      STOP
      END
```

Here, again, the loop is executed 100 times.

The counter of the DO loop, J, is not used in any of the statements within the DO loop. Instead, a counter, X, is initialized outside the DO loop and incremented within the DO loop to generate the 100 real numbers. These are the real numbers used in forming the SUM.

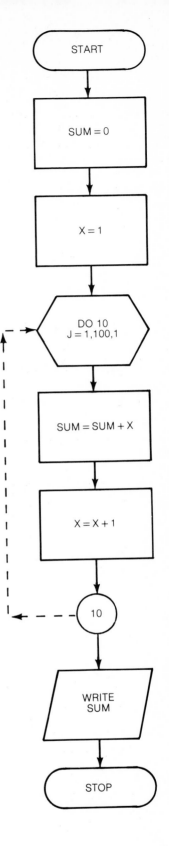

2. DO-Loop Rules

Rule 1
The first statement in the range of the DO loop must be an executable statement.

Rule 2
The last statement in the range of the DO loop must be an executable statement, but it cannot be a transfer of control statement: i.e., it cannot be

> any type of a GO TO statement
>
> Arithmetic IF statement
>
> RETURN (discussed later)
>
> STOP
>
> PAUSE
>
> DO
>
> Logical IF, containing any of the previous.

The CONTINUE statement is used as a terminal instruction to avoid conflict with rule 2. It is used when one of the transfer of control statements would otherwise occur in the last statement position. The CONTINUE statement is a dummy or "do nothing" statement that may be inserted into programs, as needed, without affecting their execution.

The use of a CONTINUE statement for all DO loops is good programming practice as it enables one to see the limits of a loop at a glance. Indentation of loop statements also adds to the readability of a program.

Rule 3
"i," "m_1," "m_2," and "m_3" must not be redefined within the range of the DO loop.

Example [2]

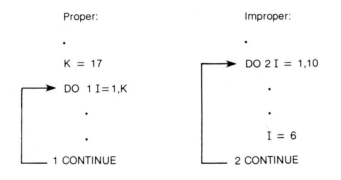

Note in the above example that the test value of the counter "I" can be defined in an arithmetic statement, "K=17," prior to the DO loop. However, it is not permissible to change the counter "I" in the range of the DO loop. Some programmers consider it good practice to define m_1, m_2, and m_3 prior to the loop. When the values of the variables m_1, m_2, and m_3 are likely to change in some future execution of the program, it is a good programming practice to read these values from a control card.

Rule 4

A transfer into the range of a DO loop is not permissible, unless it is to the DO itself.

A transfer out of the range of any DO loop is permissible, as long as the limit of the loop has not been reached. Some systems may allow this transfer to be followed by a transfer back into the DO loop.

Any departure from within the DO loop allows the control variable to be used outside the DO loop, with the value it had at the time of departure. However, the value of the index variable becomes unpredictable after the loop limit has been reached.

Example [3]

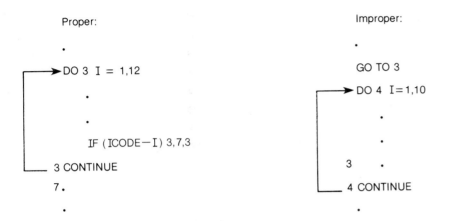

Proper:

```
    .
    .
  DO 3  I = 1,12
        .
        .
        IF (ICODE-I) 3,7,3
  3 CONTINUE
  7.
    .
    .
```

Improper:

```
      .
  GO TO 3
  DO 4  I=1,10
        .
        .
  3     .
  4 CONTINUE
      .
```

If "ICODE-I" equals ZERO "0," then control is transferred out of the range of the DO loop to the statement with label 7. The "GO TO 3" statement causes a transfer into a DO loop. This is not allowed, unless transfer was previously made out of that DO loop.

Rule 5

Indexing parameters (i, m_1, m_2, m_3) may be changed by statements outside the range of the DO loop (rule 3) only if no transfer is made back into the range of the DO loop that uses these parameters (rule 4).

Rule 6

A DO loop can be placed within the range of another DO loop, called nested loops, but all statements of the inner DO loop must be within the range of the outer DO loop.

Example [4]

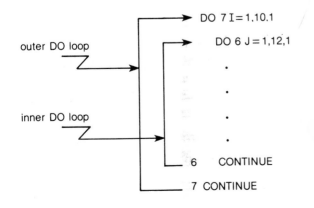

```
outer DO loop        DO 7 I=1,10.1
                     DO 6 J=1,12,1
                           .
inner DO loop              .
                           .
                           .
                    6    CONTINUE
                    7 CONTINUE
                           .
```

Here the inner DO loop is in the range of the outer DO loop, and the counters "I" and "J" are different, so that rules 3 and 5 are not violated.

Example [5]

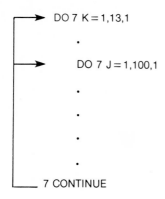

.

    DO 7 K = 1,13,1

        .

        DO 7 J = 1,100,1

          .

          .

          .

          .

    7 CONTINUE

It is quite proper that one statement is the terminal statement of several DO loops. However, this is not considered good programming practice as it does not allow one to see the limits of a particular loop.

Example [6]

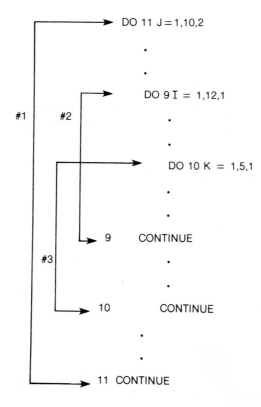

              DO 11 J = 1,10,2

                .

                .

              DO 9 I = 1,12,1

\#1   \#2

                DO 10 K = 1,5,1

        9   CONTINUE

\#3

        10   CONTINUE

        11 CONTINUE

This is not a proper construction of inner and outer DO loops since rule 6 is violated by the two inner DO loops \#2 and \#3.

Example [7]

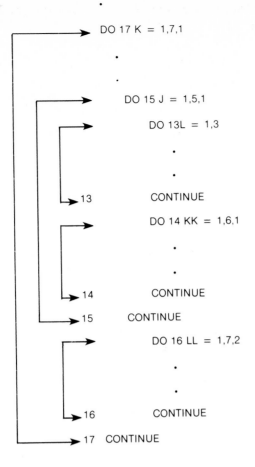

```
                    DO 17 K = 1,7,1

                        .

                    DO 15 J = 1,5,1
                        DO 13L = 1,3

                            .

                            .

             13     CONTINUE
                        DO 14 KK = 1,6,1

                            .

                            .

             14     CONTINUE
             15  CONTINUE
                        DO 16 LL = 1,7,2

                            .

                            .

             16         CONTINUE
             17  CONTINUE
```

This is a proper arrangement of nested DO loops.

Rule 7

Control must not be transferred into the range of an inner DO loop from its outer DO loop. However, it is permissible to transfer control from a statement within an inner DO loop to a statement within its outer DO loop.

Example [8]

The transfer (opposite) from the inner DO loop to the outer DO loop is correct.

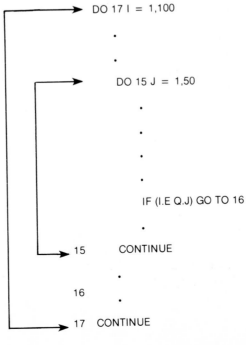

```
              DO 17 I = 1,100

                  .

              DO 15 J = 1,50

                  .

                  .

                  .

                  .

              IF (I.E Q.J) GO TO 16

                  .

        15    CONTINUE

              .

        16        .

        17    CONTINUE
```

Example [9]

The following transfer of Control to statement #18, however, is incorrect:

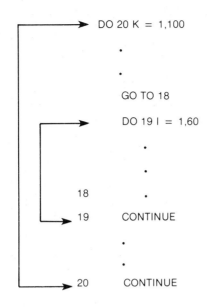

```
        DO 20 K = 1,100
              •
              •
        GO TO 18
        DO 19 I = 1,60
              •
              •
   18         •
   19   CONTINUE
              •
              •
   20   CONTINUE
```

3. Examples

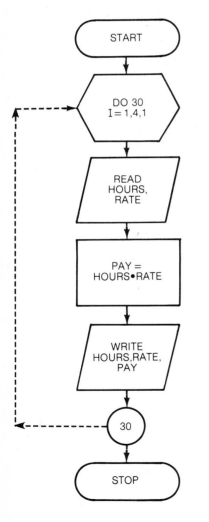

Example [10]

A DO loop can be used in example [1] of chapter 7 to generate the same output. If a DO loop is used, the flowchart is changed as shown:

```
C *** PAYROLL EXAMPLE
C *** FOLLOWING VARIABLE NAMES ARE USED
C *** HOURS: NUMBER OF HOURS WORKED
C *** RATE: HOURLY WAGE RATE
C *** PAY: AMOUNT PAID FOR HOURS WORKED
      WRITE(6,10)
   10 FORMAT(1H1,10X,'NAME',4X,'HRS',1X,
     *      'RT',1X,'INCOME',//)
C *** LOOP STRUCTURE TO CALCULATE THE PAYROLL
      DO 30 I=1,4
      READ(5,20) HOURS, RATE
   20 FORMAT(6X,'                    ',F3.0,F4.1,F7.2)
      PAY = HOURS * RATE
      WRITE(6,20) HOURS, RATE, PAY
   30 CONTINUE
      STOP
      END
```

The DO loop in example [9] is executed 4 times before the STOP statement is reached.

The counter "I" has a starting value of "1," gets incremented by "1," and has a test value of "4."

The first time the DO statement is reached, "I" is set equal to "1," and the statements of the DO loop are executed. When statement number "30" is executed, control is transferred to the DO statement, and "I" is incremented by one and therefore equals "2." As this "I" value does not exceed the test value, the DO loop is executed again. The DO loop is executed four times, until the counter value "I" exceeds the test value "4." Then control is transferred to the STOP statement in the program.

The same output is generated as in example [1] of chapter 7.

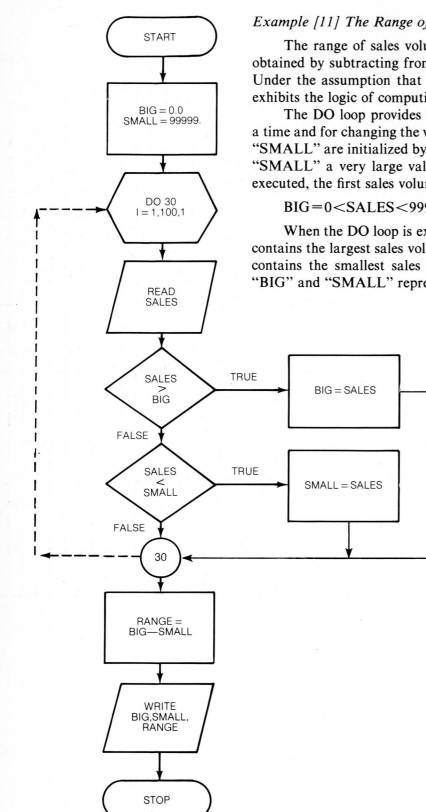

Example [11] The Range of Sales Volume

The range of sales volume is a measure of sales dispersion and is obtained by subtracting from the largest sales volume the smallest one. Under the assumption that one hundred sales are made, the flowchart exhibits the logic of computing the range of the sales volume.

The DO loop provides for reading in the 100 sales volumes one at a time and for changing the values of "SMALL" and "BIG." "BIG" and "SMALL" are initialized by giving "BIG" a very small value (zero) and "SMALL" a very large value (99999). The first time the DO loop is executed, the first sales volume is assigned to "BIG" and "SMALL":

$$BIG = 0 < SALES < 99999 = SMALL$$

When the DO loop is executed 100 times, the variable name "BIG" contains the largest sales volume, whereas the variable name "SMALL" contains the smallest sales volume. Therefore, the difference between "BIG" and "SMALL" represents the range of the sales volume.

The FORTRAN program for this flowchart is as follows:

```
C  ***  RANGE OF SALES VOLUME
C  ***  FOLLOWING VARIABLE NAMES ARE USED
C  ***  SALES: SALES VOLUME
C  ***  BIG: LARGEST SALES VOLUME
C  ***  SMALL: SMALLEST SALES VOLUME
C  ***  RANGE: DIFFERENCE BETWEEN BIG AND SMALL
   10  FORMAT(F7.2)
   20  FORMAT(1H1,//,5X,'RANGE OF SALES VOLUME,//,
      * 5X,'LARGEST SALES VOLUME=',F8.2,/,
      * 5X,'SMALLLEST SALES VOLUME=',F7.2,/,
      * 5X,'RANGE OF SALES VOLUME=',F7.2)
       BIG = 0.0
       SMALL = 99999
C  ***  ROUTINE TO FIND LARGEST AND SMALLEST
C  ***  SALES VOLUME
       DO 30 I=1,100,1
          READ(5,10)SALES
          IF(SALES.GT.BIG) BIG=SALES
          IF(SALES.LT.SMALL) SMALL = SALES
   30  CONTINUE
       RANGE = BIG - SMALL
       WRITE(6,20) BIG,SMALL,RANGE
       STOP
       END
```

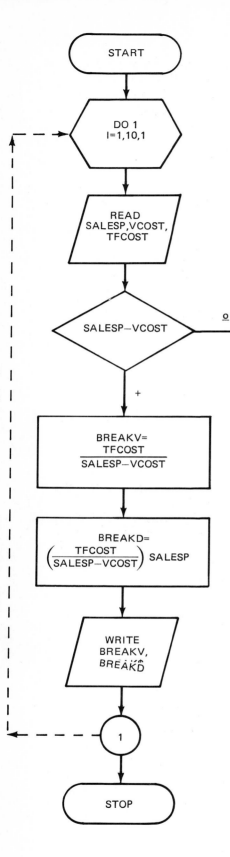

Example [12] The Break-even Analysis

The break-even point for a product (BREAK) is a function of the sales price (SALESP), the variable cost (VCOST), and the total fixed cost (TFCOST) of that product.

If the sales price is less than the total variable cost, a loss of profit will be indicated.

The break-even point can be calculated in sales volume or dollar value.

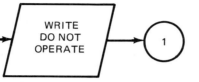

In sales volume, the break-even point is calculated as follows:

$$BREAKV = \frac{TFCOST}{SALESP - VCOST}$$

In dollar amount, the break-even point is calculated as follows:

$$BREAKD = \left(\frac{TFCOST}{SALESP - VCOST}\right) SALESP$$

The following procedure can be used to calculate the break-even point and to decide whether the operation is profitable.

1. Obtain information of product: sales price (SALESP), variable cost (VCOST), and total fixed cost (TFCOST).
2. If (SALESP−VCOST) is negative, do not operate.
3. If (SALESP−VCOST) is positive, operate.

$$BREAKV = \frac{TFCOST}{SALESP - VCOST}$$

$$BREAKD = \left(\frac{TFCOST}{SALESP - VCOST}\right) SALESP$$

4. Write out all appropriate information.

Using a DO loop to perform above procedure for ten different products, the flowchart represents the flow of operations.

Example [13] A Queueing Problem

A car wash has a single service line and a single waiting line (single line, single-station system). Arrivals at the car wash are considered to be Poisson distributed, with an arrival time of 10 minutes between one arrival and the next one. It takes an average of 3 minutes to wash a car. The probability that a car arriving at the car wash will have to wait equals the probability that the number of cars in the system is greater than zero. This probability is given by the following relation:

$$\frac{\text{Arrival Rate}}{\text{Service Rate}} = \frac{6/\text{hour}}{20/\text{hour}} = .3$$

The average number of cars waiting in line is given by the following relation:

$$\frac{(\text{Arrival Rate})^2}{\text{Service Rate (Service Rate} - \text{Arrival Rate})} = \frac{(6)^2}{20(20-6)} = .129$$

Note that a queue soon becomes saturated if the arrival rate is larger than the service rate.

The following procedure produces the above statistics for any queueing system.

Step 1. Obtain arrival rate (ARRIVL) and service rate (SERVCE).

Step 2. Compare arrival rate with service rate:
if ARRIVL≥SERVICE, then the queue is saturated
if ARRIVL<SERVICE, then proceed to the following steps:

Step 3. Calculate the probability that a car, arriving at the system has to wait.

$$PRWAIT = \frac{ARRIVL}{SERVCE}$$

Step 4. Calculate the average number of cars waiting in line as follows:

$$AVNBWT = \frac{(ARRIVL)^2}{SERVCE(SERVCE - ARRIVL)}$$

Step 5. Write out PRWAIT, AVNBWT or "the queue is saturated."

The flowchart represents the use of the DO loop in evaluating ten different queues.

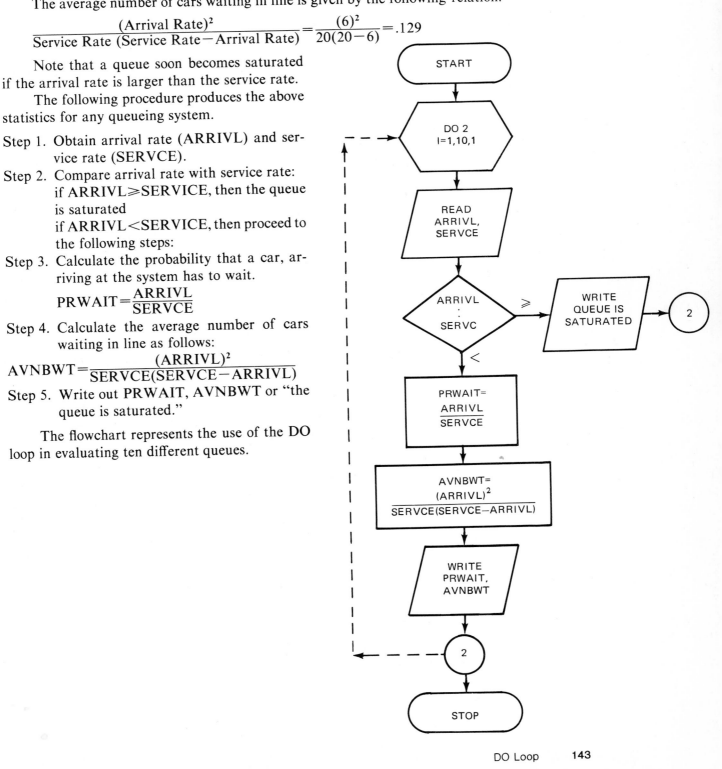

4. FORTRAN 77 Additional DO Loop Considerations

Four useful additions have been introduced by FORTRAN 77. These are briefly discussed here.

Addition #1:

An optional comma after the statement label in the DO statement is permitted, and the following two DO statements are equivalent:

    DO 10 I=1,10,2
    DO 10,I=1,10,2

Addition #2:

FORTRAN 77 permits the DO variable to be not only an integer variable, but also a real variable. In addition, it allows the initial-, test- and increment-value to be any integer or real arithmetic expression with either positive or negative values. Therefore, the FORTRAN 77 general form is:

    DO n, v=e1,e2,e3.
    where n: statement level, which is end of the range of the DO loop
         ,: optional comma
         v: Any real or integer variable name
        e1: arithmetic real or integer expression for initial value
        e2: arithmetic real or integer expression for test value
        e3: arithmetic real or integer expression for increment

In considering this extended formulation of the DO loop statement, the following statements are correct FORTRAN 77 DO statements.

    DO 10, A=B*C,1000.5,Q
    DO 20 C=B,D,R
    DO 30 L=10,1,−1

In either case, the number of times a DO loop is executed is defined by

$$\max [\text{Integer} ((m2-m1+m3)/m3),0]$$

For example the DO 30 L=10,1,−1 is executed max [Integer $((1-10-1)/-1)$, 0] or 10 times.

Addition #3:

FORTRAN 77 allows for a DO loop to be executed zero times, depending on the e_1, e_2 and e_3 values. The following DO loop is never executed:

    DO 30 K=5,2,2
      L=K
      M=K**2
    30 CONTINUE

This is also true for the following DO loop:

    DO 40 L=5,7,−1
      M=L**2
      N=2*L
    40 CONTINUE

Addition #4:

As with 1966 FORTRAN standards, FORTRAN 77 also does not allow for redefining the DO variable within the range of the DO loop. However, in FORTRAN 77, statements within the range of the DO loop may change the value of variables that appear in the expressions defining the increment and the terminal value. A change of these variables has no effect on the number of times a loop will be executed, because this is determined at the time the DO statement is executed.

Consider the following statements:

```
    M=10
    N=2
    DO 20 I=1,M+3,N/2
       L=M+7
       M=M+1
 20 CONTINUE
```

Using the above information, you can verify that the loop is executed 13 times (max [integer $((13-1+1)/1)]$, 0). After the loop has been executed 13 times the value of L equals 29 and the value of M equals 23.

5. Good Programming Style (continued)

The following four rules can now be added to the rules of good programming style:

Rule 10

It is good practice to end all DO loops with a CONTINUE statement.

Rule 11

Indent all statements within the range of the DO, except for the last CONTINUE statement. Indent all nested DO loops.

Rule 12

Comment statements before the DO statement helps explain the function of the loop.

Rule 13

It is good practice (whenever possible) to have the number of times a loop is executed as a variable in the program. It may be read from a control card at execution time. This makes the program more flexible.

Exercises

Problem No. 1

Answer each of the following questions briefly:

a) Can any of the index parameters in a DO statement be omitted? If so, which one or ones? *— yes, increment if one*

b) When a DO statement is executed normally, what statement is first executed after departure of the DO loop? *first ex after following do loop*

c) What is the mode of the index parameters? Must they be constants? *integers; variables or constants*

d) Can the DO index be incremented by fractional amounts? by negative amounts? *no*

Problem No. 2

Rewrite the following program by using an implicit transfer, rather than a Logical IF statement.

```
        SUM=0
        I=0
      2 READ(5,1)X
        IF(X)3,3,4
      4 SUM=SUM+X
      3 I=I+1
        IF(I.LT.20) GO TO 2
        WRITE(6,1) SUM
      1 FORMAT(F7.2)
        STOP
        END
```

(handwritten annotation:)
```
        Sum = 0
    2   Read(5, 1, End=100) X
        if (X) 2, 2, 4
    4   Sum = Sum + X
        Go to 2
  100   write(6, 1) sum
    1   Format (F7.2)
        Stop
        end
```

Draw up a flowchart for your rewritten program.

Problem No. 3

Rewrite the following program without the use of a DO loop.

```
        INTEGER COUNT
        COUNT=0
        DO 30 I=1,10
          DO 20 J=1,10
            DO 10 K=1,10
              COUNT=COUNT+I*J*K
     10     CONTINUE
     20   CONTINUE
     30 CONTINUE
        STOP
        END
```

(handwritten annotation:)
```
        Integer Count
        Count = 0
    1   I = I + 1
        If (I. Gt. 10) Stop
        J = 0
    2   J = J + 1
        If (J. Gt. 10) Go to 1
        K = 0
    3   K = K + 1
        If (K. Gt. 10) Go to 2
        Count = Count + I*J*K
        Go to 3
```

Problem No. 4

Peter Minuit, governor of the Dutch West India Company, is reputed to have purchased Manhattan Island from the Indians for $24 in 1626. Assume that the Indians invested their receipts at 6%, compounded annually, and write a FORTRAN program that would determine and print out the value of their investment at the end of the following years: 1676, 1726, 1776, 1826, 1926, and 1976. In your printout, identify the year associated with each investment value.

Problem No. 5

A sample of 200 people was taken to obtain income statistics. If there is one card per person, find the percentage of people sampled whose annual income is greater than $10,000, and calculate the overall average and the average income of the people whose income is above $10,000. Draw the flow diagram and write a complete program to accomplish this.

Problem No. 6

Write a FORTRAN program for the Queueing problem as exhibited in the flowchart of example #13.

Problem No. 7

Write a FORTRAN program for the Break-Even problem as exhibited in the flowchart of example #12.

Problem No. 8

Given the following data input:

1. Original cost of the investment (COST)
2. Salvage value of the investment (SALVGE)
3. Economic life of the investment (LIFE)
4. Number of years owned (NUMBER)
5. Accumulated depreciation (DEPREC)

Draw a flowchart and write a FORTRAN IV program to calculate the depreciation for the year, using sum-of-the-years-digits.

Recall that the depreciation value is given by

$$\left[\frac{LIFE - NUMBER}{\displaystyle\sum_{I=1}^{LIFE} I} \right] \quad [CAPIN]$$

Where CAPIN is the invested capital.

Problem No. 9

The input for processing the payroll of the ABC company consists of the following data items:

1. N: indicating the number of employees in the ABC company.
2. N sets of data for each employee consisting of:
   the employee's ID number (ID)
   the hourly pay rate (RATE), and
   five numbers, representing the number of hours that the employee worked each day of the previous week. (H1, H2, H3, H4, and H5).

Give the flowchart and a FORTRAN program that will:

1. Calculate the paycheck amount for each employee and output the ID, total hours (HOURS), pay rate and paycheck amount (PAY).
2. Calculate and output the total of the paychecks and the average hourly rate (AVRGE) paid to the employees (divide total pay by total hours).

Check your flowchart and program with the following data items:

```
3
2045, 2.25, 6, 8, 5, 3, 11
4678, 2.75, 8, 7, 4, 9, 5
3894, 3.75, 9, 5, 4, 10, 6
```

Problem No. 10

Process twenty sets of information. Each set contains three closing stock prices for companies A, B, and C. In this manner you are given the closing prices (per share) of the stock of three companies on twenty successive days. Give the flowchart and the FORTRAN program that will determine and output the following:

1. The number of times that Company A stock closed higher than that of either Company B or Company C.
2. The number of times that a buyer could have purchased one share of stock from each company for a total of less than $100.
3. The average price of Company B stock on the days that its stock was selling for less than Company A stock.

Problem No. 11

Calculate the checking service charge.

Give the flowchart and a FORTRAN program that calculates and prints the checking service charge and the final balance. Checking charges are calculated on the basis of the following specifics:

1. A charge of $.04 is made for each deposit.
2. A charge of $.05 is made for each withdrawal.
3. If the account becomes negative, a $3.00 charge occurs. This charge is assessed only once, regardless of the number of times the account becomes negative.
4. No charges are made if a minimum balance of $150 is maintained.
5. All checks are honored even if the balance is negative.

The input consists of: (1) one data card containing two numbers (N and B). N represents the number of transactions (deposits and checks) and B reflects the starting balance; (2) N data cards, each representing one value; if the value is positive it then represents a deposit; if the value is negative, however, it represents a withdrawal.

Problem No. 12

Consider the flowchart and the following data: 6, 7, −5, 4, 3, 4.5, 7. Process this data through the flowchart in the form of a procedure. Write a FORTRAN program and run it with the above data. Describe what the flowchart or program does.

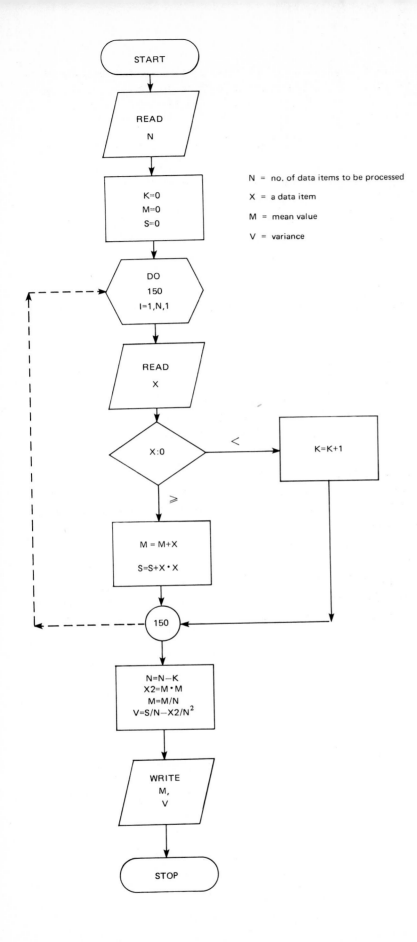

N = no. of data items to be processed

X = a data item

M = mean value

V = variance

Problem No. 13

You are asked to draw a flowchart and to write a FORTRAN program to generate a summary report for No Worry Finance Company. Your summary report should contain the following information:

1. Average balance of all accounts.
2. Average balance of all accounts which are past due for more than a month (at least 30 days).
3. Average number of days past due of all accounts.
4. Average number of days past due of all accounts with a current balance greater than $1,000.
5. Average number of days past due of all accounts with a current balance less than or equal to $1,000.
6. Number of past due accounts having a current balance greater than $1,000.
7. Number of past due accounts having a current balance less than $1,000.

Your data consists of N followed by N cards, where N denotes the number of account holders. Each of the N cards contains an account number, its current balance and the number of days that the account is past due.

Run your FORTRAN program with self-constructed data.

Problem No. 14

A major northwestern university accepts students into its MBA program based on their undergraduate grade-point average (GPA) and their quantitative (QUANT) and verbal (VERBAL) ATGSB scores.

To be accepted the student must satisfy one of the following conditions:

1. The sum of his two ATGSB scores must be greater than 1000 and his grade point average (GPA) must be greater than 3.5.
2. Each ATGSB score must be at least 600.
3. His grade point average must be at least 3.9.

For the following data draw a flowchart and write a FORTRAN program to generate a listing of all accepted students.

Name	ID	GPA	QUANT	VERBAL
Johnson, J.	1345	3.95	400	390
Adams, A.	1993	2.90	615	370
Dickson, I.	2234	3.40	480	560
Brown, C.	4566	2.50	650	700
Nelson, A.	3190	3.80	500	500

Problem No. 15

You are to write a program that processes checking account transactions. Each transaction is on a card, which contains a code C, in I1, followed by two blank columns, followed by a dollar amount A, in F6.2 (no decimal point appears on the card). The rest of the card is blank.

Before reading the cards, initialize the balance B to zero. Then read the cards, one at a time, and process them as follows:

1. If the code is 1 (i.e. C=1), the transaction is a deposit; add the amount to the balance, set the service charge to zero, and go to step 4.

2. If the code is 2, the transaction is a withdrawal (check); compute a service charge as follows:
   a. If the balance is $500.00 or more before the check is cashed, the service charge is zero.
   b. If the balance is less than $500.00 but more than $250.00, the service charge is 15¢.
   c. If the balance is $250.00 or less, the service charge is 25¢.
3. After computing the service charge, test to see if the check plus the service charge will clear; that is, make sure the balance, minus the amount, minus the service charge, is not negative. If the check is valid, update the balance and go to step 4. Otherwise, set the service charge to $4.00 and subtract it from the balance, but do not subtract the amount (i.e., don't cash the check) from the balance. Set the amount to zero and go to step 4.
4. Print, under the appropriate headers, the old balance (before the update), the code, amount, service charge, and the new balance. Then read another card and go to step 1.
5. If the code is any other digit besides 1 or 2, print "END OF JOB" and stop.

Your header line at the top of the page should be something like this:

OLD BALANCE CODE AMOUNT SERVICE CHARGE NEW BALANCE

Use of Subscripts

Subscripted variables are used when a list of similar data items must all be stored and remembered. It avoids the cumbersome creation of many unique names; instead, one variable name is used and each data item is identified by one or two subscripts as discussed in this chapter.

1. Single Subscripted Variables

The following are two examples of subscripted variables:

Example [1] The Inventory Example

Consider the mathematical notation for representing twenty sales items for a small store:

I_1 stands for the first item (PEAS),
I_2 stands for the second item (PIES),

.

.

.

I_{20} stands for the last item (MILK).

The mathematical representation of the unit price associated with each of the above items is:

P_1 stands for the price of the first item (PEAS),
P_2 stands for the price of the second item (PIES).

.

.

.

P_{20} stands for the price of the last item (MILK).

Business and science applications often use this type of shorthand to represent the elements listed above.

Example [2] The Statistical Example

In statistics, a random variable is a variable that can take on several values, called elements. The random variable is given a general name, say X. The elements of the random variable X are referred to by the use of subscripts, as follows:

X_1 is the first element,

X_2 is the second element,

X_3 is the third element,

.

.

.

X_n is the nth element.

So, if $X = $ 1,4,7,9,10,17,3   , then X is an array with:

$X_1 = 1$

$X_2 = 4$

$X_3 = 7$

$X_4 = 9$

$X_5 = 10$

$X_6 = 17$

$X_7 = 3$

FORTRAN Representation of Subscripts

The FORTRAN representation of subscripts is slightly different than the mathematical representation above. In FORTRAN we refer to the elements of an array by putting the subscript in parentheses, as follows:

Mathematical Notation	FORTRAN Notation	Meaning
X_1	X(1)	the first element in array X
X_n	X(N)	the nth element in array X
I_3	I(3)	the 3rd inventory item
I_k	I(K)	the Kth inventory item
P_{20}	P(20)	the price of the 20th inventory item

The subscript in the array must be an integer constant or a nonsubscripted integer variable name or an integer arithmetic expression that could contain the previous two. There are only seven acceptable subscript forms for arithmetic expressions. Let "v" refer to an unsigned, nonsubscripted integer variable (scalar), and "c" refer to an unsigned integer constant; then the seven forms are:

Form	Meaning	Example
v	one variable	A(I)
c	one constant	A(10)
v+c	one variable+one constant	A(I+10)
v−c	one variable−one constant	A(I−10)
c*v	one constant*one variable	A(3*I)
c*v+c′	one constant*one variable+one constant	A(3*I+10)
c*v−c′	one constant*one variable−one constant	A(3*I−10)

When variable names are used in subscripts or in arithmetic expressions of subscripts, they must be defined before the subscripted variable name is encountered in the program.

An array can be either integer or real, depending on the first letter of the name of the array. As arrays are subscripted variable names, the same rules of variable names (scalars) apply to the subscripted variable names. Integer subscripted variable names store integer constants, whereas real subscripted variable names store real constants. A zero (0) or negative subscript is not allowed.

The DIMENSION Statement

Information of the following kind must be supplied to the FORTRAN compiler when using subscripted variables in a program.

1. Which variables are subscripted?
2. How many subscripts are there for each subscripted variable?
3. What is the maximum size of each subscript?

This information can be given to the computer in a DIMENSION statement, which has the following general form:

DIMENSION v,v,v

where: v: stands for variable names followed by parentheses, enclosing up to seven integer constants, giving the maximum size of each subscript.

The appropriate DIMENSION statement for the Small Store Inventory example [1] is:

DIMENSION I(20), P(20)

When FORTRAN processes the above DIMENSION statement, it will set aside twenty (20) storage locations for the one-dimensional integer array I and twenty (20) storage locations for the one-dimensional real array P.

The INTEGER and REAL type declaration statements can be used to declare modes and dimensions for variable names as follows:

INTEGER X(7)

During the compilation of the above statement, seven (7) storage locations for the one-dimensional integer array X are set aside. For this case, notice that the DIMENSION statement is not necessary and should not be used. Conversely, if a DIMENSION statement is set up for a variable, that variable cannot be declared INTEGER or REAL in a separate statement.

Input/Output Statements Using Arrays

There are many ways to read in or write out the elements of a single subscripted variable name. Three of them are discussed here.

1. The DO Loop Technique

A DO loop can be used to read in or to write out the elements of an array one at a time. The seven elements of the random variable X= 1,4,7,9,10,17,3 in example [2] can be read in as follows:

```
      INTEGER X(7)
      DO 1 J=1,7
         READ (5,2) X(J)
    1 CONTINUE
    2 FORMAT (I3)
```

According to the INTEGER dimension statement, an integer array X is used that specifies a maximum of 7 memory locations. Since X is declared to be an integer variable, integer values will be stored in the seven (7) storage locations provided for X. The X(J) in the READ statement refers to the Jth location in the integer array X. The index of the DO statement defines that subscript. The first time the DO loop is executed J equals 1; the integer value 1 is assigned to the subscript J in X(J) and the READ statement reads in the first element and assigns it to the first storage location of the array X; and so on.

Because the DO loop is executed seven (7) times, the READ statement is also executed seven (7) times. Therefore, seven data cards, each containing one integer value for the array X, must be prepared according to the FORMAT specification of the statement that is labeled number two (2). The DO loop and the READ statement are equivalent to the following seven (7) statements:

```
READ(5,2)X(1)
READ(5,2)X(2)
READ(5,2)X(3)
READ(5,2)X(4)
READ(5,2)X(5)
READ(5,2)X(6)
READ(5,2)X(7)
```

2. The Implied DO-Loop Technique

The above partial program can be rewritten as follows:

```
      INTEGER X(7)
      READ(5,2)(X(J),J=1,7)
    2 FORMAT(7I3)
      .
      .
      .
```

Here, one statement is used to read all seven elements from one card according to the "7I3" specification in the FORMAT statement. The implied DO loop is $(X(J),J=1,7)$. Note that since the READ instruction itself is not being reexecuted by the implied DO loop, the above READ statement is equivalent to:

```
READ(5,2)X(1),X(2),X(3),X(4),X(5),X(6),X(7)
```

According to the FORMAT specifications, only one data card must be constructed as follows:

⌐bb1bb4bb7bb9b10b17bb3

Consider, however, the following set of statements:

```
      INTEGER X(7)
      READ(5,2)(X(J),J=1,7)
    2 FORMAT (4I3)
      .
      .
      .
```

Again an implied DO loop $(X(J),J=1,7)$ is used to read in all seven (7) elements of the array X. However, according to the FORMAT specification a maximum of four integer values are taken and read from one single card. Therefore, two data cards must now be prepared as follows (see chapter 4, rule 6):

Card #1 ⌐bb1bb4bb7bb9

Card #2 ⌐b10b17bb3

Therefore, when an implied DO loop is used in a READ statement, the FORMAT specifications will dictate the number of data values that must be keypunched on each data card.

An implied DO loop can also be used to simultaneously read in two (2) arrays as illustrated:

```
    DIMENSION I(20), P(20)
    READ(5,2)(I(J),P(J),J=1,20)
  2 FORMAT(A4,5X,F5.2)
        .

        .

        .
```

The DIMENSION statement specifies two arrays. The array I is an alphabetic inventory array, in which a maximum of twenty (20) alphanumeric strings can be stored. The second array, P, is the unit price array, that can contain a maximum of twenty (20) real price values. The above READ statement is equivalent to:

READ(5,2)I(1),P(1),I(2),P(2),....,I(20),P(20)

According to the FORMAT specifications, twenty (20) data cards must be prepared, each containing an inventory item (I) and its associated per unit price (P), as follows:

1st card	PEAS^{bbbbbbb}.59
2nd card	PIES^{bbbbbbb}.79
	.
	.
	.
last card	MILK^{bbbbbb}1.19

3. The Array READ/WRITE Technique

The array read statement is similar to the implied DO loop technique as illustrated:

```
    INTEGER X(7)
    READ(5,2)X
  2 FORMAT(7I3)
        .

        .

        .
```

Since the INTEGER declaration statement specifies that there is a maximum of seven elements that need to be stored under the variable name X, seven storage allocations are made during the compilation of the above program segment. During the execution of the array READ statement, all seven (7) elements are read in, according to the specifications in the FORMAT statement that is labeled 2 (seven elements from one card). Therefore the READ(5,2)X is equivalent to:

READ(5,2)X(1),X(2),X(3),X(4),X(5),X(6),X(7)

The array READ technique cannot be used when only some elements of the array are to be read, say, for example, the first five (5) elements. In this case a DO loop technique must be used, as follows:

```
    INTEGER X(7)
    READ(5,2)(X(J),J=1,5)
  2 FORMAT(7I3)
        .

        .

        .
```

Even though seven (7) elements are specified in the INTEGER dimension statement, only five (5) elements will be read, according to the list, (X(J),J=1,5), of the READ statement. All five elements are read from one data card. Another alternative is the explicit loop structure:

```
INTEGER X(7)
DO 1 J=1,5
    READ(5,2)X(J)
1 CONTINUE
2 FORMAT(I3)
```

Now, since the READ statement is executed five (5) times, five data cards must be prepared to read the first five elements of the array.

The preceding described techniques—the DO loop technique, the implied DO loop technique, and the array READ technique—can also be used to write out the values which have been assigned to array elements.

Examples of One-Dimensional Array Manipulations

Example [3] Generating Market Statistics

Consider the following estimated distribution of stainless plates in net tons by states.

ALA	173	MD	255	OREGON	152
ARIZ	33	MASS	852	PENNA	1817
ARK	32	MICH	1170	R I	103
CALIF	1418	MINN	233	S C	76
COLO	86	MISS	106	S D	11
CONN	714	MO	373	TENN	265
DEL	55	MONT	12	TEXAS	522
FLA	146	NEB	49	UTAH	59
GA	150	NEV	8	VT	15
IDAHO	14	N H	67	VA	196
ILL	1844	N J	926	WASH	217
IND	660	N M	16	W VA	71
IOWA	191	N Y	1687	WISC	816
KANSAS	118	N C	152	WYO	8
KY	227	N D	7	D C	8
LA	133	OHIO	1868		
MAINE	55	OKLA	150		

The following program generates the following statistics:

```
SUM
MEAN
VARIANCE
RANGE
```

The SUM reflects the total estimated production in net tons of stainless plates in the United States.

The MEAN is the average estimated production in net tons of stainless plates for the above forty-eight states and the District of Columbia.

The VARIANCE gives the discrepancy of the estimated production over these forty-eight states and the District of Columbia and is equal to the sum of the squared difference between the observed production and mean production, divided by the number of observations (49).

The RANGE is the difference between the largest (BIG) and the smallest observation (SMALL).

The procedure for calculating these statistics is outlined in the flowchart, where PROD-UCT is the observed production for the different states.

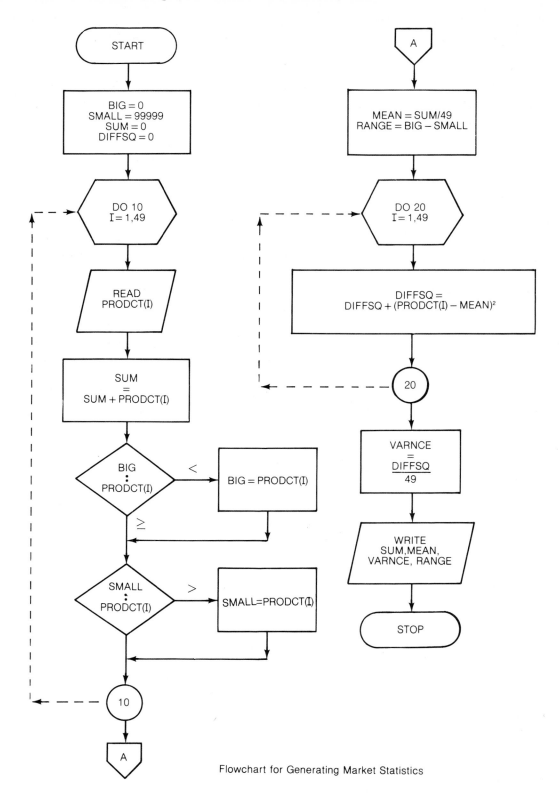

Flowchart for Generating Market Statistics

The first processing block contains four assignments:

1. BIG=0

BIG is the variable name used to store the largest production volume. This variable is initialized to zero (0) and gets reassigned in the first loop as production volumes are evaluated.

2. SMALL=99999

SMALL is a variable name used to store the smallest production volume. This variable is initialized to a very large value, 99999, and gets reassigned in the first loop as production volumes are evaluated.

3. SUM=0
4. DIFFSQ=0

SUM is the variable name used to store the total estimated production and DIFFSQ is the variable name used to store the total of the square differences between the mean production volume and the actual production volumes.

The first loop (DO 10 I=1,49) calculates the total estimated production volume and defines the largest (BIG) and smallest (SMALL) production volume as it reads and stores all production volumes one at a time.

The mean, MEAN, is calculated by dividing the total estimated production volume by forty-nine (49), whereas the range, RANGE, is defined by subtracting the smallest production volume (SMALL) from the largest production volume (LARGE).

The second loop calculates the sum of the squares differences between each production volume and the mean, DIFFSQ. The variance, VARNCE, is obtained by dividing DIFFSQ by forty-nine (49).

Note that it is necessary to remember all production volumes, as this data is used in both the first and second loop to calculate the mean and the variance respectively.

The corresponding FORTRAN program is as follows:

```fortran
C *** GENERATING MARKET STATISTICS
      DIMENSION PRODCT(50)
      REAL MEAN
C *** INITIALIZING VARIABLES
      BIG = 0
      SMALL = 99999
      SUM = 0
      DIFFSQ = 0
C *** ROUTINE FOR SUMMING AND DEFINING LARGEST
C *** AND SMALLEST VOLUME
      DO 10 I=1,49
         READ(5,30) PRODCT(I)
         SUM = SUM + PRODCT(I)
         IF(BIG.LT.PRODCT(I)) BIG=PRODCT(I)
         IF(SMALL.GT.PRODCT(I)) SMALL =PRODCT(I)
   10 CONTINUE
C *** CALCULATION OF AVERAGE AND RANGE OF VOLUME
      MEAN = SUM/49.0
      RANGE = BIG-SMALL
C *** CALCULATION OF THE VARIANCE
      DO 20 I=1,49
         DIFFSQ = DIFFSQ + (PRODCT(I)-MEAN)**2
   20 CONTINUE
      VARNCE = DIFFSQ/49.0
      WRITE(6,40) SUM, MEAN, VARNCE, RANGE
   30 FORMAT(F4.0)
   40 FORMAT(1H1,///,5X,'MARKET STATISTICS',//,
     5X,'TOTAL=',F12.2,/,
     5X,'AVERAGE=',F10.2,/,
     5X,'VARIANCE=',F9.2,/,
     5X,'RANGE=',F12.2)
      STOP
      END
```

The previous description and the comment statements fully explain the FORTRAN program. Notice, however, that when the FORTRAN compiler processes the DIMENSION statement, it will set aside fifty (50) storage locations for the one dimensional array PRODCT, even though only forty-nine (49) values get stored under that variable name.

The OUTPUT is:

```
MARKET STATISTICS

TOTAL=      18316.00
AVERAGE=      373.80
VARIANCE=281092.06
RANGE=       1861.00
```

Example [4] The Mail Order Example

The following list represents the inventory code and unit price of ten inventory items which Mr. Lucky sells by mail order.

Inventory Code (ICODE)	Unit Price (UPRICE)
AP1	12.50
AP2	7.75
LC3	112.50
LD7	13.00
AP4	5.50
DUM	1.50
TET	30.45
FED	0.75
POT	14.20
SMO	9.99

Orders are received by mail and a computer is used to bill all customers. The simplified billing procedure is as follows:

STEP 1: the inventory list (inventory code and unit price) is read into memory and stored.

STEP 2: the customer's order is keypunched and read to be processed. The customer's order contains:

Name (12 columns): NAME
Address (24 columns): ADDR
Name of product ordered (3 columns): IPRDCT
Quantity ordered (10 columns): QUANT
Discount per unit (5 columns): DISC

STEP 3: each customer's order is processed as follows:

a) unit price is looked up by equating the ordered product (IPRDCT) to the inventory code (ICODE);

b) total price (TPRICE) is calculated by multiplying the ordered quantity (QUANT) with the unit price (UPRICE);

c) total discount (TDSCT) is calculated;

d) net bill is calculated (BILL).

STEP 4: Output: name, address, product code, quantity, unit price, total price, total discount, and bill.

The following flowchart represents the above four steps:

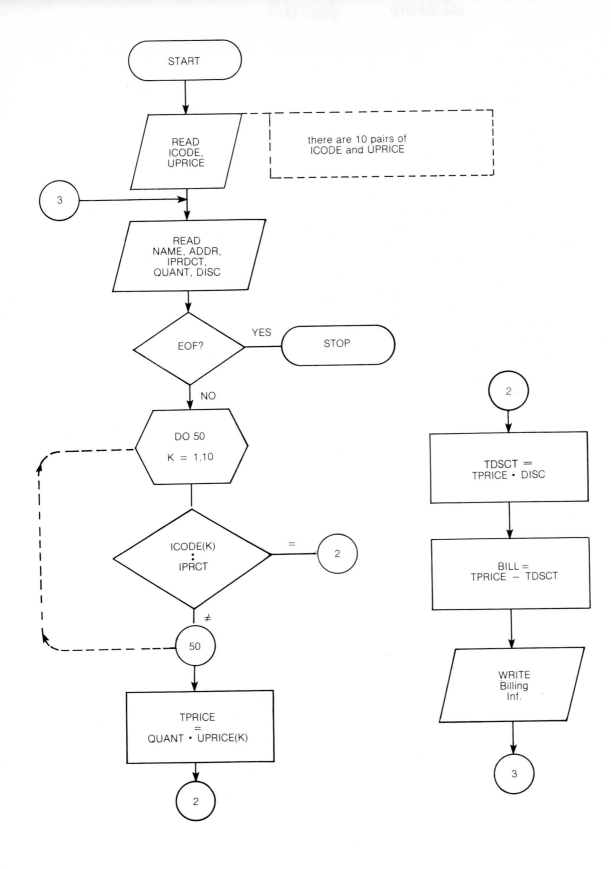

The preceding flowchart is translated in the following FORTRAN program.

```
C ***   THE MAIL ORDER EXAMPLE
        DIMENSION ICODE(10),UPRICE(10),NAME(3),
       *          ADDR(6)
        WRITE(6,10)
10      FORMAT(1H1)
C ***   READ INVENTORY CODE/UNIT PRICE AND ORDER
        READ(5,20)(ICODE(I),UPRICE(I),I=1,10)
20      FORMAT(A3,F10.2)
30      READ(5,40,END=80)(NAME(I),I=1,3),(ADDR(I),
       *          I=1,6),IPRDCT,QUANT,DISC
40      FORMAT(3A4,6A4,/,A3,F10.2,F5.3)
C ***   DEFINE THE UNIT PRICE
        DO 50 K=1,10
           IF(ICODE(K).EQ.IPRDCT) GO TO 60
50      CONTINUE
C ***   CALCULATE GROSS BILL,DISCOUNT,NET BILL
60      TPRICE = QUANT*UPRICE(K)
        TDSCT = TPRICE * DISC
        BILL = TPRICE - TDSCT
C ***   WRITE OUT BILLING INFORMATION
        WRITE(6,70)(NAME(I),I=1,3),(ADDR(I),I=1,6),
       *          IPRDCT,QUANT,UPRICE(K),TPRICE,
       *          TDSCT,BILL
70      FORMAT(5X,3A4,/,
       *       5X,6A4,//,
       *       5X,'PRODUCT CODE',3X,A3,/,
       *       5X,'QUANTITY',7X,F10.2,/,
       *       5X,'UNIT PRICE',5X,F10.2,/,
       *       5X,'TOTAL PRICE',4X,F10.2,/,
       *       5X,'TOTAL DISCOUNT',1X,F10.2,/,
       *       5X,'TOTAL BILL',5X,F10.2)
        GO TO 30
80      STOP
        END
```

Let us assume that the following DATA needs to be processed.

card	contents
card #1	AP1 12.50
card #2	AP2 7.75
card #3	LC3 112.50
card #4	LD7 13.00
card #5	AP4 5.50
card #6	DUM 1.50
card #7	TET 30.45
card #8	FED .75
card #9	POT 14.20
card #10	SMO 9.99
card #11	ADAM SMITH 12 RANCH RD, TOLEDO OHIO
card #12	LD7 19.50 .035

The **DIMENSION** statement defines four (4) single subscripted variables (ICODE, UPRICE, NAME, ADDR). During compilation ten (10) storage locations are set aside for ICODE and for UPRICE, whereas three (3) and six (6) storages are allocated to NAME and ADDR respectively.

The first READ statement:

READ(5,20)(ICODE(I),UPRICE(I),I=1,10)

inputs information from ten (10) data cards according to FORMAT statement labeled #20. It stores ten alphanumeric inventory codes (in the locations for the ICODE array) and their corresponding unit prices (in the locations for the UPRICE array) as follows:

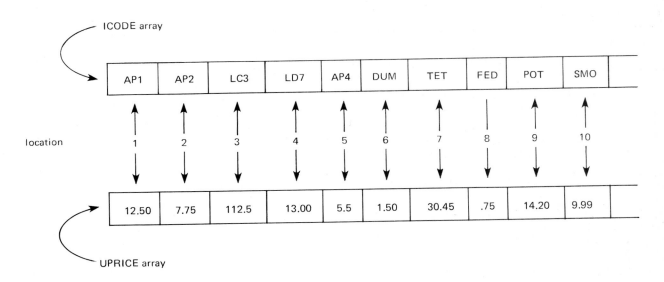

Notice how the information in both arrays match up:

the first (1st) inventory code, ICODE(1), is stored in the first (1st) location of the ICODE array and its corresponding unit price, UPRICE(1), is stored in the first (1st) location of the UPRICE array;

the second (2nd) inventory code, ICODE(2), is stored in the second (2nd) location of the ICODE array and its corresponding unit price, UPRICE(2), is stored in the second (2nd) location of the UPRICE array;

and so on. . . .

According to the FORMAT statement labeled 40, the second READ statement reads in the customer's name (NAME) and his address (ADDR) from one card and the inventory identification (IPRDCT), quantity ordered (QUANT), and the per unit discount (DISC) from a second card. Since the customer's name and address consist of more than four alphanumeric characters each, subscripted variables are used to store the complete name and address string as follows:

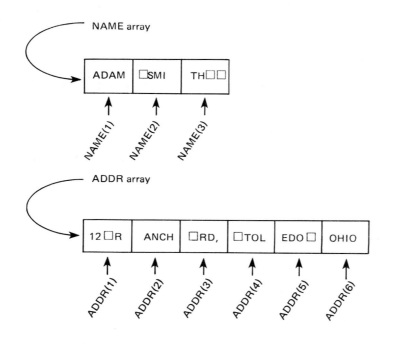

The first DO loop compares each element of the ICODE array with the content of IPRCT. When a match is found between the Kth element of the ICODE array and IPRCT, the unit price can be found in location K of the UPRICE array. Transfer is then made to the assignment statement labeled 60 to calculate the total price, TPRICE. The remainder of the program is self-explanatory.

The following output is generated by this program.

```
ADAM SMITH
12 RANCH RD, TOLEDO OHIO

PRODUCT CODE    LD7
QUANTITY              19,50
UNIT PRICE            13,00
TOTAL PRICE          253,50
TOTAL DISCOUNT         8,87
TOTAL BILL           244,63
```

2. Double Subscripted Variables

Two-dimensional tables or arrays are also permitted in FORTRAN. The following is a typical example of a two-dimensional array in mathematical notation.

Example [5] The Inventory Example with Price Breaks

Consider the mathematical notation for representing the the twenty sales items for a small store, similar to Example [1]

I_1 stands for the first item (PEAS),
I_2 stands for the second item (PIES),
.
.
.
I_{20} stands for the last item (MILK).

The following shows how three price values may be listed for each of the above inventory items: if the quantity ordered is less than or equal to three (3) units then the first price value applies; if the quantity ordered is larger than three (3) units but less than or equal to ten (10) units then there is a price break equal to the second price value for these additional units; and finally, if more than ten (10) units are ordered another price break applies to each additional unit larger than ten (10).

$P_{1,1}$, $P_{1,2}$ and $P_{1,3}$ stands for the three prices of the first item (PEAS)
$P_{2,1}$, $P_{2,2}$ and $P_{2,3}$ stands for the three prices of the second item (PIES)
.
.
.
$P_{20,1}$, $P_{20,2}$ and $P_{20,3}$ stands for the three prices of the 20th item (MILK)

The aforementioned price data can be represented in the following matrix:

$P_{1,1}$ $\quad$ $P_{1,2}$ $\quad$ $P_{1,3}$
$P_{2,1}$ $\quad$ $P_{2,2}$ $\quad$ $P_{2,3}$
$P_{3,1}$ $\quad$ $P_{3,2}$ $\quad$ $P_{3,3}$
.
.
.
.
$P_{20,1}$ $\quad$ $P_{20,2}$ $\quad$ $P_{20,3}$

A two-dimensional array has a column and a row arrangement. In the above example the columns and the rows are as follows:

	Column 1	Column 2	Column 3
Row 1→	$P_{1,1}$	$P_{1,2}$	$P_{1,3}$
Row 2→	$P_{2,1}$	$P_{2,2}$	$P_{2,3}$
Row 3→	$P_{3,1}$	$P_{3,2}$	$P_{3,3}$
.			
.			
.			
Row 20→	$P_{20,1}$	$P_{20,2}$	$P_{20,3}$

So the columns run vertically, and the rows run horizontally. The first subscript of a two-dimensional array refers to the row and the second subscript refers to the column:

$P_{2,3}$ is the element of the second row and the third column, and therefore represents the third price for the second inventory item.

In other words, the rows (twenty in total) refer to the different inventory items, whereas the columns (three in all) refer to the different prices for each of the twenty inventory items.

FORTRAN Representation of Double Subscripted Variables

When using two subscripts, both must be placed within the parentheses and separated by a comma. The first subscript refers to the row and the second refers to the column. The following are examples:

Mathematical Notation	FORTRAN Notation	Meaning
$P_{1,3}$	P(1,3)	is the price in the 1st row and the 3rd column
$P_{i,j}$	P(I,J)	is the price in the ith row and the jth column
$P_{i,2}$	P(I,2)	is the price in the ith row and the 2nd column

As for the single subscripted variable the subscripts in the double subscripted variable must be either integer constants, nonsubscripted integer variable names, or integer arithmetic expressions, containing these two. The aforementioned seven acceptable forms of arithmetic expressions also hold for each of the two subscripts of the double subscripted variable names (v, c, v+c, v−c, c∗v, c∗v+c′, c∗v−c′). Again, any variable name used in subscripts must be defined prior to the execution of the statement in which the subscripted variable is used.

Although our discussion is limited to one- and two-dimensional arrays, some versions of FORTRAN allow up to seven-dimensional arrays with the same rules applying.

The DIMENSION Statement

The same DIMENSION statements as those illustrated in the previous section are used to define which variable names are double subscripted, and to specify the size of each subscript.

The appropriate DIMENSION statement for the Inventory Example with Price Breaks in example 5 is:

DIMENSION I(20),P(20,3)

When FORTRAN processes the above DIMENSION statement, it will set aside twenty (20) storage locations for the one-dimensional integer array I and sixty (20×3) storage locations for the two-dimensional real array P. The order in which the two-dimensional array P is stored in computer memory is as follows:

P Array Subscripts

1,1	2,1	3,1	4,1	5,1	6,1	7,1	8,1	9,1	10,1	11,1	12,1
13,1	14,1	15,1	16,1	17,1	18,1	19,1	20,1	1,2	2,2	3,2	4,2
....											
....								17,3	18,3	19,3	20,3

The above arrangement indicates that the computer stores the two-dimensional arrays columnwise by rows; in other words the computer stores the consecutive columns, and the rows are stored in order within the columns. Again, the INTEGER and the REAL type declaration statement can be used to declare modes and dimensions of double subscripted variables simultaneously.

Example [6] The Customers' File

Two-dimensional arrays can also be used to store used to store alphanumeric strings. Consider the following customers' file:

Name	*Address*
Bales, James	122 W 10th, Lebanon, Indiana
Begley, Tom	Flint Drive, Connersville, Indiana
Hauks, Diane	RR2, Lafayette, Indiana
Lamberts, John	3227 Beeson Ave, Kokomo, Indiana
Overbeck, Mia	208 S Market, Liberty, Indiana

If a maximum of four (4) alphabetic characters can be held in one storage location of the computer, then a 5×4 array must be set up to store the names and a 5×9 array must be set up to store all addresses as follows:

	col1	col2	col3	col4
row 1	BALE	S, J	AMES	
row 2	BEGL	EY,	TOM	
row 3	HAUK	S, D	IANE	
row 4	LAMB	ERTS	, JO	HN
row 5	OVER	BECK	, MI	A

	col1	col2	col3	col4	col5	col6	col7	col8	col9
row 1	122	W 10	TH,	LEBA	NON,	IND	IANA		
row 2	FLIN	T DR	IVE,	CON	NERS	VILL	E, I	NDIA	NA
row 3	RR2,	LAF	AYET	TE,	INDI	ANA			
row 4	3227	BEE	SON	AV,	KOKO	MO,	INDI	ANA	
row 5	208	S MA	RKET	, LI	BERT	Y, I	NDIA	NA	

The appropriate DIMENSION statement for the above example is:

DIMENSION NAME(5,4)
INTEGER ADDRS(5,9)

When FORTRAN processes the above DIMENSION and INTEGER statements, it will set aside twenty (5×4) storage locations for the two-dimensional integer array NAME and forty-five (5×9) storage locations for the two-dimensional real array ADDRS.

Input/Output Statements

There are many ways to read in or write out the elements of a double subscripted variable name. Four of them are discussed here.

1. The Nested DO Loop Technique

The nested DO loop can be used to read in or to write out the elements of a double subscripted variable. The price breaks for example [5] can be read in as follows:

```
        DIMENSION P(20,3)
        DO 20 I=1,20
            DO 10 J=1,3
                READ(5,30) P (I,J)
10          CONTINUE
20 CONTINUE
30 FORMAT (F10.2)
        .
        .
        .
```

According to the DIMENSION statement a real two-dimensional array is used that specifies a maximum of sixty (20×3) storages. The P(I,J) in the READ statement refers to the price in the ith row and the jth column. The indexes of both DO statements define the subscripts. The first time the inner loop is executed, I equals 1 and J equals 1, therefore P(1,1) will be read in; the second time the inner loop is executed I equals 1 and J equals 2, therefore P(1,2) will be read in; . . . and so on . . . ; the last time the inner loop is executed I equals 20 and J equals 3, therefore P(20,3) will be read in.

Note that the inner DO (DO 10 J=1,3) cycles the fastest or first. In other words, each time a pass through the first loop (DO 20 I=1,20) is made, the inner loop is executed 3 times. Therefore, the inner loop is executed 3×20 or 60 times.

Because the inner loop is executed sixty (20×3) times, the READ statement is also executed sixty times. Therefore, sixty data cards, each containing one real value for the array P, must be prepared according to the FORMAT specification of the statement that is labeled number thirty (30). The DO loops and the READ statement are equivalent to the following sixty (60) statements:

```
      READ(5,30) P(1,1)
      READ(5,30) P(1,2)
      READ(5,30) P(1,3)
      READ(5,30) P(2,1)
      READ(5,30) P(2,2)
      READ(5,30) P(2,3)
            .
            .
            .

      READ(5,30) P(20,1)
      READ(5,30) P(20,2)
      READ(5,30) P(20,3)
   30 FORMAT(F10.2)
```

2. The DO and Implied DO Loop Technique

The previous program section can be rewritten as follows:

```
      DIMENSION P(20,3)
      DO 10 I=1,20
         READ(5,20) (P(I,J),J=1,3)
   10 CONTINUE
   20 FORMAT(3F10.2)
```

Since the READ instruction itself is not being reexecuted by the implied DO loop, the above READ statement is equivalent to:

```
      READ(5,20) P(I,1), P(I,2), P(I,3)
```

The DO loop index, I, defines the other subscript.
The DO loop and the implied READ statement stand for the following 20 READ statements:

```
      READ(5,20) P(1,1), P(1,2), P(1,3)
      READ(5,20) P(2,1), P(2,2), P(2,3)
      READ(5,20) P(3,1), P(3,2), P(3,3)
      READ(5,20) P(4,1), P(4,2), P(4,3)
            .
            .
            .

      READ(5,20) P(20,1), P(20,2), P(20,3)
   20 FORMAT(3F10.2)
```

Since each READ list consists of three (3) elements, and since there are three (3) FORMAT specifications in the FORMAT statement, a total of twenty data cards must be constructed, each containing three data items, as follows:

the first data card contains the price breaks for the first inventory item;

the second data card contains the price breaks for the second inventory item;

the third data card contains the price breaks for the third inventory item;

....

....

3. Nested Implied DO Loop Technique
The explicit nested DO loop technique:

```
        DO 20 I=1, 20
            DO 10 J=1,3
                READ(5,30) P(I,J)
    10      CONTINUE
    20 CONTINUE
    30 FORMAT(F10.2)
```

instructs the computing system to repeat the READ instruction sixty $(60=20\times3)$ times. Therefore, sixty data cards must be prepared.
The DO and implied DO loop technique:

```
        DO 10 I=1,20
            READ(5,20) (P(I,J), J=1,3)
    10 CONTINUE
    20 FORMAT(3F10.2)
                .
                .
                .
```

tells the computer to repeat the READ instruction only twenty (20) times. According to the above FORMAT statement, only 20 data cards need to be prepared.

Exactly the same results, as in the above example, can be obtained by the use of the nested implied DO loop technique, as follows:

```
READ(5,20) ((P(I,J),J=1,3),I=1,20)
```

outer loop (row index)
inner loop (column index)

If the same FORMAT statement is used for the previous example:

```
20 FORMAT(3F10.2)
```

twenty data cards must be prepared, each containing three (3) price break values.

The DO and implied DO loop technique, and the nested implied DO loop technique can also be used to simultaneously read in two (2) arrays, as illustrated for Example [5]—The Inventory Example with Price Breaks—in the following equivalent FORTRAN statements:
1st alternative: the DO and implied DO loop technique:

```
        DIMENSION I(20), P(20,3)
        DO 10 L=1,20
            READ(5,20) (I(L), P(L,J),J=1,3)
    10 CONTINUE
    20 FORMAT(A4,3F10.2)
                .
                .
                .
```

2nd alternative: the nested implied DO loop technique:

```
        DIMENSION I(20), P(20,3)
        READ(5,20) (I(L), P(L,J), J=1,3), L=1,20)
    20 FORMAT(A4, 3F10.2)
                .
                .
                . .
```

For both alternatives the data must be prepared as follows:

Specifications:	A4	F10.2	F10.2	F10.2
data card 1 :	I(1)	P(1,1)	P(1,2)	P(1,3)
data card 2 :	I(2)	P(2,1)	P(2,2)	P(2,3)
data card 3 :	I(3)	P(3,1)	P(3,2)	P(3,3)
data card 4 :	I(4)	P(4,1)	P(4,2)	P(4,3)
.				
.				
.				
data card 19 :	I(19)	P(19,1)	P(19,2)	P(19,3)
data card 20 :	I(20)	P(20,1)	P(20,2)	P(20,3)

4. The Array READ/WRITE Technique

When a two-dimensional array is read in or written out by the use of a simple array READ/WRITE technique, the elements of the entire array are read in or written out columnwise as is illustrated for the following data:

The integer VALUE array:

	Col.1	Col.2	Col.3	Col.4	Col.5
Row 1	1	2	3	4	5
Row 2	6	7	8	9	10
Row 3	11	12	13	14	15
Row 4	16	17	18	19	20

can be stored by the use of the following program segment:

```
      INTEGER VALUE(4,5)
      READ(5,10) VALUE
   10 FORMAT(4I5)
       .
       .
       . .
```

Since the data will be read in columnwise, and since four items will be read from each card (4I5), the data must be keypunched as follows:

	1	6	1 1	1 6	2 1	
Data Card #1	1	6	11	16		1st Column
Data Card #2	2	7	12	17		2nd Column
Data Card #3	3	8	13	18		3rd Column
Data Card #4	4	9	14	19		4th Column
Data Card #5	5	10	15	20		5th Column

Similarly, if this program segment were executed once the array was in memory:

.
.
.

```
    WRITE(6,30) VALUE
30 FORMAT(1X,4I5)
```

.
.
.

then the output would be:

```
1   6  11  16
2   7  12  17
3   8  13  18
4   9  14  19
5  10  15  20
```

The above described techniques—the nested DO loop technique, the DO and the implied DO loop technique, the nested implied DO loop technique, and the array READ/WRITE technique—can also be used to write out the values which have been assigned to array elements.

Examples of Two-Dimensional Array Manipulations

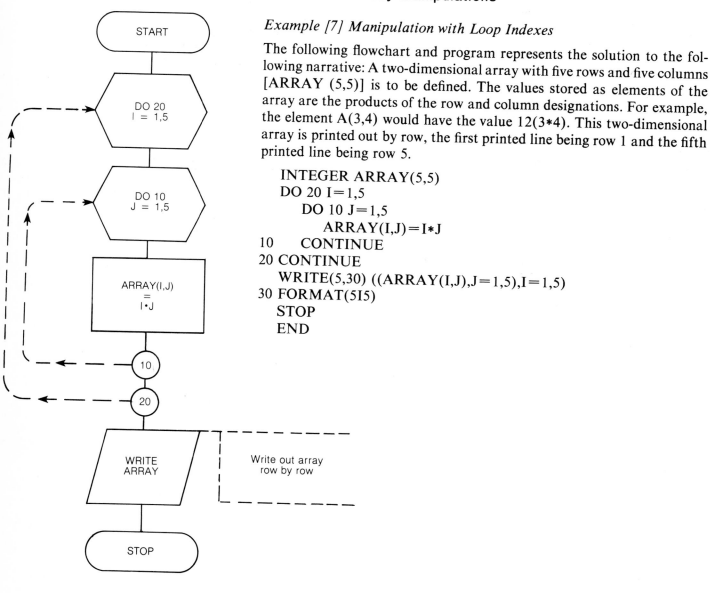

Example [7] Manipulation with Loop Indexes

The following flowchart and program represents the solution to the following narrative: A two-dimensional array with five rows and five columns [ARRAY (5,5)] is to be defined. The values stored as elements of the array are the products of the row and column designations. For example, the element A(3,4) would have the value 12(3*4). This two-dimensional array is printed out by row, the first printed line being row 1 and the fifth printed line being row 5.

```
    INTEGER ARRAY(5,5)
    DO 20 I=1,5
        DO 10 J=1,5
            ARRAY(I,J)=I*J
10      CONTINUE
20  CONTINUE
    WRITE(5,30) ((ARRAY(I,J),J=1,5),I=1,5)
30  FORMAT(5I5)
    STOP
    END
```

Notice the efficient and powerful use of the loop indexes (I and J) in the assignment statement.

$$ARRAY(I,J) = I*J$$

Example [8] The Mail Order Example with Price Breaks

The Mail Order Example [4] is reconsidered here. Mr. Lucky tags three (3) price values to each of his ten inventory items as follows.

Inventory Code ICODE(I)	Base Price UPRICE(I,1)	First Price Break UPRICE(I,2)	Second Price Break UPRICE(I,3)
AP1	12.50	12.00	11.50
AP2	7.75	7.50	7.25
LC3	112.50	109.50	107.50
LD7	13.00	12.50	12.00
AP4	5.50	5.25	5.00
DUM	1.50	1.40	1.30
TET	30.45	39.75	39.10
FED	.75	.70	.65
POT	14.20	13.70	13.20
SMO	9.99	9.75	9.50

The base price applies to the first ten units purchased; the first price break applies to the next additional ten units ordered; and the second and final price applies to all units ordered in excess of twenty. These price considerations are incorporated in the following revised flowchart and program.

The variable names used in the flowchart and in the program, along with their meaning and dimensions, are summarized in the following table:

Program Variable Names	Definition	Mode	Dimension
ICODE	Product Code	Integer	1
UPRICE	Unit Price Breaks	Real	2
NAME	Customer Name	Integer	1
ADDR	Address	Real	1
IPRDCT	Product Ordered	Integer	0
QUANT	Quantity Ordered	Real	0
BILL	Customer's Bill	Real	0

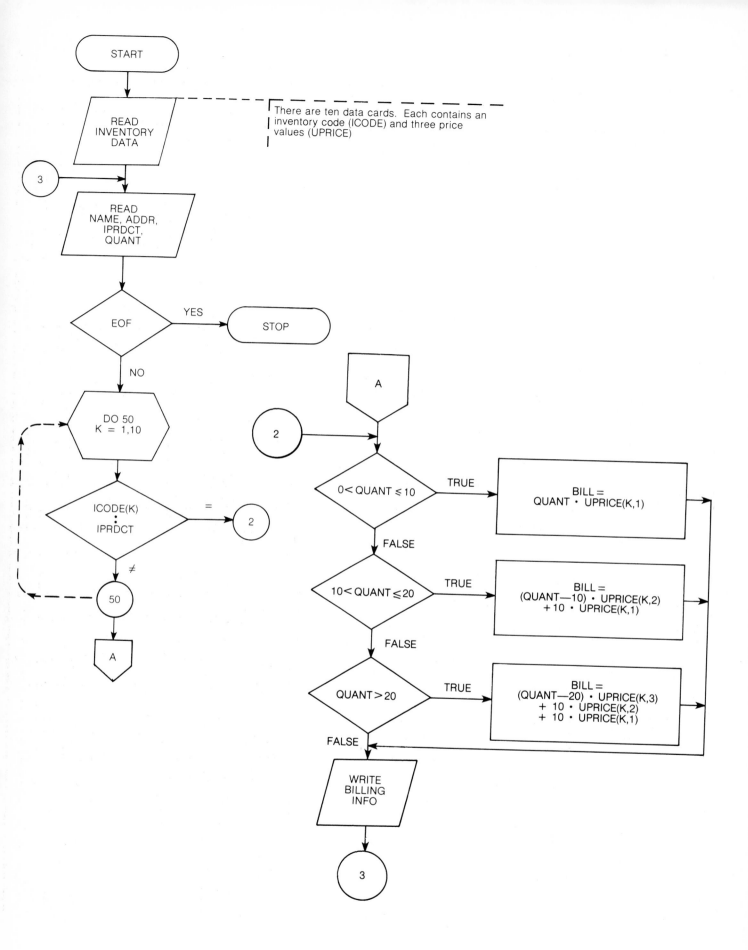

The FORTRAN Program:

```
C *** THE MAIL ORDER EXAMPLE
      DIMENSION ICODE(10), UPRICE(10,3), NAME(3),
     *          ADDR(6)
      WRITE(6,10)
   10 FORMAT(1H1)
C *** READ THE INVENTORY (CODE AND PRICE BREAKS)
      READ(5,20)(ICODE(I),(UPRICE(I,J),J=1,3),
     *          I=1,10)
   20 FORMAT(A3,3F10.2)
C *** READ CUSTOMER'S ORDER
   30 READ(5,40,END=80)(NAME(I),I=1,3),
     *          (ADDR(I),I=1,6),IPRDCT,QUANT
   40 FORMAT(3A4,6A4,/,A3,F10.2)
C *** ROUTINE TO IDENTIFY THE PRICE BREAKS
      DO 50 K=1,10
      IF(ICODE(K).EQ.IPRDCT) GO TO 60
   50 CONTINUE
C *** CALCULATE NET BILL, USING PRICE BREAKS
   60 IF(QUANT.LE.10.0)BILL=QUANT*UPRICE(K,1)
      IF(QUANT.GT.10.0.AND.QUANT.LE.20.0)
     *   BILL=(QUANT-10.)*UPRICE(K,2)+
     *        10*UPRICE(K,1)
      IF(QUANT.GT.20)BILL=(QUANT-20.0)*UPRICE(K,3)
     *        +10.*UPRICE(K,2)+10.*UPRICE(K,1)
C *** WRITE OUT BILLING INFORMATION
      WRITE(6,70)(NAME(I),I=1,3),(ADDR(I),I=1,6),
     *        IPRDCT,QUANT,(UPRICE(K,I),I=1,3),BILL
   70 FORMAT(5X,3A4,/,
     *        5X,6A4,//,
     *        5X,'PRODUCT CODE',3X,A3,/,
     *        5X,'QUANTITY',7X,F10.2,/,
     *        5X,'PRICE VALUES',3X,3F10.2,/,
     *        5X,'TOTAL BILL',5X,F10.2)
      GO TO 30
   80 STOP
      END
```

The following data needs to be processed.

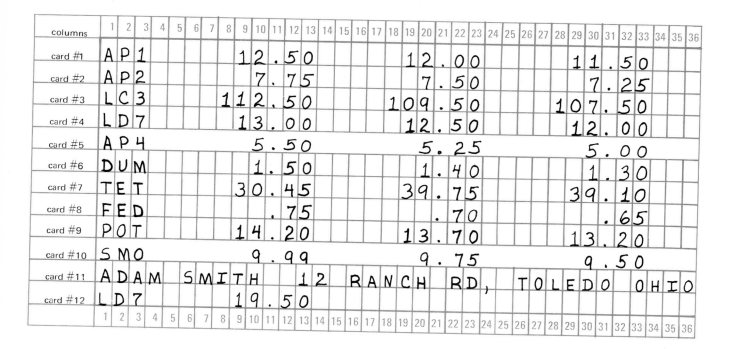

While viewing the program of this reconsidered Mail Order Example, one notices three major changes. These are:

1. change in the DIMENSION statement (line 2)
2. change in the READ statement (line 7)
3. change in the calculation of the net bill (lines 19–24)

The DIMENSION statement defines a two-dimensional array for the UPRICE variable. The array consists of ten (10) rows, referencing the inventory items, and three (3) columns, referencing the three price levels for each inventory item. A total of thirty (10×3) storage allocations are made for the double subscripted variable UPRICE.

A variation of the Nested Implied DO Loop Technique is used to read in the inventory code and price values, as follows:

READ(5,20)(ICODE(I),(UPRICE(I,J),J=1,3),I=1,10)

implied inner loop

implied outer loop

Because the format specification for the above READ statement (FORMAT statement labeled 20) specifies that each data card contains 4 constants:

1st alphanumeric constant: A3

2nd, 3rd, and 4th real constant: 3F10.2

the following set of statements could replace the above single READ statement:

```
        DO 15 I=1,10
            READ(5,20) ICODE(I), (UPRICE(I,J), J=1,3)
    15 CONTINUE
    20 FORMAT(A3, 3F10.2)
```

Finally, lines 19 through 24 contain several logical IF statements to insure proper calculation of the final BILL. Again the correct price levels are defined in the DO loop of the program. Here, the DO loop subscript, K, identifies the appropriated price row in the UPRICE matrix.

The output for this program is as follows:

```
ADAM SMITH
12 RANCH RD, TOLEDO OHIO

PRODUCT CODE    LD7
QUANTITY            19.50
PRICE VALUES        13.00      12.50      12.00
TOTAL BILL         248.75
```

Three-Dimensional Arrays

A three-dimensional array is nothing more than a logical extension of a two-dimensional array. Suppose, for example, it was necessary to tabulate the number of individuals holding a given degree in a given department at a university. This would provide a typical two-dimensional array such as:

	Faculty		
Department	BA	MA	PhD.
1	4	16	22
2	3	18	35
3	2	15	19
4	1	19	26
5	6	12	25

In this case, Department 1 has four members holding the B.A. degree, which would be referenced in the FACLTY array by (1,1) with the first subscript referring to row and the second to column. The four faculty members in Department 1 who hold the M.A. degree would be referenced by (1,2) and so forth to the 25 faculty members in Department 5 who hold the Ph.D. and would be referenced by (5,3).

Now, suppose it becomes necessary to tabulate not only the number of faculty members holding a given degree in a given department but to record the sex of those faculty members as well. We could now generate a three-dimensional array as follows:

	Faculty					
	Male			Female		
Department	B.A.	M.A	Ph.D	B.A.	M.A	Ph.D
1	3	9	12	1	7	10
2	1	9	15	2	9	20
3	1	8	10	1	7	9
4	1	9	13	0	10	13
5	4	8	13	2	4	12

In this case, Department 1 has three members holding the B.A. degree who are males and 1 member holding the B.A. degree who is female. The former would be referenced by (1,1,1), and the latter would be referenced by (1,1,2) with the third subscript 1 denoting male and the third subscript 2 denoting female. The nine faculty members in Department 1 holding the M.A. degree who are males would be referenced by (1,2,1) while the seven faculty members in Department 1 holding the M.A. degree who are females would be referenced by (1,2,2) and so forth to the twelve faculty members in Department 5 who hold a Ph.D. who are female and would be referenced by (5,3,2).

An appropriate DIMENSION statement to declare the number of storage locations necessary to hold the data in this last example would be:

DIMENSION FACLTY(5,3,2)

where FACLTY is the name of the array and 5 refers to the departments, 3 refers to the degrees and 2 refers to the sex—male or female. This would serve to allocate 30 positions of storage ($5 \times 3 \times 2 = 30$) for the accumulated data. In this case it would be twice the storage that was necessary to tabulate simply the department and degrees of our two-dimensional array ($5 \times 3 = 15$). It should be obvious that large multi-dimensional arrays will typically consume a large amount of storage.

While it would be rare to encounter an array that goes beyond three levels, it does occasionally happen. When it becomes necessary, the basic logic, though extended, remains the same. Suppose, for example, one wanted to compare the data in our three-dimensional array with similar data from another university. This may be illustrated as:

			Faculty				
			Male			Female	
	Department	B.A.	M.A	Ph.D	B.A.	M.A	Ph.D
University A	1	3	9	12	1	7	10
	2	1	9	15	2	9	20
	3	1	8	10	1	7	9
	4	1	9	13	0	10	13
	5	4	8	13	2	4	12
University B	1	3	4	10	4	7	15
	2	4	7	11	6	6	20
	3	5	9	2	4	9	5
	4	6	7	3	5	6	7
	5	0	4	5	0	3	5

In this case, the 3 faculty members at University A in Department 1 who hold a B.A. degree and are male are referenced by (1,1,1,1) while the 5 faculty members at University B in Department 5 who hold the Ph.D. and are female would be referenced by (2,5,3,2). The first subscript, in this case, refers to the university (1 for University A and 2 for University B) while the next three subscripts are the same as in the previous example.

3. FORTRAN 77 Additional Subscript Considerations

As was the case with the 1966 FORTRAN standard, FORTRAN 77 allows for a maximum of seven dimensions. However, FORTRAN 77 allows for a greater flexibility in defining the subscripts of arrays. These additions are discussed briefly here.

FORTRAN 77 allows for specifying an integer lower bound for any dimension. If that lower bound is omitted, the default is one. This is illustrated in the following array declaration examples.

[1]   DIMENSION A(0:4)

This dimension statement specifies a one-dimensional array A consisting of the following five elements: A_0, A_1, A_2, A_3, A_4.

[2]   DIMENSION B(4)

This dimension statement specifies a one-dimensional array B consisting of the following four elements: B_1, B_2, B_3, B_4.

[3]   DIMENSION D(0:4,3)

This third dimension statement specifies a two-dimensional array D consisting of the following elements:

$$\begin{bmatrix} D_{0,1} & D_{0,2} & D_{0,3} \\ D_{1,1} & D_{1,2} & D_{1,3} \\ D_{2,1} & D_{2,2} & D_{2,3} \\ D_{3,1} & D_{3,2} & D_{3,3} \\ D_{4,1} & D_{4,2} & D_{4,3} \end{bmatrix}$$

[4]   DIMENSION E(−2:4)

Here, the dimension statement specifies a one-dimensional array E containing the following elements: E_{-2}, E_{-1}, E_0, E_1, E_2, E_3, E_4.

An array element must be referenced by a subscript that is an integer expression. That expression may contain array elements and even special function references. Care must be exercised that the value of the integer subscript expression is within the bounds specified by the DIMENSION statement.

Exercises

Problem No. 1

Consider the following questions and give brief answers.

1. What, if anything, is wrong with the following statements?
   a) DIMENSION X(I,K), APE(8)
   b) ABC=A(K,I)*12.0*I
   c) TOT=VALUE(K)+VALUE(I,J)

2. For each of the following three questions, consider the following two-dimensional array, NOTE

$$NOTE = \begin{bmatrix} 2 & 4 & 3 & 5 & -2 \\ -1 & 8 & 0 & 2 & 9 \\ 3 & 1 & -1 & 6 & 2 \end{bmatrix}$$

This array is arranged so that, for example, NOTE(1,3)=3
   a) If I=NOTE(3,2) and if J=3, what is the value of NOTE(I,J)?
   b) If K=NOTE(2,3) and J=NOTE(2,4), what is the value of NOTE(K,J)?
   c) If K=NOTE(3,1), I=NOTE(K,1) and N=NOTE(I,K−1), what is the value of NOTE(I,N)?

3. Are the following subscripts correct (C) or illegal (I), and why?
   a) X(MNO∗3)
   b) X(MIN,MAX)
   c) X(LIA+1)
   d) X(K12345,K123456,L123)

4. Consider the following programs and determine how many data cards must be prepared

   a)
```
        DIMENSION A(20)
        READ(5,1)(A(I),I=1,20)
      1 FORMAT(10F5.0,/,5F5.0)
        STOP
        END
```

   b)
```
        DIMENSION A(20)
        READ(5,1)(A(I),I=1,20)
      1 FORMAT(/,10F5.0,/,5F5.0,/,5F5.0)
        STOP
        END
```

   c)
```
        DIMENSION A(20)
        DO 10 I=1,2
           READ(5,20)(A(J),J=1,20)
     10 CONTINUE
     20 FORMAT(5F5.0)
        STOP
        END
```

5. Consider the following partial programs and assume that each is used with the same set of data cards as shown below.

   DATA cards:
1st card	7432981065
2nd card	8923475610
3rd card	1324798056
4th card	6879035421
5th card	4987635012

   a)
```
     DIMENSION M(5)
     READ(5,70)(M(J),J=1,5)
  70 FORMAT(I2)
```
   b)
```
     DIMENSION M(5)
     READ(5,80)M
  80 FORMAT(6I2)
```

```
c)      DIMENSION M(5)
        DO 10 I=1,5
           READ(5,20)M(I)
     10 CONTINUE
     20 FORMAT(3I2/2I3)
d)      DIMENSION M(5),N(5)
        READ(5,10)(M(K),N(K),K=1,5)
     10 FORMAT(5I2)
e)      DIMENSION M(5),N(5)
        READ(5,10)M,N
     10 FORMAT(5I2)
f)      DIMENSION M(5),N(5)
        READ(5,10)(M(K),K=1,5),(N(J),J=1,5)
     10 FORMAT(2I2)
```

Indicate the stored value for the M and N arrays in the table.

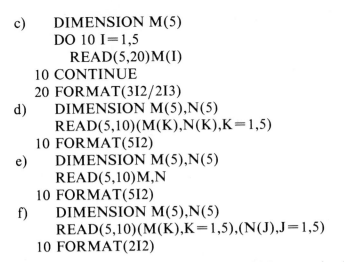

	M(1)	M(2)	M(3)	M(4)	M(5)	N(1)	N(2)	N(3)	N(4)	N(5)
a)										
b)										
c)										
d)										
e)										
f)										

6. Consider the following program segments. Assume that each uses the same set of data cards. Indicate the stored value for L array in the table.

Data cards:
   1st card   496409876530
   2nd card   743296484392
   3rd card   846263987431

```
        DIMENSION L(2,3)
a) 10 FORMAT (3I2)
        READ(5,10) ((L(I,J),J=1,3), I=1,2)
        DIMENSION L(2,3)
b) 12 FORMAT (2I2)
        READ(5,12)((L(I,J), I=1,2), J=1,3)
        DIMENSION L(2,3)
c) 14 FORMAT (3I2)
        READ(5,14)L
```

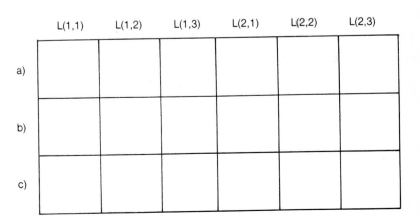

	L(1,1)	L(1,2)	L(1,3)	L(2,1)	L(2,2)	L(2,3)
a)						
b)						
c)						

Problem No. 2

Rewrite the following program without the use of a DO loop (the implied DO loops need not be changed).

```
      DIMENSION A(10,20),B(20,5),C(10,5)
      READ(5,2)((A(I,K),I=1,10),K=1,20)
      READ(5,2)((B(K,J),K=1,20),J=1,50)
    2 FORMAT(10F5.2)
      DO 5 I=1,10
        DO 4 J=1,5
          C(I,J)=0
          DO 3 K=1,20
            C(I,J)=C(I,J)+A(I,K)*B(K,J)
    3     CONTINUE
    4   CONTINUE
    5 CONTINUE
      WRITE(6,6)((C(I,J),J=1,5),I=1,10)
    6 FORMAT(5F11.4)
      STOP
      END
```

What matrix operation is accomplished in the above program?

Problem No. 3

NOTE is a two-dimensional array consisting of six rows and six columns. Assume that all elements in NOTE have been initialized to zero. Determine the content of NOTE after the following sequence of instructions have been executed.

```
      DO 30 I=1,6
        DO 20 J=1,6
          NOTE(I,J)=NOTE(J,I)+2*I+J+2
   20   CONTINUE
   30 CONTINUE
```

	Column 1	Column 2	Column 3	Column 4	Column 5	Column 6
Row 1						
Row 2						
Row 3						
Row 4						
Row 5						
Row 6						

Problem No. 4

Write a complete FORTRAN program to set all the values of an array, A(80,8) to the same value, 7.563. Then print the array, 8 values per line (each in F6.3), 80 lines altogether.

Problem No. 5

Write a program segment that will sum all elements of a two-dimensional array named DATA. The maximum value of the first subscript is given as MAXROW and the maximum value of the second subscript is given as MAXCOL. You can assume that the values for MAXROW, MAXCOL and DATA are already loaded. You do not have to either input or output information. The result must be stored in the variable name TOTAL.

Problem No. 6

Write a FORTRAN segment that will count the number of elements in array HURRAY, which are greater than 2345. Assume that the array HURRAY is defined by the following: DIMENSION HURRAY(50,30).

Problem No. 7

Write a program that will count the number of even numbers in an array named N. All the values in the array are positive and less than 100. Assume N is defined by DIMENSION N(50,100).

Problem No. 8

Write a segment of a program that will write out, on the third line of a new page, the first ten elements of an array named X, where X is defined by DIMENSION X(50). Assume that all elements are positive and less than 1000 and that four decimal places are required in the output. Include the FORMAT statement used.

Problem No. 9

Give the flowchart and the FORTRAN program that inputs a two-dimensional array PRICE (matrix) and that loads the content of matrix PRICE into a one-dimensional array VALUES (vector), such that the last column of the matrix, PRICE, is at the beginning of the vector, VALUES, followed by the next-to-last column, etc., up to the first column. Finally output the vector, VALUES.

Run your FORTRAN program for the following data:

$$\text{Matrix PRICE} = \begin{pmatrix} 6 & 2 & 5 & 6 \\ 9 & 1 & 8 & 9 \\ 5 & 2 & 3 & 2 \end{pmatrix}$$

The resulting Vector, VALUES, will be:

(6 9 2 5 8 3 2 1 2 6 9 5)

Problem No. 10

Give the flowchart and the FORTRAN program that will input an N position vector A, and that will create two new vectors: B and C. Vector B should contain all odd elements of A and vector C should contain all even elements of A. The one-dimensional array A contains positive integer constants.

Problem No. 11

Write a FORTRAN program that will input twenty values into a one-dimensional array A and that will interchange these elements pairwise, that is:

A(1) is to contain A(2) and A(2) is to contain A(1),

A(3) is to contain A(4) and A(4) is to contain A(3)

....

....

A(19) is to contain A(20) and A(20) is to contain A(19)
Print out the rearranged array.

Problem No. 12

Input twenty values in a one-dimensional array B and do the following:

1. Make the sum of all elements of B which have an even subscript, and call this sum SUM1.
2. Make the sum of all elements of B which have an odd subscript, and call this sum SUM2.
3. Make the difference between SUM1 and SUM2 (SUM1−SUM2), and call this difference DIFF.
4. Print the array B, SUM1, SUM2, and DIFF.

Problem No. 13

An array A(100,10) contains the scores of 100 students on 10 exams. Each score is between 0 and 100. Draw a flowchart and write a program for a procedure that does the following:

(1) compute and print the average score for each of the 100 students. In this calculation drop any scores below 10.
(2) using the averages calculated in (1), find the average score of the remaining 98 students, after the highest and lowest average are dropped.

Problem No. 14

An instructor gives a 30-question multiple-choice exam. There are five possible answers given for each question (1,2,3,4, or 5). Write a FORTRAN program to grade the exam. The data consists of:

1. One DATA card containing 30 integers separated by commas reflecting the 30 correct answers to the 30 questions (ANSWER).
2. One DATA card indicating the number of students in the class who took the exam (N).
3. N Data cards each containing the student's Social Security number (S) and 30 answers ("0" indicates that the student did not answer the question).

Your FORTRAN program should generate the following information:

1. A listing of the student's Social Security number, the number of wrong (WRONG) and correct (CORRCT) answers and his final grade based on the following formula: 2(CORRCT−WRONG/5). If the grade has a fraction larger than or equal to .5, then round the grade up to the next integer, otherwise drop the fraction.
2. The class average (AVRGE).
3. A listing indicating for each question the percentage of the students who answered it correctly (C1), incorrectly (W1), or left blank (B1).

More Advanced Business Programs 10

In this chapter, four advanced business programs are developed in order to illustrate the following FORTRAN features:

1. DIMENSION statement and use of arrays
2. INTEGER and REAL statements
3. Arithmetic assignment statements
4. Transfer of control statements
5. Explicit DO loops
6. INPUT/OUTPUT statements with implicit DO loops

But first, let us restate the rules, previously presented, that enhance good programming style. They are:

Rule 1
Explain the meaning of important program variable names in a table outside the program.

Rule 2
Use comment statements to identify routines and flows within the program.

Rule 3
Spell out important variable names to their fullest extent possible. Use the INTEGER/REAL type declaration statement rather than changing the first letter of the variable name to accommodate for the mode.

Rule 4
Attempt to keep statement numbers in ascending order. Initially, when constructing the program, try to use multiples of 10, 50, 100, etc. and, if at all possible, avoid using digits 1 thru 9 in the units position.

It is preferred to right-justify statement numbers in their five-column field, so that it is easier to reference statements.

Rule 5
Place all the FORMAT statements either after the corresponding READ or WRITE statements, or in the beginning of the program, or at the end of the program before the END statement. This will help you to locate any FORMAT statement quickly.

Rule 6
Indent all continuation statements by at least five spaces.

Rule 7

If more than one line of output is shown in a FORMAT statement, it is preferred to indent each separate line and start the specifications for each new output line on a separate continuation card.

Rule 8

Avoid using the GO TO statement. FORTRAN 77 provides ways of avoiding GO TO statements. Therefore, if a FORTRAN 77 compiler is available, use FORTRAN 77 control structures, rather than FORTRAN 66 structures.

Rule 9

Indent control structures in order to identify the various control levels and to make programs more readable.

Rule 10

It is good practice to end all DO loops with a CONTINUE statement.

Rule 11

Indent all statements within the range of the DO, except for the last CONTINUE statement. Indent all nested DO loops.

Rule 12

Comment statements before the DO statement help to explain the function of the loop.

Rule 13

Whenever reasonable, it is good practice to control the number of times a loop is to be performed from a control card.

1. Calculating the Monthly Payment of a Loan

The monthly payment of a loan equals the sum of the principal value of the loan plus the monthly interest. If the loan is for financing a new car, the monthly interest is based on the total amount borrowed and therefore does not change from month to month.

The data used as input to the FORTRAN program to calculate the monthly payment of a loan are:

1. customer's name
2. number of the loan
3. amount of the loan
4. interest rate
5. term of loan

The interest rate is the yearly interest for a loan of $100. The term of the loan is the number of months over which it is paid. It is assumed that any number of months may be agreed upon, and that the monthly payments are all equal to each other.

The procedure used to calculate the monthly payment of a loan for several customers is illustrated in the next flowchart. The variable names used in the flowchart and in the program, their meaning, dimension, and mode follow:

Program Variable Name	Definition	Mode	Dimension
CUNUM	Number of the loan	Integer	1
INTER	Total interest to be paid on a loan	Real	1
INTMON	Monthly interest to be paid on a loan	Real	1
INTRT	Yearly interest rate	Real	0
LOAN	Amount of the loan	Real	1
NAME	Name of the person who is taking the loan	Alpha	2
PAYMT	Monthly payment	Real	1
PRINC	Principal value of the loan	Real	1
TERM	Number of equal payments to be made to pay off the loan	Real	1

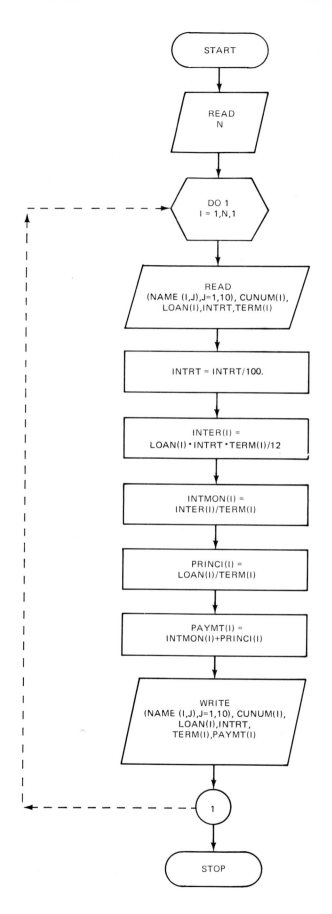

Flowcharting the Calculations of
the Monthly Payment of a Loan

1. Read in the number of loans
   to be processed

2. Read in name, customer's
   number, amount of loan,
   yearly interest, and number
   of equal payments

3. Calculation of yearly interest
   for $1.00.

4. Calculation of the total
   amount of interest

5. Calculation of the monthly
   interest

6. Calculation of the principal
   value

7. Calculation of the monthly
   payment

8. Write out, name, customer's
   number, amount of loan,
   yearly interest, number of
   equal payments, and
   monthly payment.

```
C *** CALCULATION OF THE MONTHLY PAYMENT OF A LOAN
      INTEGER CUNUM(50), NAME(50,10)
      REAL PRINCI(50), INTER(50), LOAN(50), INTRT, TERM(50)
      REAL PAYMT(50), INTMON(50)
C *** READ IN THE NUMBER OF LOANS TO BE PROCESSED
      READ(5,20) N
C *** PROCESS ALL LOANS
      DO 10 I = 1, N
         READ(5,30) (NAME(I,J), J = 1, 10), CUNUM(I), LOAN(I),
     *              INTRT, TERM(I)
         INTRT = INTRT / 100.
         INTER(I) = LOAN(I) * INTRT * TERM(I) / 12.0
         INTMON(I) = INTER(I) / TERM(I)
         PRINCI(I) = LOAN(I) / TERM(I)
         PAYMT(I) = INTMON(I) + PRINCI(I)
         INTRT = INTRT * 100.0
         WRITE(6,40) (NAME(I,J), J = 1,10), CUNUM(I), LOAN(I), INTRT,
     *               TERM(I), PAYMT(I)
   10 CONTINUE
   20 FORMAT(I3)
   30 FORMAT(10A4,10X,I6,/,
     *        6X,3F10.2)
   40 FORMAT(1H1,///,1X,'MONTHLY STATEMENT FOR'/,
     *        1X,10A4,/,
     *        1X,I6,//,
     *        1X,'AMOUNT OF LOAN',F10.2,/,
     *        1X,'INTEREST RATE ',1X,F10.2,/,
     *        1X,'TERM',11X,F10.2,/,1X,'PAYMENT DUE ',3X,F10.2,/,1H1)
      STOP
      END
```

Program Input is:

```
   3
HENRY M. MILLER JUNIOR                            123456
123456     567.89       6.        12.
JOHN B. WHALEY                                    654321
654321     567.89       6.5       12.
BERTRAM H. WILDER                                 123654
123654     567.89       6.75      12.
```

The Program Output is:

```
MONTHLY STATEMENT FOR
HENRY M. MILLER JUNIOR
123456

AMOUNT OF LOAN        567.89
INTEREST RATE           6.00
TERM                   12.00
PAYMENT DUE            50.16
```

```
MONTHLY STATEMENT FOR
JOHN B. WHALEY
654321

AMOUNT OF LOAN        567.89
INTEREST RATE           6.50
TERM                   12.00
PAYMENT DUE            50.40
```

```
MONTHLY STATEMENT FOR
BERTRAM H. WILDER
123654

AMOUNT OF LOAN        567.89
INTEREST RATE           6.75
TERM                   12.00
PAYMENT DUE            50.52
```

2. Updating the Inventory Stock

A number (N) of different article groups is held in stock. Each time one or more of these articles is withdrawn from the stock, a data card is punched with the quantity withdrawn, resulting in one card per inventory item. These cards accumulate and are processed in batches by a computer.

Management has set up a minimum or safety stock level for each inventory group which should not be diminished by withdrawals. Each time inventory has dropped beyond the safety level, or each time the safety level is reached, an order is placed to fill up the safety stock plus a certain constant minimum order quantity (economical quantity). When the ordered quantity exceeds a certain level, there is a price break. This level exists for all articles held in stock but is different for each article.

A printout for all ordered articles is the purpose of this program. The printout consists of the stock number, quantity ordered, price per unit, and total price. The following program is designed to use as many basic FORTRAN features as possible and does not show the most elegant way to compute the desired output. The program contains:

Declarations	REAL, INTEGER, and DIMENSION, and shows that all three can be used to dimension arrays
Input/Output	READ and WRITE statements for the conventional card and printer I/O FORMAT statements using /,X, and I,F,A conversion, and literals in the output to write an appropriate text to the computed numbers
DO-loops	1. implicit DO loops in I/O statements
	2. explicit DO loops in computing and output
GO TO	1. the unconditional GO TO statement
	2. the computed GO TO statement
IF statements	the logical IF statement
Dummy statement	the dummy CONTINUE statement
STOP	
END	

The flowchart, comment statements in the program, and the definition of the variable names used in the flowchart and the program fully explain the programming procedure.

Program Variable Name	Definition	Mode	Dimension
INVENT	Quantity in Inventory	Real	1
IQUANT	Inventory Quantity withdrawn	Real	1
ITOLER	Inventory Safety-stock quantity	Real	1
JQUANT	Price-jump quantity	Integer	1
KONST	Economical order quantity	Integer	1
TPRICE	Total price to be paid	Real	1
SPRICE	Unit price for small orders	Real	1
LPRICE	Unit price for large orders	Real	1
N	Number of different stock items	Integer	0
ORDER	Order quantity	Real	1

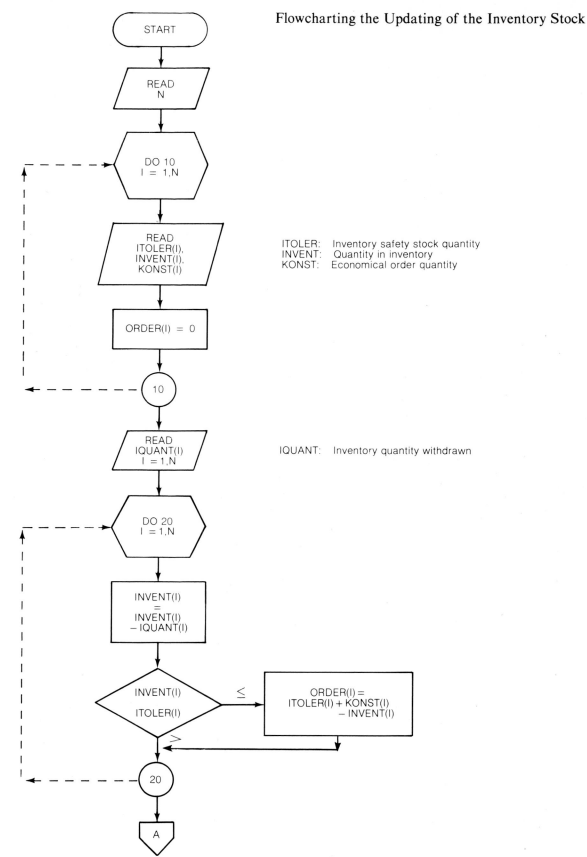

ITOLER: Inventory safety stock quantity
INVENT: Quantity in inventory
KONST: Economical order quantity

IQUANT: Inventory quantity withdrawn

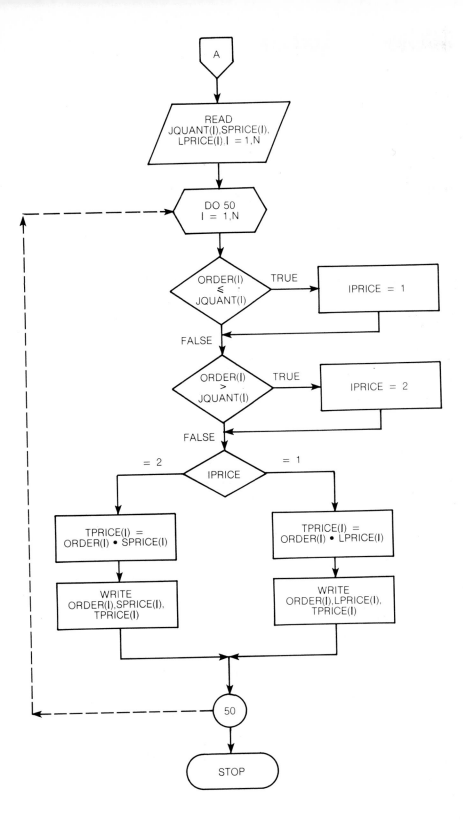

```
C *** UPDATING THE INVENTORY
      INTEGER IPRICE, KONST(100), JQUANT(100)
      REAL SPRICE(100), TPRICE(100), LPRICE(100)
      REAL ITOLER(100), INVENT(100), IQUANT(100)
      DIMENSION ORDER(100)
      READ(5,60) N
C *** READ ALL INVENTORY DATA: SAFETY STOCK, INVENTORY
C *** QUANTITY AND ECONOMIC ORDER QUANTITY
      DO 10 I = 1, N
         READ(5,70) ITOLER(I), INVENT(I), KONST(I)
         ORDER(I) = 0
   10 CONTINUE
C *** READ QUANTITIES WITHDRAWN
      READ(5,80) (IQUANT(I), I = 1, N)
C *** DEFINE QUANTITY TO BE ORDERED
      DO 20 I = 1, N
         INVENT(I) = INVENT(I) - IQUANT(I)
         IF(INVENT(I) .LE. ITOLER(I))
     *           ORDER(I) = ITOLER(I) = KONST(I) - INVENT(I)
   20 CONTINUE
      READ(5,100) (JQUANT(I), SPRICE(I), LPRICE(I), I=1,N)
      WRITE(6,90)
C *** CALCULATION OF THE TOTAL PRICE OF QUANTITY ORDERED
      DO 50 I = 1, N
         IF(ORDER(I) .LE. JQUANT(I))    IPRICE = 1
         IF(ORDER(I) .GT. JQUANT(I))    IPRICE = 2
         GOTO(30,40), IPRICE
   30    TPRICE(I) = ORDER(I) * SPRICE(I)
         WRITE(6,110) I, ORDER(I), SPRICE(I), TPRICE(I)
         GOTO 50
   40    TPRICE(I) = ORDER(I) * LPRICE(I)
         WRITE(6,110) I, ORDER(I), LPRICE(I), TPRICE(I)
   50 CONTINUE
   60 FORMAT(I3)
   70 FORMAT(2F10.2,I10)
   80 FORMAT(2F10.2)
   90 FORMAT(1H1,'UPDATING INVENTORY STOCKS',///,
     *          1X,'NUMBER OF ARTICLE',2X,'TOTAL PRICE')
  100 FORMAT(I10,2F10.2)
  110 FORMAT(1X,I3,16X,2(F10.2,8X),F10.2)
      STOP
      END
```

The first read statement, READ(5,60) N, reads in the number of different inventory items. The first DO loop

```
DO 10 I=1,N
    READ(5,70) ITOLER(I), INVENT(I), KONST(I)
    ORDER(I)=0
10 CONTINUE
```

reads for each article group the safety stock level, the inventory on hand, and the economical order quantity. It also provides for equating all orders to zero.

The quantity withdrawn from each article group is read in by the implicit DO loop:

READ(5,80)(IQUANT(I),I=1,N)

The quantity to be ordered for each article group is defined in the second explicit DO loop:

```
DO 20 I=1,N
    INVENT(I)=INVENT(I)-IQUANT(I)
    IF(INVENT(I).LE.ITOLER(I)).....
20 CONTINUE
```

It includes an arithmetic assignment statement that defines the inventory level for each article after the inventory is diminished by the quantity ordered. It also checks whether the new inventory level is below or equal to the safety-stock level and defines the order quantity if the inventory is less than or below the safety stock level.

The read statement

READ(5,100)(JQUANT(I),SPRICE(I),LPRICE(I),I=1,N)

defines for each article group the price break when the ordered quantity exceeds a certain level (JQUANT).

The last DO loop, DO 50 I=1,N, checks the quantity to be ordered to define whether there will be a price break or not. If the quantity to be ordered is larger than JQUANT, then the total price equals ORDER(I)*LPRICE(I). If the quantity ordered is smaller than JQUANT, the total price equals ORDER(I)*SPRICE(I).

The Program Input is:

```
3
   100.      200.      150
   150.      250.      200
   200.      300.      250
   175.
   225.
   275.
      190      20.      10.
      240      70.      60.
      290     120.     110.
```

The Program Output is:

```
UPDATING INVENTORY STOCKS

NUMBER OF ARTICLE   QUANTITY ORDERED   PRICE OF ARTICLE   TOTAL PRICE
       1                225.00              10.00           2250.00
       2                325.00              60.00          19500.00
       3                425.00             110.00          46750.00
```

3. Term Revolving Credit Plan

The objective of this program is to generate customers' monthly payments based on the end-of-the-month balance of their accounts.

The input to the program consists of a master file and a sales file. The master file contains a set of data cards for each customer, containing the customer's number, name and address, and old balance. The customer's file is arranged in increasing order of the customer number.

The sales file contains for each customer a set of cards which are the copies of the customer's sales slips. Each sales slip copy contains the customer's number and the amount of the sale. The last card of the set for each customer repeats the customer's number and contains the alphanumeric character @ as an indicator of the last sales slip. These sales slips are arranged in increasing order of the customer number. It is assumed that there are no more than 100 sales slips to be processed.

The steps used for computing the minimum payment are as follows:

Step 1: Read from the master file all customers' numbers, names, addresses, and old balances.

Step 2: Read sales slips for all customers (there are no more than 100).

Step 3: For each customer:
   a) add the sales to the old balance to obtain the new balance;
   b) calculate the minimum monthly payment as follows:
      if the new balance is less than or equal to $10, the payment equals the balance
      if the new balance is larger than $10, but $100 or less, the payment equals $10
      if the new balance is larger than $100, but $150 or less, the payment equals $15
      if the new balance is larger than $150, but $200 or less, the payment equals $20
      if the new balance is larger than $200, the payment equals 10% of the new balance;
   c) write out the customer's bill.

The variable names used in the flowchart and the program, their meaning, dimension, and mode follow:

Program Variable Names	Definition	Mode	Dimension
BAOH	Balance of the customer's account	Real	1
CUADD1	Customer's street address	Alpha	2
CUADD2	Customer's city address	Alpha	2
CUNAM	Customer's name	Alpha	2
CUNUM	Customer's number in master file	Integer	1
DUDATE	Payment due date	Alpha	1
INDIC	Indicator: @ or 2084585536 is the indicator on the last sales slip	Alpha	1
L	Number of customers	Integer	0
PAYME	Monthly minimum payment	Real	1
SALES	Sales value on the sales slip	Real	1
SCUNUM	Customer's number on the sales slip	Integer	1

Flowcharting the Term Revolving Credit Plan:

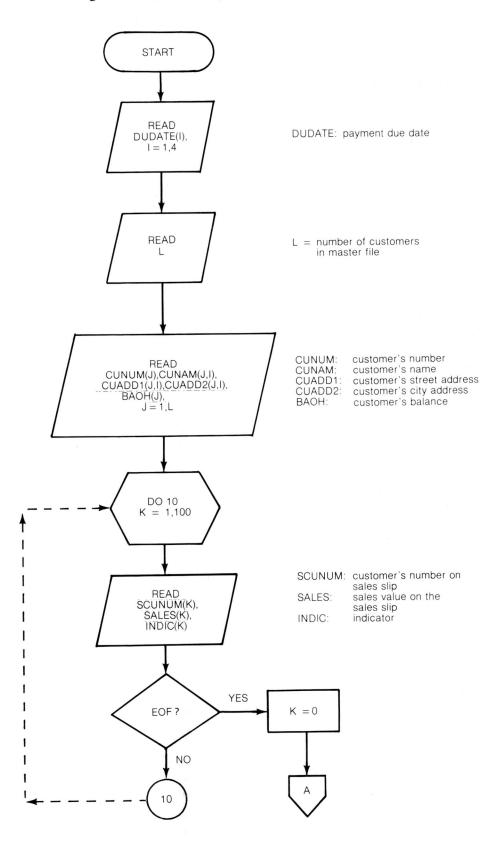

DUDATE: payment due date

L = number of customers
in master file

CUNUM: customer's number
CUNAM: customer's name
CUADD1: customer's street address
CUADD2: customer's city address
BAOH: customer's balance

SCUNUM: customer's number on
sales slip
SALES: sales value on the
sales slip
INDIC: indicator

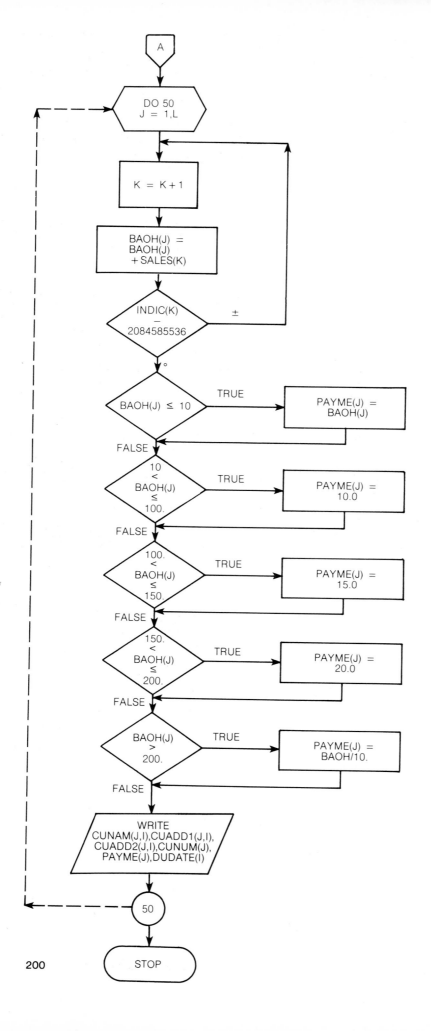

200

```
C *** TERM REVOLVING CREDIT PLAN PROGRAM
      INTEGER CUNUM(10), SCUNUM(100)
      DIMENSION DUDATE(4), CUNAM(10,20), CUADD1(10,20), CUADD2(10,17),
     1          SALES(100), INDIC(100), BAOH(100), PAYME(100)
      READ(5,90) (DUDATE(I), I = 1,4)
      READ(5,100) L
C *** READ IN CUSTOMERS' FILE
      READ(5,60) (CUNUM(J), (CUNAM(J,I), I=1,20), (CUADD1(J,I) I=1,20),
     *           (CUADD2(J,I), I=1,17), BAOH(J), J=1,L)
C *** READ IN ALL SALES SLIPS (THERE ARE NO MORE THAN 100)
      DO 10 K=1,100
         READ(5,70,END=20) SCUNUM(K), SALES(K), INDIC(K)
   10 CONTINUE
   20 K = 0
C *** ACCUMULATE ALL SALES SLIPS AND CALCULATE MINIMUM PAYMENT
      DO 50 J=1,L
   30    K = K + 1
         BAOH(J) = BAOH(J) + SALES(K)
         IF(INDIC(K) - 2084585536) 30, 40, 30
   40    IF(BAOH(J) .LE. 10.0)  PAYME(J) = BAOH(J)
         IF(BAOH(J) .GT. 10.00 .AND. BAOH(J) .LE. 100.0)  PAYME(J) = 10.0
         IF(BAOH(J) .GT. 100.0 .AND. BAOH(J) .LE. 150.0)  PAYME(J) = 15.0
         IF(BAOH(J) .GT. 150.0 .AND. BAOH(J) .LE. 200.0)  PAYME(J) = 20.0
         IF(BAOH(J) .GT. 200.0)  PAYME(J) = BAOH(J) / 10.0
         WRITE(6,80) (CUNAM(J,I), I=1,20), (CUADD1(J,I), I=1,20),
     *               (CUADD2(J,I), I=1,17), CUNUM(J), PAYME(J),
     *               (DUDATE(I), I=1,4)
   50 CONTINUE
   60 FORMAT(I6,20A2,/,
     *        6X,20A2,17A2,/,
     *        6X,F10.2)
   70 FORMAT(I6,F10.2,A1)
   80 FORMAT(1H1,'CUSTOMER BILL FOR',///,
     *        2(1X,20A2,/),
     *        1X,17A2,//,
     *        1X,'CUSTOMER NUMBER',1X,I6,///,
     *        1X,'THE AMOUNT OF',F10.2,' WILL BE DUE ON ',4A4,//,
     *        1X,'THANK YOU FOR YOUR ORDERS')
   90 FORMAT(4A4)
  100 FORMAT(I3)
      STOP
      END
```

The FORTRAN features used in this program are:

INTEGER declaration statement

DIMENSION statement

READ statements with implicit DO loops

Common READ statement

DO loops

Assignment statements

Arithmetic IF statements

Logical IF statement

GO TO statements

WRITE statement with implicit DO loops.

The first READ statement

READ(5,90)(DUDATE(I),I=1,4)

reads from one data card the payment due date into four memory words, by the use of an implicit DO loop (DUDATE(I),I=1,4).

The second READ statement

READ(5,100)L

reads the number of customers in the master file.

The third READ statement

    READ(5,60)(CUNUM(J),(CUNAM(J,I)I=1,20),(CUADD1(J,I),I=1,20),
*   (CUADD2(J,I),I=1,17),BAOH(J),J=I,L

reads in the master file. Each customer's information is contained on four cards.

The sales slips are read in through the use of the DO loop:

    DO 10 K=1,100
        READ(5,70,END=20)SCUNUM(K),SALES(K),INDIC(K)
    10 CONTINUE

Each sale is indicated on one data card, containing the customer's number, the sales value, and an indicator. The indicator equals @ on the last sales card of each customer. On all other sales cards, the indicator is blank (absence of indicator).

The major DO loop:

DO 50 J=1,L

calculates for all customers the minimum monthly payment.

The new balance is calculated in the assignment statement:

BAOH(J)=BAOH(J)+SALES(K)

The arithmetic IF statement:

IF(INDIC(K)−2084585536)30,40,30

controls for adding sales slips of the same customer to obtain the correct new balance of that customer.

The remaining IF statements, and assignment statements of that major DO loop accomplish step 3 of the Term Revolving Credit Plan algorithm.

Finally, the WRITE statement:

    WRITE(6,80)(CUNAM(J,I),I=1,20),(CUADD1(J,I),I=1,20),
*   (CUADD2(J,I),I=1,17),CUNUM(J),PAYME(J),
*   (DUDATE(I),I=1,4)

uses implicit DO loops to generate the appropriate output, containing the customer's name, address, number, minimum monthly payment, and the due date.

The data input is as follows:

```
DECEMBER 31.1971
     2
123456HENRY MILLER
1234561234 WEST MORELAND DRIVE          CINCINNATI   OHIO 45000
123456     10.30
123457JOHN A. WRIGHLEY
123457202 HIGHLAND                       CARLSBAD CA 92008
123457     20.75
123456     67.89
123456     67.89
123456     67.89
123456           @
123457     67.89
123457     67.89
123457           @
```

The FORTRAN program generates the following output:

```
CUSTOMER BILL FOR


HENRY MILLER
1234 WEST MOCRLAND DRIVE
CINCINNATI   OHOI 45000


CUSTOMER NUMBER 123456


THE AMOUNT OF      21.40 WILL BE DUE ON DECEMBER 31.1971

THANK YOU FOR YCUR ORDERS
```

```
CUSTOMER BILL FOR


JOHN A. WRIGHLEY
202 HIGHLAND
CARLSBAD CA 92008


CUSTOMER NUMBER 123457


THE AMOUNT OF      20.00 WILL BE DUE ON DECEMBER 31.1971

THANK YOU FOR YCUR ORDERS
```

4. Savings Accumulation: Single-Premium Life Insurance Policy

This example illustrates how to generate the savings accumulations for a single-premium life insurance policy. The single premium of $339.65 for $1,000 insurance is paid at the beginning of age 25 and accumulates 2½% interest. A net single premium of $339.65 for a $1,000 insurance is chosen since it results from a 2½% guaranteed interest.

Under the assumption that the premium is paid at age 25, at the beginning of the policy year, and that the death claims are paid at the end of the policy year, the accumulated fund at the end of any policy year, I, equals:

$$ENDCA(I) = INCAP(I) + INTER(I) + SURVI(I) - MOCOS(I)$$

where:

ENDCA(I) = the accumulated fund at the end of year I
INCAP(I) = the accumulated fund at the beginning of year I
INTER(I) = the interest of INCAP(I) at the end of year I
SURVI(I) = the survivor benefit at the end of year I
MOCOS(I) = the mortality cost during year I

The accumulated fund at the beginning of the year equals the fund at the end of the previous year.

$$INCAP(I) = ENDCA(I-1) \qquad [1]$$

At age 25 the fund at the beginning of the year equals the premium or $339.65:

$$INCAP(INAGE) = PREMI, \qquad [2]$$

where:

INAGE = 25
PREMI = $339.65

At the end of the policy year the interest accumulated during one year equals 2½% of the fund at the beginning of the year, or:

$$INTER(I) = INCAP(I) * .025 \qquad [3]$$

The mortality cost can be obtained from the 1958 CSO (commissioners 1958 Standard Ordinary Table) and is read in as data for the years 25 up to and including 75.

Since the CSO death rate at age 44 equals 4.92 people out of 1000, and since $1000 benefits are paid for each death claim, the mortality cost per person at age 44 equals:

$$\frac{\$1000 \times 4.92 \text{ people}}{1000 \text{ people}} \text{ or } \$4.92$$

Therefore the death rates per thousand people of the Commissioners 1958 Standard Ordinary Table equals the mortality cost for $1000 of life insurance.

The survivor benefit equals:

$$SURVI(I) = \frac{[INCAP(I) + INTER(I) - MOCOS(I)]DEATH(I)}{LIVING(I+1)} \qquad [4]$$

where:

LIVING(I+1) = number of people living at the end of the year I, or at the beginning of year (I+1), as per 1958 CSO table
DEATH(I) = LIVING(I) - LIVING(I+1)

All people who die during YEARI(DEATH(I)) cannot claim any of the accumulated savings (INCAP(I)+INTER(I)−MOCOS(I)). This results in a total sum of

$$(INCAP(I)+INTER(I)-MOCOS(I))DEATH(I)$$

relinquished savings, that becomes available to the survivors at the end of year I. Each survivor obtains, therefore, a survivor benefit equal to the total of the relinquished savings divided by the number of survivors at the end of year I, which is the above survivor benefit equation [4].

The variable names used in the flowchart and the program, their meaning, dimension, and mode are:

Program Variable Names	Definition	Mode	Dimension
DEATH	Number of people dying during a policy year	Integer	1
ENAGE	Ultimate age for which to calculate the accumulated savings for a single premium life insurance policy	Integer	0
ENAGEM	ENAGE+1	Integer	0
ENDCA	Accumulated fund at the end of the policy year	Real	1
INAGE	Initial age for which to calculate the accumulated savings for a single-premium life insurance policy	Integer	0
INCAP	Accumulated fund at the beginning of the policy year	Real	1
INTER	Interest in INCAP at the end of the policy year	Real	1
INTRT	Interest rate per unit	Real	0
LIVING	Number of people living at the beginning of the policy year	Integer	1
MOCOS	Mortality cost during the policy year	Real	1
PREMI	Single premium payment	Real	0
SURVI	Survivor benefit at the end of a policy year	Real	1

Flowcharting the Savings Accumulation for the Single-Premium Life Insurance Policy:

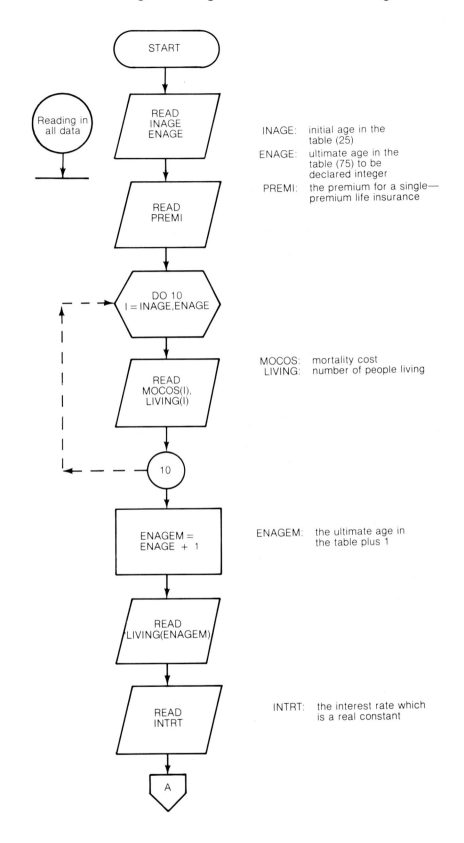

INAGE: initial age in the table (25)

ENAGE: ultimate age in the table (75) to be declared integer

PREMI: the premium for a single—premium life insurance

MOCOS: mortality cost
LIVING: number of people living

ENAGEM: the ultimate age in the table plus 1

INTRT: the interest rate which is a real constant

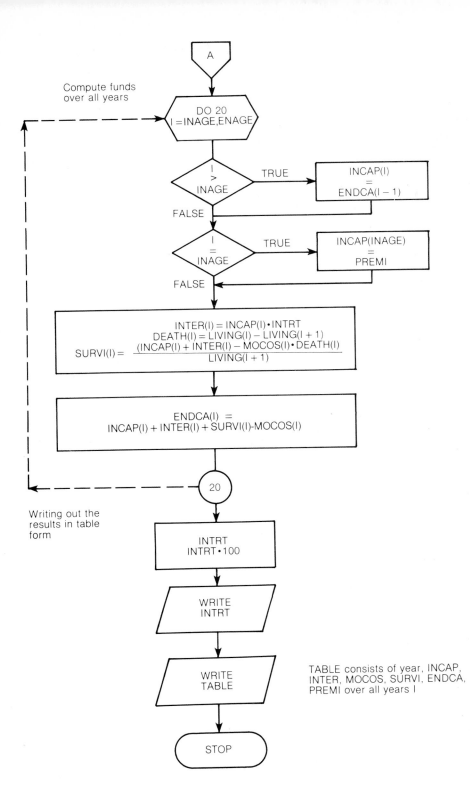

Compute funds over all years

A

DO 20
I = INAGE,ENAGE

$$\frac{I}{>}$$
$$INAGE$$

TRUE → INCAP(I) = ENDCA(I − 1)

FALSE

$$\frac{I}{=}$$
$$INAGE$$

TRUE → INCAP(INAGE) = PREMI

FALSE

$$INTER(I) = INCAP(I) \cdot INTRT$$
$$DEATH(I) = LIVING(I) − LIVING(I + 1)$$
$$SURVI(I) = \frac{(INCAP(I) + INTER(I) − MOCOS(I) \cdot DEATH(I)}{LIVING(I + 1)}$$

$$ENDCA(I) = INCAP(I) + INTER(I) + SURVI(I)-MOCOS(I)$$

20

Writing out the results in table form

INTRT
INTRT · 100

WRITE
INTRT

WRITE
TABLE

TABLE consists of year, INCAP, INTER, MOCOS, SURVI, ENDCA, PREMI over all years I

STOP

```
C *** SAVINGS ACCUMULATION FOR SINGLE PREMIUM LIFE
C *** INSURANCE
      INTEGER DEATH(100), LIVING(100), ENAGE, ENAGEM
      REAL INTRT, MOCOS(100), INCAP(100), INTER(100)
      DIMENSION SURVI(100), ENDCA(100)
C *** READ IN THE INITIAL AND FINAL AGE OF TABLE
      READ(5,100) INAGE, ENAGE
C *** READ IN PREMIUM FOR SINGLE PAYMENT
      READ(5,110) PREMI
C *** READ MORTALITY COSTS AND NUMBER LIVING
      DO 10  I = INAGE, ENAGE
        READ(5,120) MOCOS(I), LIVING(I)
   10 CONTINUE
      ENAGEM = ENAGE + 1
      READ(5,130) INTRT
C *** COMPUTE FUNDS OVER ALL YEARS
      DO 20  I = INAGE, ENAGE
        IF(I .GT. INAGE) INCAP(I) = ENDCA(I-1)
        IF(I .EQ. INAGE) INCAP(I) = PREMI
        INTER(I) = INCAP(I) * INTRT
        DEATH(I) = LIVING(I) - LIVING(I+1)
        SURVI(I) = ((INCAP(I)+INTER(I)-MOCOS(I)*DEATH(I))/LIVING(I+1)
        ENDCA(I) = INCAP(I) + INTER(I) + SURVI(I) - MOCOS(I)
   20 CONTINUE
C *** WRITE OUT HEADINGS AND TABLE
      INTRT = INTRT * 100
      WRITE(6,140) INTRT
      DO 30  I = INAGE, ENAGE
        WRITE(6,150) I, INCAP(I), INTER(I), MOCOS(I),
     *               SURVI(I), ENDCA(I), PRIMI
   30 CONTINUE
      WRITE(6,160)
      STOP
  100 FORMAT(2I3)
  110 FORMAT(F6.2)
  120 FORMAT(F6.2,I8)
  130 FORMAT(F5.3)
  140 FORMAT(1H1,9X,'SAVINGS ACCUMULATIONS',/,
     *       10X,'SINGLE PREMIUM LIFE INSURANCE POLICY',/,
     *       10X,'1958 CSO AT ',F5.2,' PERCENT',//,
     *       10X,263('*'),/,
     *       10X,'AGE',2X,'FUND AT',4X,'INTEREST',2X,'MORTAL',3X,
     *          'SURVI',3X,'FUND AT',4X,'PREMIUM',/,
     *       15X,'JAN. 1.',32X,'DEC. 31.',/,
     *       10X,63('*'))
  150 FORMAT(10X,I3,2X,'$',F7.2,2X,'$',F6.2,2X,'$',F5.2,
     *       2X,'$',F5.2,2X,'$',F7.2,2X,'$',F6.2)
  160 FORMAT(10X,63('*'))
  170 FORMAT(I8)
      END
```

This FORTRAN program exhibits many FORTRAN features and is very efficiently written.

The declaration statements INTEGER and REAL are used to declare variable names to be integer or real, respectively, regardless of their first letter. These two declaration statements also provide dimensions for some variable arrays. The DIMENSION statement declares two additional arrays: SURVI and ENDCA. The Input/Output statements are the READ and the WRITE statements for the conventional card and printer I/O.

The first read statement

READ(5,100)INAGE,ENAGE

provides for reading in two integer constants from the first data card, according to FORMAT statement label 100.

The second read statement

READ(5,110)PREMI

reads from a second card the single-premium payment from the first six columns as specified in FORMAT 110

An explicit DO loop

DO 10 I=INAGE,ENAGE

results in reading in the next 51 cards, each containing a real constant, (the mortality cost for a policy year) and an integer constant (the number of people living at the beginning of the policy year) according to FORMAT number 120.

The next two READ statements are Self-explanatory.

In the DO loop:

DO 20 I=INAGE,ENAGE

all necessary calculations are made for the Single-Premium Life Insurance Table, as explained before.

The two IF statements provide for calculating the accumulated fund at the beginning of the policy year. This fund equals the premium during the first policy year and equals the accumulated fund at the end of the previous year during all other policy years.

The WRITE statements print a table containing a heading, the interest rate, column headings, and all generated values for all policy years.

The data input is as follows:

```
      25  75
      339.65
        1.93 9575636
        1.96 9557155
        1.99 9538423
        2.03 9519442
        2.08 9500118
        2.13 9480358
        2.19 9460165
        2.25 9439447
        2.32 9418208
        2.40 9396358
        2.51 9373807
        2.64 9350279
        2.80 9325594
        3.01 9299482
        3.25 9271491
        3.53 9241359
        3.84 9208737
        4.17 9173375
        4.53 9135122
        4.92 9093740
        5.35 9048999
        5.83 9000587
        6.36 8948114
        6.95 8891204
        7.60 8829410
```

```
        8.32 8762306
        9.11 8689404
        9.96 8610244
       10.89 8524486
       11.90 8431654
       13.00 8331317
       14.21 8223010
       15.54 8106161
       17.00 7980191
       18.59 7844528
       20.34 7698698
       22.24 7542106
       24.31 7374370
       26.57 7195099
       29.04 7003925
       31.75 6800531
       34.74 6584614
       38.04 6355865
       41.68 6114088
       45.61 5859253
       49.79 5592012
       54.15 5313586
       58.65 5025855
       63.26 4731089
       68.12 4431800
       73.37 4129906
        3826895
      0.025
```

The FORTRAN program generates the following table:

```
SAVINGS ACCUMULATIONS
SINGLE PREMIUM LIFE INSURANCE POLICY
1958 CSO AT  2.50 PERCENT


****************************************************************
AGE   FUND AT      INTEREST   MORTAL     SURVIV     FUND AT      PREMIUM
      JAN. 1.                                       DEC. 31.
****************************************************************
 25  $  339.65   $   8.49   $  1.93   $  0.67   $  346.88   $ 339.65
 26  $  346.88   $   8.67   $  1.96   $  0.69   $  354.29   $ 339.65
 27  $  354.29   $   8.86   $  1.99   $  0.72   $  361.87   $ 339.65
 28  $  361.87   $   9.05   $  2.03   $  0.75   $  369.64   $ 339.65
 29  $  369.64   $   9.24   $  2.08   $  0.79   $  377.59   $ 339.65
 30  $  377.59   $   9.44   $  2.13   $  0.82   $  385.72   $ 339.65
 31  $  385.72   $   9.64   $  2.19   $  0.86   $  394.03   $ 339.65
 32  $  394.03   $   9.85   $  2.25   $  0.91   $  402.54   $ 339.65
 33  $  402.54   $  10.06   $  2.32   $  0.95   $  411.24   $ 339.65
 34  $  411.24   $  10.28   $  2.40   $  1.01   $  420.12   $ 339.65
 35  $  420.12   $  10.50   $  2.51   $  1.08   $  429.19   $ 339.65
 36  $  429.19   $  10.73   $  2.64   $  1.16   $  438.44   $ 339.65
 37  $  438.44   $  10.96   $  2.80   $  1.25   $  447.86   $ 339.65
 38  $  447.86   $  11.20   $  3.01   $  1.38   $  457.42   $ 339.65
 39  $  457.42   $  11.44   $  3.25   $  1.52   $  467.12   $ 339.65
 40  $  467.12   $  11.68   $  3.53   $  1.68   $  476.95   $ 339.65
 41  $  476.95   $  11.92   $  3.84   $  1.87   $  486.91   $ 339.65
 42  $  486.91   $  12.17   $  4.17   $  2.07   $  496.98   $ 339.65
 43  $  496.98   $  12.42   $  4.53   $  2.30   $  507.17   $ 339.65
 44  $  507.17   $  12.68   $  4.92   $  2.55   $  517.48   $ 339.65
 45  $  517.48   $  12.94   $  5.35   $  2.82   $  527.89   $ 339.65
 46  $  527.89   $  13.20   $  5.83   $  3.14   $  538.40   $ 339.65
 47  $  538.40   $  13.46   $  6.36   $  3.49   $  548.99   $ 339.65
 48  $  548.99   $  13.72   $  6.95   $  3.89   $  559.65   $ 339.65
 49  $  559.65   $  13.99   $  7.60   $  4.33   $  570.38   $ 339.65
 50  $  570.38   $  14.26   $  8.32   $  4.84   $  581.15   $ 339.65
 51  $  581.15   $  14.53   $  9.11   $  5.39   $  591.96   $ 339.65
 52  $  591.96   $  14.80   $  9.96   $  6.00   $  602.80   $ 339.65
 53  $  602.80   $  15.07   $ 10.89   $  6.68   $  613.67   $ 339.65
 54  $  613.67   $  15.34   $ 11.90   $  7.43   $  624.54   $ 339.65
 55  $  624.54   $  15.61   $ 13.00   $  8.26   $  635.41   $ 339.65
 56  $  635.41   $  15.89   $ 14.21   $  9.18   $  646.27   $ 339.65
 57  $  646.27   $  16.16   $ 15.54   $ 10.21   $  657.10   $ 339.65
 58  $  657.10   $  16.43   $ 17.00   $ 11.35   $  667.88   $ 339.65
 59  $  667.88   $  16.70   $ 18.59   $ 12.62   $  678.60   $ 339.65
 60  $  678.60   $  16.97   $ 20.34   $ 14.02   $  689.25   $ 339.65
 61  $  689.25   $  17.23   $ 22.24   $ 15.56   $  699.80   $ 339.65
 62  $  699.80   $  17.49   $ 24.31   $ 17.27   $  710.25   $ 339.65
 63  $  710.25   $  17.76   $ 26.57   $ 19.15   $  720.58   $ 339.65
 64  $  720.58   $  18.01   $ 29.04   $ 21.22   $  730.78   $ 339.65
 65  $  730.78   $  18.27   $ 31.75   $ 23.52   $  740.82   $ 339.65
 66  $  740.82   $  18.52   $ 34.74   $ 26.08   $  750.68   $ 339.65
 67  $  750.68   $  18.77   $ 38.04   $ 28.92   $  760.33   $ 339.65
 68  $  760.33   $  19.01   $ 41.68   $ 32.08   $  769.74   $ 339.65
 69  $  769.74   $  19.24   $ 45.61   $ 35.53   $  778.90   $ 339.65
 70  $  778.90   $  19.47   $ 49.79   $ 39.22   $  787.80   $ 339.65
 71  $  787.80   $  19.70   $ 54.15   $ 43.13   $  796.48   $ 339.65
 72  $  796.48   $  19.91   $ 58.65   $ 47.21   $  804.95   $ 339.65
 73  $  804.95   $  20.12   $ 63.26   $ 51.45   $  813.26   $ 339.65
 74  $  813.26   $  20.33   $ 68.12   $ 55.96   $  821.43   $ 339.65
 75  $  821.43   $  20.54   $ 73.37   $ 60.86   $  829.45   $ 339.65
****************************************************************
```

Problem No. 1

Write a program to read in an input card file containing the following fields of data:

Column   1–4   Inventory part number

           11–16   Quantity (in units)

           21–25   Cost per unit

There are no more than fifty cards of data. The inventory cost for each part is to be determined as well as the cost of the total inventory. This information must be printed in the following format:

Column   7–10   Inventory Part Number

           14–20   Quantity

           25–30   Cost per Unit

           31–45   Inventory Cost

For those parts which exceed 4% of the cost of the total inventory, the part number and the percent of the total inventory (to the nearest tenth of a percent) are to be printed in columns 11–14 and 21–25 of a single spaced list.

Problem No. 2

The fees at an airport parking lot are established as follows:

fifty cents for the first half hour of parking;

an additional 25 cents is charged for each additional hour to a maximum of $2.50 per day for up to five days;

after the fourth day the rate drops to $1.25 per day for a maximum of two weeks.

Create a flowchart and a program which compute the amount due for each car parked in the lot. Each parking ticket (input) contains the total parking time in hours and minutes.

Problem No. 3

A wholesale firm grants customer discounts which depend on the size of the sale. The following discount table is used:

Sale Amount (SALES)	Discount (DISC)
less than $250.00	0%
$250.00–$499.00	2%
$500.00–$999.99	5%
$1000.00 and over	8%

You are asked to design a computer program for processing the following customer sales. The program will read customer cards, each of which contains the following fields of data:

Column   1–5   customer's identification number (ID)

           10–15   number of units sold (NUNITS)

           20–25   sales price per unit for the product sold (UPRICE)

The program is to calculate the gross amount of each sale, the discount allowed (if any), and the net sale amount (gross sale—discount). The program must also compute the total sales, total discounts, and the total net sales for the firm. Finally, write out the following:

For each Customer Sale: customer identification
number of units sold
sale price per unit
gross sale amount
discount amount
net sale amount

For Company Totals: total gross sales
total discounts allowed
total net sales

Appropriately label all output.

Problem No. 4

The MATCH-MAKER, a computer dating company, administers the following questionnaire to its clients. The questionnaire collects twenty data items related to each person. This data has to do with physical appearance, interests, values, personality, etc. You are supposed to write a computer program that:

1. reads the answers of all girls and boys;
2. considers the answer of each girl and compares it with that of each boy;
3. computes for each question the difference between all the girls' and the boys' answers and squares it.
4. sums these twenty squared data item responses as a measure of compatibility of a girl and a boy
5. prints for each girl the name of the boy who is best fitted and the name of the boy who is most poorly suited.

Questionnaire:

Sex: 1. Male   2. Female

Name _____ (20 characters)

1. Physical appearance
   (1) attractive   (2) average   (3) unattractive
2. Height
   (1) tall   (2) average   (3) short
3. Weight
   (1) slim   (2) average   (3) fat
4. Intelligence
   (1) above average   (2) average   (3) below average
5. Dress habits
   (1) stylish   (2) average   (3) unimportant
6. Your need to excel
   (1) high   (2) average   (3) unimportant
7. Interest in athletics
   (1) high   (2) average   (3) low
8. How do you feel about cheating?
   (1) never   (2) occasionally   (3) why not?
9. Do you smoke?
   (1) never   (2) occasionally   (3) steadily

10. Should our young men be drafted into the armed forces?
    (1) yes   (2) reluctantly   (3) no

11. How many nights a week do you go out?
    (1) one or two   (2) three or four   (3) more than four

12. Do you want to own a pet?
    (1) yes   (2) maybe   (3) no

13. What is your economic background?
    (1) upper class   (2) middle class   (3) lower class

14. What music do you prefer?
    (1) rock   (2) popular   (3) classical

15. How about equal rights for women?
    (1) no   (2) maybe   (3) yes

16. Your personality
    (1) exuberant   (2) average   (3) shy

17. The respect of others is:
    (1) vital   (2) important   (3) unimportant

18. On charity:
    (1) important   (2) maybe   (3) a racket

19. How about early marriage?
    (1) interested   (2) maybe   (3) no

20. Is it important to live in a neat home?
    (1) definitely   (2) yes   (3) no

Problem No. 5

Write a FORTRAN program which will do the following:

a) Enter data into two arrays in storage from punched cards in the following format:
   Cols. 2–4   is the alphanumeric code of an inventory item
         6–10 is the per unit rate of the above inventory item
   There are fifteen such cards to be read, one for each inventory item.

b) Read in a second set of punched cards that contain customer usage data as follows:
   Cols. 2–40 is the customer's name and address
        42–43 is a two-digit customer code
        45–47 is the alphanumeric code of the inventory item that the customer orders
        49–56 is the ordered quantity.
   There are twenty such cards to be read, one for each customer.

c) Print a line for each customer containing name, address, and amount due according to the quantity used, the rate, and the customer code as explained below.

Customer Code	Meaning
00	normal rate
01	3% discount
02	first 100 units at no charge
03	service temporarily discontinued, no goods are sent but a minimum charge of $2.50 to be billed to the customer
04	no charge

d) Print the total amount due the company (for all customers).

INPUT

a)

Inventory Code	Rate/Unit
APL	7.05
PER	11.15
GUM	2.00
LIP	33.27
DUM	5.02
APE	17.50
MOM	12.33
DAD	1.00
SON	99.00
ANN	10.00
POT	0.15
LOL	0.10
NOD	65.02
COT	50.00
ROT	2.50

Name and Address	CCode	UCODE	Quantity
Woods RR1 Lipton Ind	00	PER	999.95
Young 503 Vine Glenwood Ind	01	NOD	950.00
Bennett 1205 W 10th Lebanon Ind	00	APE	703.50
Begley Flint Dr Connersv Ind	03	DAD	734.45
Bales 122 W 8th Connersv Ind	04	NOD	2.50
Craig 821 Fayette Denver Col	01	APL	4532.00
Creamer 604 Ranch Rd Connersv Ind	02	ROT	201.00
Hauk RR2 Lafayette Ind	02	LIP	95.50
Harris RR2 Connersv Ind	00	SON	220.00
Hansell 2251 Grand Ave Oxford Oh	01	APE	25.00
Dorris 17 Grates Av Lola NY	01	ANN	715.00
Heeb 1517 Virginia Av Kokomo Ind	01	LOL	55.55
Liberty 3227 Beeson Av Cincinnati Oh	03	DUM	172.50
Kreep 1515 Conwell Buffalo NY	01	SON	12.50
Lambert 211 W 5th Lipton NJ	02	APE	717.50
Benson 3 County Rd Teapot Wy	00	COT	1215.20
Leming 17 Grand Av Connersv Ind	00	LIP	1300.00
Overbeck 208 S Market Liberty Ind	04	POT	500.00
Newell 13 Huston New Castle Ind	01	COT	123.00
Grimsel 1112 Burton Capetown Fl	00	GUM	7254.50

Hints

(1) Use subscripted variables.

(2) Use the following names
   (a) to call information from the first set of punched cards
      KUD(I): *inventory code
   (b) to call information from the second set of punched cards
      URATE(I): rate per unit
      ICODE(J): customer code
      JUD(J): *code of the ordered inventory item
      UQUANT(J): quantity ordered

(3) Read in name and address using A-format specification; however, remember that you cannot read in more than four characters under the name.
   Use (an) integer variable name(s) to read in the name and address.

(4) Before writing the statements, think this problem out very carefully, and perhaps write out in your own words how you would solve it; then draw a flowchart to aid you in writing your program.

*note different name (this will be necessary!)

Problem No. 6

Program the Savings Accumulation of a 20-year Premium Life Insurance Policy. During years 25 to 44 a premium of $21.68 is paid to the company at the beginning of each year.

All other data is identical to the data used in Example 4.

Subprograms in FORTRAN

Much time and effort in programming can be saved by using modules of code which have been previously prepared and tested by others. These "canned" modules are called subprograms and are used for calculations that many programmers need. Once an efficient method for doing a task has been determined, its equivalent FORTRAN program can be written and placed in a library, where other users can take advantage of it by calling for it within their own programs. Any such user is then in a position to concentrate their programming efforts on those portions of their program which are unique to their own specific problem.

These subprograms are of particular advantage if they are needed repeatedly in the same program, for example, the calculation of square roots, logs, absolute values, factorials, minima, maxima, etc. In the case of large programs, the savings in memory space or in complexity of programming are most significant. A subprogram is inserted into the total program only once, even though it may be called upon to be used at many points within the program.

This chapter will explore and explain the manner in which subprograms are written in the FORTRAN language. Basically, subprograms fall into one of four major groups: (1) the built-in functions or the library functions, (2) the arithmetic statement function. (3) the function subprogram, and (4) the subroutine subprogram.

Built-in functions or library functions are designed by the FORTRAN language composer and are provided with the FORTRAN compiler for use in FORTRAN expressions; arithmetic statement functions, on the other hand, are created in the FORTRAN program by the user or the programmer.

Function and subroutine subprograms are separate FORTRAN programs. The reasons for using them can be illustrated as follows:

1. A problem may call for the repetition of a procedure. In such an instance, one single subprogram may contain the instructions for that procedure, and the main program can then invoke that subprogram as many times as necessary.
2. A large program can be written by various people. In this case, individual tasks are defined in terms of assigning subprograns to the individual programmers. The main program, then, must call for the subprograms in the appropriate order.
3. It is easier to debug sets of subprograms than to debug an entire complex program.

There are several versions of FORTRAN in use and they differ in subprogram capability. The discussion here assumes a fairly complete FORTRAN as might be used on intermediate and large machines.

The predefined process symbol is used in flowcharting to define arithmetic statement functions and to refer to a subprogram function or subprogram subroutine. A separate flowchart is then developed to specify all steps and operations for the function or subroutine program. In this case the START block carries the name of the subprogram.

Name of
Function
or
Subroutine

1. Built-In Functions or Library Functions

Most FORTRAN compilers have a family of built-in functions that are part of the FORTRAN language. They are used to generate, in an efficient way, commonly used mathematical factors.

Specific variable names are used to call these library functions, such as:

SQRT   can be used to calcuate the square root
$$[SQRT(13.2) \rightarrow \sqrt{13.2}]$$

ALOG   to calculate the natural log
$$[ALOG](14.23) \rightarrow \log_e(14.23)]$$

SIN   to calculate the trigonometric sine of an angle in radians
$$[SIN(3.14) \rightarrow \sin 180°]$$

COS   to calculate the trigonometric cosine of an angle in radians
$$[COS(3.14) \rightarrow \cos 180°]$$

FLOAT   to convert an integer to a real value
$$[FLOAT(17) \rightarrow 17.]$$

IFIX   to convert a real to an integer value
$$[IFIX(17.5) \rightarrow 17]$$

ABS   to calculate the absolute value
$$[ABS(A) \rightarrow |A|]$$

Tables 11.1 and 11.2 provide a listing of library functions used in mathematical and business problems.

Table 11.1 Mathematical FORTRAN Functions

External Function Name	FORTRAN Name	Mathematical Definition	Number of Arguments	Type of Arguments	Type of Function
Arcsine	ARSIN	arcsin (a), argument	1	Real	Real
	DARSIN	in radians	1	Double	Double
Arccosine	ARCOS	arcsin (a), argument	1	Real	Real
	DARCOS	in radians	1	Double	Double
Arctangent	ATAN	arctan (a), argument	1	Real	Real
	DATAN	in radians	1	Double	Double
	ATAN2	arctan(a_1/a_2),	2	Real	Real
	DATAN2	arguments in radians	2	Double	Double
Trigonometric Sine	SIN	sin(a), argument in	1	Real	Real
	DSIN	radians	1	Double	Double
	CSIN		1	Complex	Complex
	CDSIN		1	Db. Compl.	Db. Compl.
Trigonometric Cosine	COS	cos(a), argument in	1	Real	Real
	DCOS	radians	1	Double	Double
	CCOS		1	Complex	Complex
	CDCOS		1	Db. Compl.	Db. Compl.
Trigonometric Tangent	TAN	tan(a), argument in	1	Real	Real
	DTAN	radians	1	Double	Double
Trigonometric Cotangent	COTAN	cotan(a), argument in	1	Real	Real
	DCOTAN	radians	1	Double	Double
Hyperbolic Sine	SINH	sinh(a), argument in	1	Real	Real
	DSINH	radians	1	Double	Double
Hyperbolic cosine	COSH	cosh(a), argument in	1	Real	Real
	DCOSH	radians	1	Double	Double
Hyperbolic Tangent	TANH	tanh(a), argument in	1	Real	Real
	DTANH	radians	1	Double	Double

Table 11.2 Library Functions Used in Business Problems

External Function Name	FORTRAN Name	Mathematical Definition	Number of Arguments	Type of Arguments	Type of Function
Square Root	SQRT	$\sqrt{a}$	1	Real	Real
	DSQRT		1	Double	Double
	CSQRT		1	Complex	Complex
	CDSQRT		1	Db. Compl.	Db. Compl.
Exponential	EXP	e^a	1	Real	Real
	DEXP		1	Double	Double
	CESP		1	Complex	Complex
	CDEXP		1	Db. Compl.	Db. Compl.
Absolute Value	ABS	$\lvert a \rvert$	1	Real	Real
	DABS		1	Double	Double
	IABS		1	Integer	Integer
Natural Logarithm	ALOG	$\log_e(a)$	1	Real	Real
	DLOG		1	Double	Double
	CLOG		1	Complex	Complex
	CDLOG		1	Db. Compl.	Db. Compl.
Common Logarithm	ALOG10	$\log_{10}(a)$	1	Real	Real
	DLOG10		1	Double	Double
Largest Value	AMAX0	$\max(a_1, a_2, \ldots)$	≥ 2	Integer	Real
	AMAX1			Real	Real
	DMAX1			Double	Double
	MAX0			Integer	Integer
	MAX1			Real	Integer
Smallest Value	AMINO	$\min(a_1, a_2, \ldots)$	≥ 2	Integer	Real
	AMIN1			Real	Real
	DMIN1			Double	Double
	MIN0			Integer	Integer
	MIN1			Real	Integer
Float	FLOAT	convert integer→real	1	Integer	Real
	DFLOAT		1	Integer	Double
Fix	IFIX	convert real→integer	1	Real	Integer

A typical FORTRAN statement that uses a FORTRAN built-in function is:

EOQ=SQRT(2.*AUSAGE*ORDERC/CARRYC)

The arithmetic assignment statement uses the square root library function to calculate the economic order quantity (EOQ). The argument of the function is:

2.*AUSAGE*ORDERC/CARRYC

where AUSAGE stands for annual usage, ORDERC stands for order cost, and CARRYC stands for carrying cost. Note that the argument is placed in parentheses after the name of the function.

An argument of a built-in function may be a constant, a variable name, or an arithmetic expression with or without built-in functions; however, a built-in function may not be an argument of itself. Examples of correct built-in functions are:

EOQ=SQRT(2.*AUSAGE*ORDERC/CARRYC)
OUT=ABS(A)
VALUE=ALOG(1725.2)

Examples of incorrect built-in functions are:

A=SQRT(2.5+B*SQRT(C)) no built-in function may be an argument of itself.
SMALL=AMIN1(A,B,2.5,J,D) the arguments of the AMIN1 function must all be real.

2. Arithmetic Statement Functions

The programmer can define a function which is not available from the list of library functions. This function is called the arithmetic statement function. As this function appears in the FORTRAN program, it is compiled along with the main program, and therefore cannot be used in any other program.

As with library functions, the arithmetic statement functions save considerable storage space and simplify writing statements. They are of great help when they are complex statements, have many parameters, and are used many times in the same program.

In arithmetic statement functions, dummy variables are placed in parenthesis following the name of the function. These dummy variables must be unsubscripted variables. The expression following the equal sign may be any valid FORTRAN expression, excluding subscripted variables.

An example of an arithmetic statement function is:

CUM(A,N)=A*(1.+B)**N

This definition must appear in the beginning of the FORTRAN program preceding the first executable statement and following the DIMENSION statement. This arithmetic statement function can be used in any of the following ways:

```
CAP=CUM(CAP,NYEARS)
CAP=CUM(CAP1+CAP2,NYEARS)
CAP=CUM(CAP,7)
```

The dummy variables A and N are replaced by the actual arguments CAP, and NYEARS or CAP1 + CAP2 and NYEARS or CAP and 7. When, in the calling statements, arguments are assigned specific values, they cease to be dummy arguments. Notice, as in the above examples, that actual arguments may be variable names, arithmetic expressions, or constants. Keep in mind, however, that the actual arguments must be of the same mode (integer or real) and in the same order as the dummy argument.

Note that in the above function, B is not listed as an argument of the arithmetic statement function CUM(A,N). The variables that appear in the statement, but not in the argument list, are the parameters of that function. So B is a parameter.

The current values of the actual arguments and the parameters are used when an arithmetic statement function is called. Therefore one can change the values of the parameters or the arguments between calls of the function.

The following short program illustrates the use of the arithmetic statement function.

```
C*** ILLUSTRATION OF ARITHMETIC-STATEMENT FUNCTION
C*** DEFINING THE FUNCTION
     CUM(A,N)=A*(1.+B)**N
C*** DEFINING THE INTEREST RATE B (5.50%)
  20 B=0.055
C*** PROCESSING THE FIRST SET OF DATA
     READ(5,40)CAP,NYEARS
  40 FORMAT(F10.2,I4)
  50 CAP=CUM(CAP,NYEARS)
     WRITE(6,70)CAP
  70 FORMAT(5X,'ACCUMULATED INVESTMENT',F12.2)
C*** PROCESSING THE NEXT DATA SET
     READ(5,90)CAP1,CAP2,NYEARS
  90 FORMAT(2F10.2,I4)
 100 CAP=CUM(CAP1+CAP2,NYEARS)
     WRITE(6,70)CAP
```

```
C*** PROCESSING THE LAST DATA SET
      READ(5,130)CAP
130   FORMAT(F10.2)
140   CAP=CUM(CAP,7)
      WRITE(6,180)CAP
      STOP
      END
```

The statement $CUM(A,N)=A*(1.+B)**N)$ defines an arithmetic statement function. This function appears in the beginning of the program and precedes the first executable statement. It has two arguments: A and N. The variable name B is not an argument but a parameter. The value of the parameter B is defined through an assignment in statement #20.

Assignment statement #50 calls for the statement function. Note that this statement function is invoked in the same way that a library function is invoked. The actual arguments used are CAP and NYEARS.

The arithmetic statement function is invoked a second time in statement #100. The first actual argument is the expression CAP1+CAP2. The second argument is NYEARS.

Finally, the arithmetic statement function is called for a third time in statement #140.

In conclusion, the arithmetic statement function is called upon in the same manner as we call upon a library function. The difference between the two, however, is that an arithmetic statement function must be defined within the program, while a library function is not.

3. The FORTRAN Function Subprogram

The structure of the FORTRAN function subprogram is quite different from the arithmetic statement function or the library function. The function subprogram is used when the subprogram cannot be expressed by a single FORTRAN statement due to its complexity, and when only a single value needs to be returned to the main or calling program.

The function is a separate FORTRAN program and is compiled independently of the program in which it is called. It is, however, called in the same manner as a library or an arithmetic statement function as outlined before.

The following rules govern the structure of the function subprogram:

1. The first statement must name the function and identify all arguments. A real function name is used if a real constant needs to be returned to the calling program; an integer function name is used if an integer constant is to be returned to the calling program.
2. At least one arithmetic assignment statement of the function subprogram must contain the name of the function on the left side.
3. The number of actual arguments in the calling statement must be equal to the number of dummy arguments in the function definition statement of the function subprogram. These arguments must also agree in mode, order, and dimension. If the actual argument is an array, the corresponding dummy argument must also be an array and identical dimensions are necessary. Dummy arguments must be unsubscripted variables even though array names are permitted.
4. A function subprogram cannot contain a STOP statement, but must have a RETURN and an END statement. The RETURN statement returns control to the calling program. Like the STOP statement in a main program, there may be more than one RETURN statement in the function subprogram. The last statement before the END statement need not be a RETURN statement; it can be a transfer statement that transfers control to an earlier statement in the function subprogram.
5. Since FUNCTION subprograms are separate programs, their variable names and statement numbers may be the same as those found in the main program.

Consider the following main program and function subprogram:

Main Program
```
    DIMENSION ARRAY(20)
    READ(5,10)ARRAY
10  FORMAT(20F4.1)
    I=LARGE(ARRAY,20)
    WRITE(6,20)I
20  FORMAT(5X,I4)
    STOP
    END
```

Function Subprogram
```
    FUNCTION LARGE(A,L)
    DIMENSION A(20)
    GREAT=A(1)
    LARGE=1
    DO 10 I=2,L
        IF(A(I).LT.GREAT)GO TO 10
        GREAT=A(I)
        LARGE=I
10  CONTINUE
    RETURN
    END
```

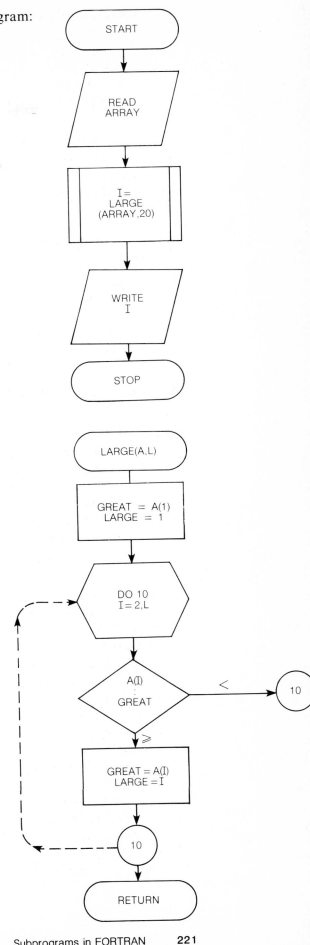

The main program calls for a function subprogram in the statement: I= LARGE(ARRAY,20). The name of the subprogram is LARGE. This function determines which of the elements of the array ARRAY is the largest or, if more than one are of equal magnitude, the largest subscript of those that are tied for the maximum. ARRAY is a real array and contains 20 elements. The first statement of the function contains the name of the function, LARGE, and the dummy arguments are A and L. LARGE is an integer name and therefore reflects that an integer constant will be returned to the calling program. At execution time, the dummy argument, A, will be replaced by the actual argument, ARRAY. Both A and ARRAY are arrays and are dimensioned in both programs. The dummy argument, L, will be replaced by the actual argument 20. Note that the ARRAY in the main program is a one-dimensional array of 20 elements and that its corresponding argument A is identically dimensioned in the FUNCTION.

The routine of determining which element is the largest starts with two statements: the first statement sets GREAT equal to the first element of the array A, and the second one sets LARGE equal to 1. The DO loop redefines GREAT and LARGE as successively equal or larger elements of the array are encountered.

When, finally, the DO loop is finished, LARGE equals the largest index of the largest value of the real array, ARRAY, and control is returned to the calling program through the RETURN statement.

Notice that the function name LARGE appears twice on the left-hand side of an arithmetic assignment statement and that the dummy arguments A and L are not redefined. The subroutine function does not contain a STOP statement, but instead a RETURN statement that transfers control to the main program.

Additional Examples of FORTRAN Function Subprograms

Example [1] Conversion of degrees, minutes, seconds to radians

```
FUNCTION RADIAN(D,FM,S)
D=D+FM/60.+S/3600.
RADIAN=D*3.14/180
RETURN
END
```

The function name, RADIAN, is real. Therefore, a real constant will be returned to the calling program. The dummy arguments, D, FM, and S, are real and are redefined in the function subprogram.

Example [2] Computation of N! (N factorial).

```
    FUNCTION NFACT(N)
    NFACT=1
    IF(N.LE.1)GO TO 20
    DO 10 I=2,N
        NFACT=NFACT*I
10 CONTINUE
20 RETURN
    END
```

Note that the integer function NFACT is put equal to 1, before the DO loop is executed $(1!=0!=1)$.

Example [3] Computation of the average of N elements of data.

```
      FUNCTION AVRAGE(A,N)
      DIMENSION A(100)
      SUM=0
      DO 10 I=1,N
        SUM=SUM+A(I)
   10 CONTINUE
      AN=N
      AVRAGE=SUM/AN
      RETURN
      END
```

Example [4] Computation of the variance where the function subprogram VARNCE makes use of another function subprogram AVRAGE.

```
      FUNCTION VARNCE(A,N)
      DIMENSION A(100)
      TOT=0
      ABAR=AVRAGE(A,N)
      DO 10 I=1,N
        TOT=TOT+(ABAR-A(I))**2
   10 CONTINUE
      AN=N
      VARNCE=TOT/AN
      RETURN
      END

      FUNCTION AVRAGE(B,M)
      DIMENSION B(100)
      SUM=0
      DO 20 I=1,M
        SUM=SUM+B(I)
   20 CONTINUE
      BM=M
      AVRAGE=SUM/BM
      RETURN
      END
```

4. The FORTRAN Subroutine Subprogram

The subroutine subprogram is similar to a function subprogram: it is compiled separately from the main program and consists of more than one statement. Subroutines, however, may transmit either many values or no values to the main program, whereas function subprograms return only one value.

1. A subroutine subprogram is headed by a SUBROUTINE statement containing the name of the subroutine and the list of all its arguments. It must contain at least one RETURN and the last statement must be an END.
2. There is no value or mode associated with the name of the subroutine; therefore, the results of the subroutine are passed via the dummy arguments. No argument, variable, or array, defined within the subroutine, may be the same name as the subroutine.
3. More than one variable and/or array must be returned to the calling program by the subroutine.

4. There are three types of dummy arguments: input arguments, output arguments, and mixed arguments. The input arguments furnish data to the subroutine and are not modified by statements in the subroutine. The output arguments are calculated within the subroutine and returned to the calling program. The mixed arguments furnish data to the subroutine, are modified by the subroutine, and are finally returned to the calling program.

5. The number of actual arguments in the CALL statement must be equal to the number of dummy arguments in the SUBROUTINE statement. These arguments must also agree in mode, order, and dimension. If the actual argument is an array, the corresponding dummy argument must also be an array, and identical dimensions are necessary.

6. The subroutine is called by a special CALL statement in the calling program that identifies the name of the subroutine and defines the arguments.

The same variable, array names or statement numbers may be used in a main program and in all the Functions or Subroutine subprograms because the values associated with the names in the main and subprograms are completely independent since the programs are compiled separately.

Consider the following main program and subroutine:

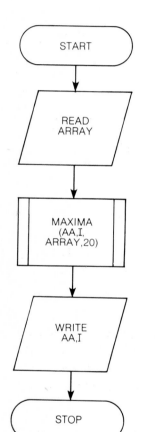

```
        Main Program
        DIMENSION ARRAY(20)
        READ(5,10)ARRAY
   10   FORMAT(20F4.1)
        CALL MAXIMA(AA,I,ARRAY,20)
        WRITE(6,20)AA,I
   20   FORMAT(F5.2,I4)
        STOP
        END
```

Subroutine Subprogram
```
       SUBROUTINE MAXIMA(GREAT,LARGE,A,L)
       DIMENSION A(20)
       GREAT=A(1)
       LARGE=1
       DO 10 I=2,L
          IF(A(I).LT.GREAT)GO TO 10
          GREAT=A(I)
          LARGE=I
   10 CONTINUE
       RETURN
       END
```

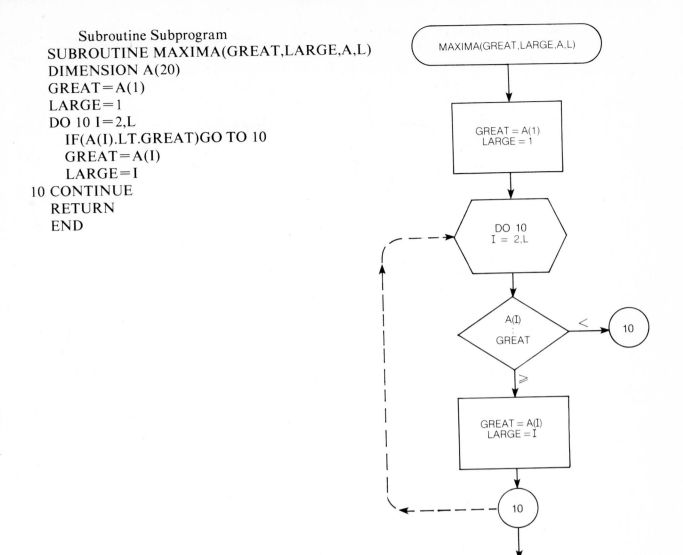

The above subroutine subprogram determines which of the elements of the array ARRAY is the largest or, if more than one are of equal magnitude, the largest subscript of those that are tied for the maximum. In addition to the index of the largest number, the largest number itself is returned to the calling program. The subroutine is called by a CALL statement:

CALL MAXIMA(AA,I,ARRAY,20),

where AA,I,ARRAY, and 20 are the actual arguments from the calling program, which will replace during execution of the subroutine the dummy arguments GREAT, LARGE, A, and L, respectively.

The input arguments, A and L, furnish data to the subprogram and are not modified in the subprogram. The arguments GREAT and LARGE are the output arguments, and their values are calculated within the subprogram and returned to the calling program.

When the SUBROUTINE is executed, all the arguments are returned to the calling program with the values they had when the RETURN statement returned control to the calling program.

Additional Examples of FORTRAN Subroutine Subprograms

Example [1] Computation of N! (N factorial)

```
SUBROUTINE NFACT(NFCT,N)
    NFCT=1
    IF(N.LE.1)GO TO 20
    DO 10 I=2,N
      NFCT=NFCT*I
10 CONTINUE
20 RETURN
    END
```

The input argument is N and the output argument is NFCT.

Example [2] Conversion of radians to degrees, minutes, and seconds (rounded to the nearest second)

```
SUBROUTINE CONVT(RAD,DEG,MIN,SEC)
INTEGER DEG,SEC
DEG=57.29578*RAD
MIN=60.*(57.29578*RAD—FLOAT(DEG))
SEC=60.*(60.*(57.29578*RAD—FLOAT(DEG))—FLOAT(MIN))+.5
RETURN
END
```

The input statement is RAD, and the output arguments are DEG, MIN and SEC. DEG and SEC are declared as integer variable names.

A library function, FLOAT, is used to convert the integer constant of DEG to a real constant.

Example [3] Calculating the product of 2 matrixes

```
C*** MAIN PROGRAM
    DIMENSION X(10,10),Y(10,10),Z(10,10)
10 FORMAT(4I3)
20 FORMAT(10F7.2)
30 FORMAT(10F10.3)
40 FORMAT(1X,'THE MATRIXES CANNOT BE MULTIPLIED')
    READ(5,10)M,N,K,L
    IF(N.EQ.K)THEN
      DO 50 I=1,M
        READ(5,20)(X(I,J),J=1,N)
50    CONTINUE
      DO 60 I=1,N
        READ(5,20)(Y(I,J),J=1,L)
60    CONTINUE
      CALL MULTPL(M,N,K,L,X,Y,Z)
      DO 70 I=1,M
        WRITE(6,102)(Z(I,J),J=1,L)
70    CONTINUE
      STOP
    ELSE
      WRITE(6,40)
      STOP
```

```
        END IF
        END
C*** SUBROUTINE
        SUBROUTINE MULTPL(MM,NN,KK,LL,A,B,C)
        DIMENSION A(MM,NN),B(KK,LL),C(MM,LL)
        DO 30 I=1,MM
          DO 20 J=1,LL
            C(I,J)=0.0
            DO 10 J1=1,NN
              C(I,J)=C(I,J)+A(I,J1)*B(J1,J)
   10       CONTINUE
   20     CONTINUE
   30 CONTINUE
        RETURN
        END
```

Note that FORTRAN 77 is used for this example.

The order of placement of the main program followed by subroutine, is the logical, acceptable order for submitting this FORTRAN program.

In the main program, two matrixes are read in. Matrix X has M rows and N columns. Matrix Y has K rows and L columns. The matrixes can only be multiplied if N and K are equal (the number of colunns of matrix X equals the number of rows in matrix Y). This is checked in the main program. If the matrix can be multiplied, the resulting matrix has M rows and L columns. The multiplication is performed in the subroutine MULTPL.

The following observations for a typical subroutine can be made:

1. there are 7 arguments in the CALL and SUBROUTINE statements
2. they correspond in mode; that is, the first four variables are in integer mode and the last three are in real mode
3. the variable names of the dummy arguments are different from the variable names of the real arguments
4. FORTRAN 77 allows for dummy array declarations:
        DIMENSION A(MM,NN),B(KK,LL),C(MM,LL)
   Note that the dummy integer arguments are used to define the array size.

5. The Common Statement and Variable Dimensions

The list of arguments provides for the communication between a main program and its subprograms. The COMMON statement is another means of communication between main program and subprograms. By using the COMMON statement, it is possible to reduce or eliminate the number of arguments in the subprogram. This statement allows storage to be shared by the main program and subprogram. For example, in the case of the SUBROUTINE MAXIMA of the previous section, we can have the following two statements:

        COMMON GREAT,LARGE
        COMMON AA,I

The first one is in the SUBROUTINE and the second one in the main program. Then GREAT and AA, and LARGE and I share the same physical storage locations. Then it is possible to have only two dummy argunents A and L in the definition of the SUBROUTINE and the simplified call statement.

        CALL MAXIMA(ARRAY,20)

as any variable listed in the COMMON statement need not be mentioned as arguments for either functions and subroutines. However, for some computers, it is necessary to have at least one argument for each FUNCTION and each SUBROUTINE.

Arguments transmitted in a common statement must follow the same rules as arguments transmitted in an argument list. This means that the mode, order, and number of variables must agree.

A COMMON statement can also include dimensions. If we wish to fix the number of elements in the dummy and actual argument arrays and specify that it is 20, then we can have the following COMMON statements

```
COMMON AA,I,ARRAY(20)
COMMON GREAT,LARGE,A(20)
```

in the main and the SUBROUTINE program, respectively, leaving the number of elements to be examined, L, as the only argument. Also, a variable can not be entered in both a common statement and an argument list.

According to chapter 9, only integer constants can be used in dimension or type declaration statements that define the size of arrays. This is certainly true for all arrays used in a main program. This rule does not apply to arrays in FUNCTION or SUBROUTINE subprograms. Integer variables can be used to define the size of arrays in subprograms, as long as these variables are contained in the list of the input arguments of the subprogram FUNCTION or SUBROUTINE.

The possibility for using variable dimensions in the FUNCTION and SUBROUTINE subprograms makes these programs very general and flexible in use. In this way, the subprograms can be called by any main program. The SUBROUTINE MAXIMA can be rewritten with variable dimensions as follows:

```
      SUBROUTINE MAXIMA(GREAT,LARGE,A.L)
      DIMENSION A(L)
      GREAT=A(1)
      LARGE=1
      DO 10 I=2,L
        IF(A(I).GE.GREAT)THEN
          GREAT=A(I)
          LARGE=I
        END IF
   10 CONTINUE
      RETURN
      END
```

6. Good Programming Style with Subprograms

SUBROUTINE and FUNCTION subprograms are essential in building structured or modular programs. It is important that the program designer be able to identify the various modules of the algorithm, or procedure that is about to be programmed. In very general terms, a module can be defined as a set of operations that are necessary to perform a specific task. When a problem is split into specific modules, then the programmer can design a FUNCTION or SUBROUTINE program for each of these modules, and the interface between the modules can be accomplished through the main program and arguments. It is preferable to use arguments rather than COMMON statements, because with arguments the subprogram is completely self-contained.

Let us look at a specific task to define modules and discuss their interface with the main program. Assume that basic statistics must be calculated for a simple array of no more than 100 data elements. In other words, basic statistics such as the average, the variance, and the range must be defined. Here, one may want to use three modules. The first one calculates the average, the second one calculates the variance, and the third one calculates the range. Another programmer may suggest more than three modules, realizing that defining the largest element and smallest element in an array (which is necessary to find the range) could be two distinct modules. In the case of three modules (case I), the general structure of our program is as follows:

```
C****MAIN PROGRAM
     DIMENSION SAMPLE(100)
     READ(5,10)N
  10 FORMAT(I3)
     READ(5,20)(SAMPLE(I),I=1,N)
  20 FORMAT(10F8.2)
C****CALL THE MODULE TO CALCULATE THE AVERAGE
     CALL AVRGE(SAMPLE,N,AVR)
     WRITE(6,30)AVR
  30 FORMAT(5X,'THE SAMPLE AVERAGE=',F10.2)
C****CALL THE MODULE TO CALCULATE THE VARIANCE
     CALL VARNCE(SAMPLE,N,AVR,VAR)
     WRITE(6,40)VAR
  40 FORMAT(5X,'THE SAMPLE VARIANCE=',F16.2)
C****CALL THE MODULE TO CALCULATE THE RANGE
     CALL RANGE(SAMPLE,N,RNG)
     WRITE(6,50)RNG
  50 FORMAT(5X'THE SAMPLE RANGE=',F10.2)
     STOP
     END
C****MODULE THAT CALCULATES THE AVERAGE
     SUBROUTINE AVRGE(A,L,EXP)
     DIMENSION A(L)
     .
     .
     .

     RETURN
     END
C****MODULE THAT CALCULATES THE VARIANCE
     SUBROUTINE VARNCE(A,L,EXP,VRNCE)
     DIMENSION A(L)
     .
     .
     .

     RETURN
     END
C****MODULE THAT CALCULATES THE RANGE
     SUBROUTINE RANGE(A,L,WIDTH)
     DIMENSION A(L)
     .
     .
     .

     RETURN
     END
```

Note how well this program is structured. Each module (SUBROUTINE) performs a specific task and is called for in the MAIN program. Also, note that each of these modules are defined in a very general way and contain a variable dimension statement. This makes the module transportable. In other words, if another program asks for the calculation of the average, and/or variance, and/or range, there is no need to change any of these modules. The programmer simply transports the code of the appropriate SUBROUTINE(S) and links it to the main program by the use of an appropriate CALL statement and list of arguments.

Even though it is feasible to enter a SUBROUTINE at various points via the ENTRY statement, the reader is urged not to use the ENTRY statement. Multiple ENTRY points defeats the advantages of structured programming. What is said about the ENTRY statements can be said about the multiple RETURN statements. It is true that FORTRAN allows for alternate return points into the main program. However, the programmer is encouraged not to use this feature, since it makes the program hard to understand and leads to poor structure. For these reasons, multiple ENTRY and alternate RETURN(s) are not discussed in this text. In conclusion, there should be only one entry point into the subprogram (the beginning), one returning point in the main program (the statement following the calling statement), and all communication between the main program and subprograms must take place through arguments rather than COMMON statements.

Exercises

Problem No. 1

Consider the following questions and give appropriate answers.

1. Identify which of the following statements describe the characteristics of FORTRAN subroutine subprograms.
   a) It may have more than one statement, more than one calling argument, but it may return more than one value.
   b) It may have more than one statement, more than one calling argument, and it may return only one value.
   c) It may have more than one statement, may have only one calling argument, but may return more than one value.
   d) It may have more than one statement, but may have only one calling argument and one return argument.
2. Identify the incorrect statement with respect to subroutine subprograms:
   a) RETURN statement is the last statement in the subroutine to be executed before control is transferred to the main program.
   b) Subprogram arguments can contain arrays.
   c) Special memory locations are assigned to the variable names in a subroutine. These variables cannot be referenced from the main program.
   d) The number of actual arguments in the calling statement must be equal to the number of dummy arguments in the subprogram definition statement. The arguments must agree in mode and dimension.

3. Which of the following statements about subroutines is true?
    a) Subroutines calculate no values.
    b) Subroutines calculate only one value.
    c) No more than two values can be calculated in a subroutine.
    d) Any number of values can be calculated in a subroutine.

Problem No. 2

Write a single FORTRAN-IV statement for each of the following:

1. $y = \left(\dfrac{a+b}{a-b}\right)^2 + 2k$

2. $48(m+n)(m-g) = y$

3. $y = \sqrt{\dfrac{(a+b)^2 - 1}{i(c+d)^2}}$

4. $y = \sqrt{\tan\varnothing - \dfrac{1}{2}}$

5. $y = 4\cos^2 x + 2\sin x$

Problem No. 3

Consider the following main program and subroutine:

```
      READ(5,1)A,B,
    1 FORMAT(2F3.0)
      CLARA=A*B
      CALL CLOWN(A,B,CLARA,C)
      BOZO=C-1.0
      WRITE(6,4)BOZO,CLARA
    4 FORMAT (3X,'BOZO=',F8.0,'CLARA=',F8.0)
      STOP
      END

      SUBROUTINE CLOWN(E,F,H,G)
      X=E+F+H
      G=X**2.0
      RETURN
      END
```

and determine the output when the following data is used:

    card #1 ⌐4.02.08.0
    card #2 ⌐3.01.06.0

Problem No. 4

Write a subroutine that sums all of the elements of a two-dimensional array. The arguments used consist of the array name, the size of each dimension, and the variable used to store the sum.

Problem No. 5

Suppose that SQRT is missing from our library functions. Newton's algorithm for computing the square root of a number, N, is:

$$\text{let } A_{i+1} = \frac{1}{2}(A_i + N/A_i)$$

where: $A_i = N$

$A_{i+1} \approx \sqrt{N}$ when $|A_{i+1} - A_i| < 0.0001$

Write a subroutine subprogram called AQROOT to compute square roots, using Newton's algorithm.

Problem No. 6

The function

$$Z = \frac{n \tan^2 \emptyset}{\sqrt{n+x^2}} \; |e^{x/n} + e^{-x/n}| \; \text{where} \; \emptyset = 60°$$

is to be evaluated for all combinations of

n:1.0(0.1)5.0   i.e. n=1.0,1.1,1.2,...,4.9,5.0
x:−1.0)0.05)1.0   i.e. x=−1.0,−0.95,−0.90,...0.95,1.0

For each combination of n and x, write a line giving the value of n, x, and Z. Write a complete program to do this.

Problem No. 7

The function

$$f = \frac{\sin x + \cos y}{\log_e(x+y)}$$ is to be evaluated for all combinations of

x:−1.0(0.05)0.0
y:10.0(0.5)25.0

For each combination of x and y, a line giving x, y, and f is to be written. Write a complete program to do this.

Problem No. 8

Write a main program and two subroutines to calculate the range of the sales volume, which is equal to the difference between the largest and the smallest sales volume. The main program calls for two subroutines: the first subroutine defines the largest sales volume, and the second subroutine defines the smallest sales volume.

Problem No. 9

Write a program that calculates the following statistics for the yield of corn obtained by several farmers.

1. The average yield, which is a measure of central tendency, a value around which the yields tend to center. The average equals:

$$\overline{X} = \frac{\sum_{i=1}^{N} X_i}{N} \; \text{where}$$ $\overline{X}$ is the sample mean

$\sum_{i=1}^{N} X_i$ is the sum of all N yields

N is the sample size, or the number of yields

2. The standard deviation in yield is a measure of deviation from the mean. It measures the relative extent to which the yields are concentrated about the mean, and this measure becomes larger as a data becomes more dispersed.

The standard variation equals:

$$s = \sqrt{\dfrac{N \sum\limits_{i=1}^{N} X_i^2 - \left(\sum\limits_{i=1}^{N} X_i \right)^2}{N(N-1)}}$$

where: s: is the standard deviation
        N: is the sample size

$\sum\limits_{i=1}^{N} X_i$ is the sum of the N values of the yield

$\sum\limits_{i=1}^{N} X_i^2$ is the sum of the N values of the yield squared.

In the development of the program, provide a subroutine to calculate the mean and the standard deviation.

12 Type Declaration and Data Statements

Some type declaration statements have been introduced in chapter 4, such as the INTEGER and the REAL declaration statements. There are six type declaration statements: the integer, the real, the logical, the complex, the double-precision, and the implicit. The real and integer declaration statements are used to specify that certain variable names are real or integer, regardless of the first letter of the variable name. Variable names are declared to be logical variable names through the logical declaration statement. Since each complex quantity and each double-precision quantity requires two storage registers, this information must be supplied to the compiler in order to provide for the necessary storage. This can be accomplished by the use of the complex and the double-precision declaration statements respectively. All type declaration statements are nonexecutable statements, and they inform the computer at the time of compilation about the nature of the variable names used in the program, which is the reason why type declarations are not flowcharted.

Initial values can be assigned to variable names at the time of compilation by the use of a DATA statement. DATA statements can be flowcharted by the use of a process block, since actual processing occurs during the assignment of values.

1. Integer Declaration

The general form of the integer declaration statement is:

INTEGER $a_1, a_2, a_3, \ldots$

The variable names $a_1, a_2, a_3, \ldots$ are explicitly declared to be integer (fixed-point) variables regardless of the first letter of their names. Also, arrays together with their sizes may be included in the statement.

A full word of memory is necessary to store an integer variable. The binary form is used to store an integer constant, which can be of the range from -2^{31} to $2^{31}-1$ (-2147483648 to 2147483647) for the IBM 360. If an integer computation results in an integer constant which is larger than 2147483647 or smaller than -2147483648, the result cannot be stored in a full word of memory, and the overflow is ignored. As the compiler does not indicate an overflow, the programmer has no way of knowing whether the integer result is correct or incorrect. Consider the following program:

```
      INTEGER A
      DO 10 I=1,20,1
        A=9**I
        WRITE(6,20)I,A
   10 CONTINUE
   20 FORMAT(5X,I3,I20)
      STOP
      END
```

This program generates the following output:

1	9
2	81
3	729
4	6561
5	59049
6	531441
7	4782969
8	43046721
9	387420489
10	-808182895
11	1316288537
12	-1038305055
13	-754810903
14	1796636465
15	-1010140999
16	-501334399
17	-217042295
18	-1953380655
19	-400556711
20	689956897

The overflow occurs when 9 is raised to a power of 10 or higher. When calculating the 10th power of 9, we obtain 3486784401, which is larger than 2147483647, the largest integer that can be stored on the IBM 360. All outputs beyond the 9th power are incorrect, since overflow occurs. When this program was run, no error messages referrring to the overflow were given.

2. Real Declaration

The general form of the real declaration statement is:

REAL $a_1, a_2, a_3, \ldots$

The variable names $a_1, a_2, a_3, \ldots$ are explicitly declared to be real (floating-point) variables, regardless of the first letter of their names. Arrays may also be included.

A full word of memory is used to store a real variable. Internally the hexadecimal form is used to store real constants, which can range from approximately $.5397605 \times 10^{-78}$ to $.7237005 \times 10^{76}$ for the IBM 360. On all IBM computers, FORTRAN prints out at most 7 significant decimal digits from a real value; however, the computations are executed with slightly higher accuracy.

3. Double-Precision Declaration

The general form of the double-precision declaration statement is:

DOUBLE PRECISION $a_1, a_2, a_3, \ldots$

The variable names $a_1, a_2, a_3, \ldots$ are declared to be real double-precision variables. The variables can also be arrays.

Two full words of memory are used to store a double-precision variable. As the FORTRAN compiler stores only 7 significant decimal digits for a single precision real constant, computation errors, such as round-off errors, occur. These can be reduced considerably by assigning two storage locations for the real constant through the double-precision declaration statement. Double precision variables are stored (and can be printed) with 17 significant decimal digits on all IBM computers.

This statement should then be used in programs requiring greater accuracy than is available with real variables.

Examples of double precision constants are:

8.12D0
24324.967231
.17D−6
−9432.2493525D−02
252D1

Notice that an integer constant is not allowed and that a maximum of 17 digits are allowed with decimal points, signs, and D character included.

A double-precision constant can be printed out under the regular floating-point form by the use of the F specification in the format statement. However, a D specification can also be used for the INPUT/OUTPUT of double-precision quantities. The general form of the D specification is:

Dw.d
where: w: is an integer that specifies the complete field length including sign, decimal point, a minimum of one place to the left of the decimal point, and a four-digit exponent part.
d: is an integer designating the number of places to the right of the decimal point, not including the 4-digit exponent.

Full benefit can be gained from double-precision constants and variable names by using them in double-precision expressions and statements. If A, B, and C are defined in a double-precision declaration statement, then the following examples are double-precision statements:

A = 2.35D+5+A*B   [1]
A = B*(1+.05)**N   [2]

In the first example, the constant and the variable names are in double precision. The second example contains an expression in mixed mode, which is perfectly acceptable on the IBM 360. If one of the operands of an operator is in double precision and the other in integer, the integer is converted. If one of the operands of an operator is in double precision and the other in single real precision, the single-real precision constant is filled out with zeros. The result of the double precision expression can be stored in double-precision floating point if it is assigned to a double precision variable name.

The merits in using double-precision constants are clearly illustrated in the following example:

Example [1]

A bank wishes to compute the balance in the customers' checking accounts at the end of the month, so it may send a statement to each customer.

The data that is read in for each customer is: (1) the customer's name and account number, (2) total amount of the withdrawals, (3) the total amount of deposits into the checking account, (4) the total number of checks written, (5) the balance in the account at the beginning of the month, (6) the service charge for each check written. The output consists of all inputs, plus the total service charge and the ending balance.

The following flowchart and programs are written for one customer.

The input values are: total amount of withdrawals: 1234567.89
beginning balance: 1234567.89
total amount of deposits: 1234567.89
number of checks written: 123456
charge per check written: .12

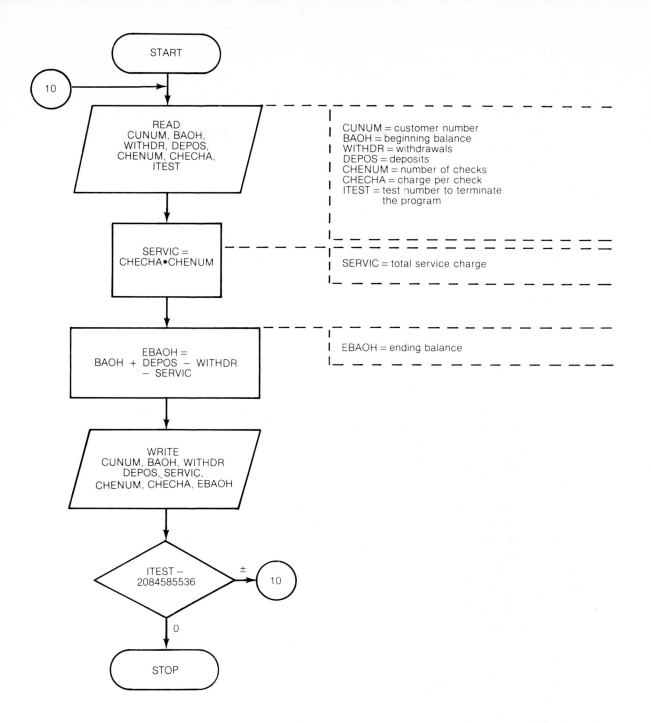

Two programs are written, the first one with single-precision and the second one with double-precision variables. Identical data were used as input to both programs. The programs and respective outputs follow.

The first program with single-precision variables:

```
C *** UPDATE CHECKING ACCOUNT
      INTEGER CHENUM, CUNUM
C *** READ IN CHECKING INFORMATION
   10 READ(5,20) CUNUM, BOAH, WITHDR, DEPOS, CHENUM,
      *              CHECHA, ITEST
   20 FORMAT(I6,3F10.2,I6,F3.2,A1)
C *** CALCULATE SERVICE CHARGE, NEW BALANCE
C ***    AND WRITE OUT RESULTS
      SERVIC = CHECHA * CHENUM
      EBAOH = BAOH + DEPOS - WITHDR - SERVIC
      WRITE(6,30) CUNUM, BAOH, WITHDR, DEPOS, SERVIC,
      *              CHENUM, CHECHA, EBAOH
   30 FORMAT(1H1,'CUSTOMER NUMBER ',I6,//,
      *       1X,'BEGINNING BALANCE ',F11.2,/
      *       1X,'WITHDRAWALS ',6X,F11.2,/,
      *       1X,'DEPOSITS ',10X,F11.2,/,
      *       1X,'SERVICE CHARGES ',2X,F11.2,5X,
      *       '(=NUMBER OF CHEQUES ',I6,
      *       ' * CHARGE ',F3.2,' )',/,
      *       1X,'ENDING BALANCE',4X,F11.2)
      IF (ITEST - 2084585536) 10,40,10
   40 STOP
      END
```

The output in single precision:

```
CUSTOMER NUMBER 123456

BEGINNING BALANCE   1234567.00
WITHDRAWALS         1234567.00
DEPOSITS            1234567.00
SERVICE CHARGES       14814.71    (=NUMBER OF CHEQUES 123456 * CHARGE .12 )
ENDING BALANCE      1219752.00
```

The second program with double-precision variables:

```
C ***  UPDATE CHECKING ACCOUNT
       INTEGER CHENUM, CUNUM
       DOUBLE PRECISION  BAOH, WITHDR, DEPOS, EBAOH, CHECHA
C ***  READ IN CHECKING INFORMATION
   10 READ(5,20) CUNUM, BAOH, WITHDR, DEPOS, CHENUM,
      *           CHECHA, ITEST
   20 FORMAT(I6,3F10.2,I6,F3.2,A1)
C ***  CALCULATE SERVICE CHARGE, NEW BALANCE
C ***   AND WRITE OUT RESULTS
       SERVIC = CHECHA * CHENUM
       EBAOH = BAOH + DEPOS - WITHDR - SERVIC
       WRITE(6,30) CUNUM, BAOH, WITHDR, DEPOS, SERVIC,
      *           CHENUM, CHECHA, EBAOH
   30 FORMAT(1H1,'CUSTOMER NUMBER ',I6,//,
      *        1X,'BEGINNING BALANCE ',F11.2,/
      *        1X,'WITHDRAWALS ',6X,F11.2,/,
      *        1X,'DEPOSITS ',10X,F11.2,/,
      *        1X,'SERVICE CHARGES ',2X,F11.2,5X,
      *        '(=NUMBER OF CHEQUES ',I6,
      *        ' * CHARGE ',F3.2,' )',/,
      *        1X,'ENDING BALANCE',4X,F11.2)
       IF (ITEST - 2084585536) 10,40,10
   40 STOP
       END
```

The output in double precision:

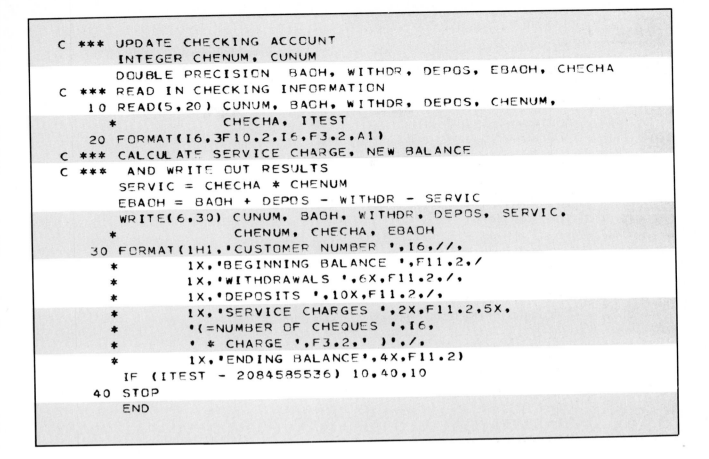

```
CUSTOMER NUMBER 654321

BEGINNING BALANCE   1234567.89
WITHDRAWALS         1234567.89
DEPOSITS            1234567.89
SERVICE CHARGES       14814.72     (=NUMBER OF CHEQUES 123456 * CHARGE .12 )
ENDING BALANCE      1219753.17
```

4. Logical Declaration

The general form of the logical declaration statement is:

LOGICAL $a_1,a_2,a_3,...$

The variable names $a_1,a_2,a_3, . . .$ are declared to be logical and can only assume the values ".TRUE." or ".FALSE." A full word of memory is necessary to store a FORTRAN logical variable. A logical assignment statement has the general form of:

a = b
where: a is a logical variable $a_1,a_2,...$
        b is a logical expression

Examples of logical expressions are:

LOGICAL L1,L2,L3,L4,L5,L6
L1 = .TRUE.
L2 = .FALSF.
L3 = A.GT.25.0
L4 = L3
L5 = D.LT.EPS.OR.ITEM.GT.20
L6 = BIG.GT.TOL.OR.L5

The above statements can be rewritten as follows:

LOGICAL L1,L2,L3,L4,L5,L6
L1 = T
L2 = F
L3 = A.GT.25.0
L4 = L3
L5 = D.LT.EPS.OR.ITEM.GT.20
L6 = BIG.GT.TOL.OR.L5

This alternative version illustrates that T and F are acceptable FORTRAN abbreviations for .TRUE. and .FALSE. when initializing logical variables.
Logical data can also be used in compound logical IF statements as follows:

IF(D.LT.50.5.AND.D.GE.25.0.AND.L3) GO TO 10

The L specification is used for INPUT/OUTPUT of logical quantities. The general form of the L specification is:

Lw
where: w is the width of the field

On the output medium either a right justified T or F is printed, depending upon whether the logical value is .TRUE. or .FALSE. On input, a field of w columns gets scanned from left to right until T or F is encountered. If the entire field is blank, the value of the logical variable name will equal F.

Logical variables and constants are most often used in programs requiring logical type operations as opposed to mathematical calculations.

5. The IMPLICIT Statement

As discussed earlier in the text, if the symbolic name of a constant, variable, array, FUNCTION, or arithmetic statement function in a program starts with the letters I, J, K, L, M, or N, then the data type associated with that name is integer; otherwise it is real. This FORTRAN convention can be changed by the use of the IMPLICIT statement.
The general form of the implicit statement is

IMPLICIT type(letter, letter, . . .), type(letter, letter, . . .), . . .

In this form, variable names starting with a single alphabetic letter, will be of a certain type as indicated by its preceding specification. The type can be followed by an optional *s, where s stands for length. The range of letters may also be indicated by the use of a minus sign between two letters.

For example:

```
IMPLICIT INTEGER(Q-T),LOGICAL(A-E)
*        DOUBLE PRECISION(F,K,L,U-Z)
*        REAL(H,J),CHARACTER*10(O)
*        INTEGER FUNCTION(G)
```

The following table shows the type associated with the variable names of the preceding example.

Type of Name	First Letter of Variable Name	Length (Optional) of Constant)
INTEGER	Q,R,S,T	
LOGICAL	A,B,C,D,E	
DOUBLE PRECISION	F,K,L,U,V,W,X,Y,Z	
REAL	H,J	
CHARACTER	O	10
INTEGER FUNCTION	G	
(other non-mentioned letters follow the convention)		
INTEGER	I,M,N	
REAL	P	

6. Rules in Using Type-Declaration Statements

The following general rules apply to all compilers using type-declaration statements:

1. The type-declaration statements are nonexecutable and must appear in a FORTRAN program preceding all executable statements.
2. A variable array may have its dimension specified in a type-declaration statement. If this is the case, then a DIMENSION statement is not necessary. The following shows the correct and incorrect combinations of DIMENSION and type-declaration statements:

DIMENSION X(10)
INTEGER X   incorrect

INTEGER X
DIMENSION X(10)   correct

INTEGER X(10)   correct

3. Once the type of a variable is specified, it may not be changed in the program.
4. A variable may appear in only one type-declaration statement.

7. Data Statement

There are several ways of assigning values to variable names, such as by reading in the values from data cards, by assigning values in assignment statements, or by the use of a data statement. The data statement is a nonexecutable statement and is used to assign values to variables at the time of compilation. During execution of the object program, if the variables are redefined they will take on the new values regardless of the DATA statement. The general form of the DATA statement is:

DATA list/$d_1,d_2,d_3,...d_n$/,list/$d_1,K_2*d_2,...$/

where: **list:** contains the name of the variables to receive values

$d_1,d_2,...$ are the values of the variables in the list

K: if it is used, is an integer constant.

The first variable in the list is assigned the first data value, the second variable in the list is assigned the second data value, etc., until the last variable in the list gets assigned the last data value. The values in the list of the data statement can be: fixed point, floating point, logical, double precision, complex, alphanumeric, etc.

Example [2]

```
DIMENSION A(2)
LOGICAL ALPHA,BETA
INTEGER APE(4)
DATA A,ALPHA,BETA/2*10.0,.TRUE.,.FALSE./,APE/1,2,3,4/
```

The following table explains the above example in terms of variable names, type of constants, and assignments:

Table 12.1

Variable	Type of Constants	Assignment
A	Real array	A(1)=10. A(2)=10.
ALPHA	Real logical	.TRUE.
BETA	Real logical	.FALSE.
APE	Integer array	APE(1)=1 APE(2)=2 APE(3)=3 APE(4)=4

Note that A and APE are arrays and may not appear in the list with subscripts. Therefore their dimensions need to be defined in a DIMENSION statement or a type-declaration statement.

There must be a one-to-one correspondence between the variables in the list and the values of the variables in the list: real variables correspond to real constants, integer variables to integer constants, logical variables to logical constants. As T and F can be used for .TRUE. and .FALSE. respectively, the above DATA statement can be rewritten as follows:

```
DATA A,ALPHA,BETA/2*10.,T,F/,APE/1,2,3,4/
```

Example [3]

```
DIMENSION TITLE(5)
DATA A/75.3/,(TITLE(I),I=1,5)/4HTHIS,4H IS ,4HAN E,4HXAMP,4HLE /
```

OR

```
DIMENSION TITLE(5)
DATA A/75.3/,(TITLE(I),I=1,5)/'THIS','IS', 'AN E','XAMP','LE'/
```

OR

```
DIMENSION TITLE(5)
DATA A/75.3/,(TITLE(I),I=1,5)/'THIS IS AN EXAMPLE'/)*
```

Notice that it is allowed to use an implied DO loop, even for alphanumeric data. A maximum of 4 characters can be included in a single alphanumeric variable (some systems allow 6, and others 8). Five full words of memory are used to store the alphanumeric constants of the array TITLE in the IBM 360, as follows:

---

*This does not work on all systems.

THIS		IS		AN E		XAMP		LE
TITLE(1)		TITLE(2)		TITLE(3)		TITLE(4)		TITLE(5)

Type-declaration statements can also be used to assign values to variables at the time of compilation.

Example [4]

REAL INTRST,YEARS/20./,CAP/2000./

In the above example, the variables are not only declared to be real, but some get initialized: YEARS equal 20. and CAP equals 2000. Note that all declared variables need not be initialized. In the above statement, INTRST is not initialized.

Exercises

Problem No. 1

Use a DATA statement and a write statement to picture Charley Brown, as outlined in problem #3 of chapter 6.

Problem No. 2

Rework exercises #1, #2, and #4 of chapter 6. Use a DATA statement to assign values to the variables in the list of the real statement. Do not use any data cards.

Problem No. 3

Resubmit exercise #5 of chapter 10, but have all calculations done in double precision.

Problem No. 4

Resubmit the "Single-Premium Life Insurance" example of chapter 10, but have all calculations done in double precision. Compare the results.

In the literature of computer programming languages and numerical methods, the activity of sorting (the process of ordering data) is an essential subject. One can sort from the smallest element to the largest one, or from the largest element to the smallest one. Numerous techniques have been developed in an attempt to sort efficiently. Two sorting programs are discussed here. The first is considerably less efficient than the second, as will be obvious after the development. Both programs sort unordered numerical constants in an increasing order and print out the ordered array in which the numbers will be stored.

1. The First Program: The Selection Sort

The sorting problem can be formulated as follows:

Given a one-dimensional array A(I);

The array needs to be ordered, beginning with the smallest element and ending with the largest one;

The ordered set has to be placed in another one-dimensional array B(I)

In the first program, the smallest element of the array A must be picked first and placed at the beginning of the B array. Choosing the same (smallest) element over and over again can be avoided by reassigning an arbitrary large value to that element of the A array after its value is placed in order in the B array. The reassigned value has to be larger than any value in the random list of the A array.

The flowchart and the program accomplish this procedure:

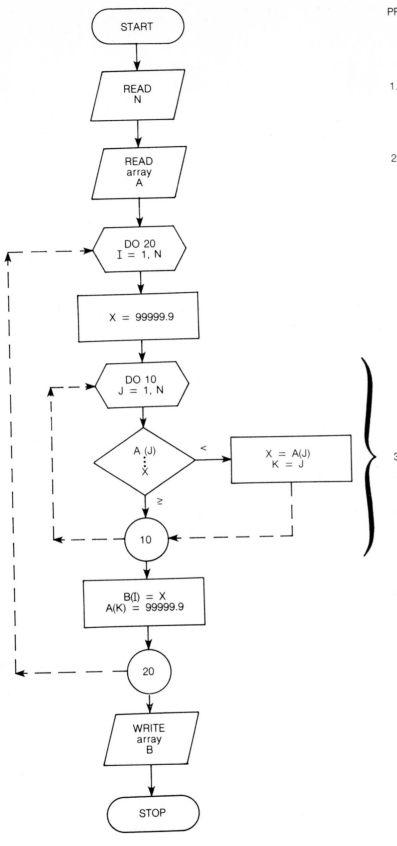

1. Read in the size of the array

2. Read in the unsorted array A

3. Select next smallest element of unsorted array

4. Assign the above defined element to the next element of array B

5. Print out the sorted array B

```
C ***  THE SELECTION SORT
       DIMENSION  A(50), B(50)
C ***  READ IN THE SIZE OF THE ARRAY
       READ (5,30)N
C ***  READ IN THE UNSORTED ARRAY A
       READ (5,40) (A(I), I = 1, N)
C ***  SORTING PROCEDURE
       DO 20  I = 1, N
         X = 99999.9
         DO 10  J = 1, N
           IF (A(J) .LT. X) THEN
             X = A(J)
             K = J
           END IF
10       CONTINUE
         B(I) = X
         A(K) = 99999.9
20     CONTINUE
       WRITE (6,40) (B(I), I = 1, N)
30     FORMAT (I2)
40     FORMAT (5F10.2)
       STOP
       END
```

According to the DIMENSION statement, it is assumed that the A-array does not contain more than 50 elements. Considering the second READ statement, and its corresponding FORMAT statement (statement labeled #40), the following input is appropriate:

25				
19.9	52.9	28.6	62.0	87.5
29.4	91.5	46.3	84.8	86.0
25.2	97.7	23.9	11.1	86.8
24.3	42.1	96.9	19.6	29.1
77.2	35.1	92.0	67.5	67.6

The generated output is:

11.10	19.60	19.90	23.90	24.30
25.20	28.60	29.10	29.40	35.10
42.10	46.30	52.90	62.00	67.50
67.60	77.20	84.80	86.00	86.80
87.50	91.50	92.00	96.90	97.70

The average number of passes through the most inner DO loop equals N^2.

In Table 13.1, an example of a program is illustrated for a one dimensional array A(5) containing the following 5 elements:

A(1)=7
A(2)=1
A(3)=10
A(4)=12
A(5)=9

Table 13.1 Illustrating the First Sorting Program

PROGRAM REFERENCE	I	J	X	K	B(I)	CHANGES IN A(I)
DO 20 I=1,N,1	1				[B(1)]	
X=99999.9			99999.9			
DO LOOP		1	7	1		A(1)=7
DO 10 J=1,N,1		2	1	2		A(2)=99999.9
—		3	1	2		A(3)=10
—		4	1	2		A(4)=12
10 CONTINUE		5	1	2		A(5)=9
B(I)=X					1	
DO 20 I=1,N,1	2				[B(2)]	
X=99999.9			99999.9			
DO LOOP		1	7	1		A(1)=99999.9
DO 10 J=1,N,1		2	7	1		A(2)=99999.9
—		3	7	1		A(3)=10
—		4	7	1		A(4)=12
10 CONTINUE		5	7	1		A(5)=9
B(I)=X					7	
DO 20 I=1,N,1	3				[B(3)]	
X=99999.9			99999.9			
DO LOOP		1	99999.9			A(1)=99999.9
DO 10 J=1,N,1		2	99999.9			A(2)=99999.9
—		3	10	3		A(3)=10
—		4	10	3		A(4)=12
10 CONTINUE		5	9	5		A(5)=99999.9
B(I)=X					9	
DO 20 I=1,N,1	4				[B(4)]	
X=99999.9			99999.9			
DO LOOP		1	99999.9			A(1)=99999.9
DO 10 J=1,N,1		2	99999.9			A(2)=99999.9
—		3	10	3		A(3)=9999.9
—		4	10	3		A(4)=12
10 CONTINUE		5	10	3		A(5)=99999.9
B(I)=X					10	
DO 20 I=1,N,1	5				[B(5)]	
X=99999.9			99999.9			
DO LOOP		1	99999.9			A(1)=99999.9
DO 10 J=1,N,1		2	99999.9			A(2)=99999.9
—		3	99999.9			A(3)=99999.9
—		4	12	4		A(4)=99999.9
10 CONTINUE		5	12	4		A(5)=99999.9
B(I)=X					12	

2. The Second Program: The Bubble Sort

This more efficient sorting technique cuts the average number of passes to $N^2/2$. It is illustrated in the second program. The program algorithm for sorting from the smallest element to the largest is summarized in the following three steps:

Step #1 Compare the first and the second element. If the first is the larger one, switch the order of the elements.

Step #2 Proceed to the next element in the array, and compare that element with the previous element, climbing up towards the first element until no switch can be made.

Step #3 If no switch can be made, or if the top of the array is reached, proceed to the next element in the array, go back to Step #2, and proceed to Step #3, until the last element in the array is considered and is put into place.

The flowchart and the FORTRAN program for this procedure follows.

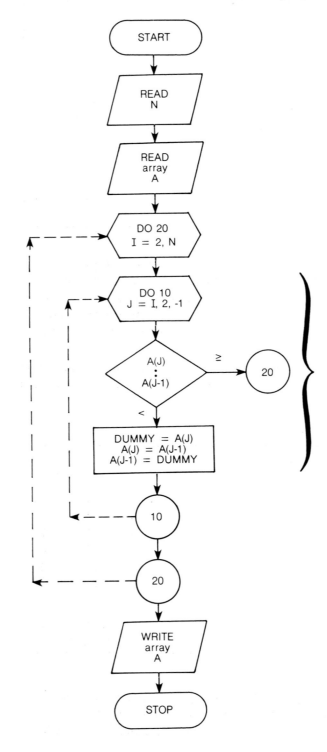

1. Read size of the array

2. Read in the unsorted array A

3. Evaluate each array element:

If the Jth element is smaller than the (J - 1st) element move it upwards in the array; repeat this until upward movement seizes because either the Jth element is no longer smaller than the previous one, or the Jth element is placed on top of the array.

4. Print out the sorted array A

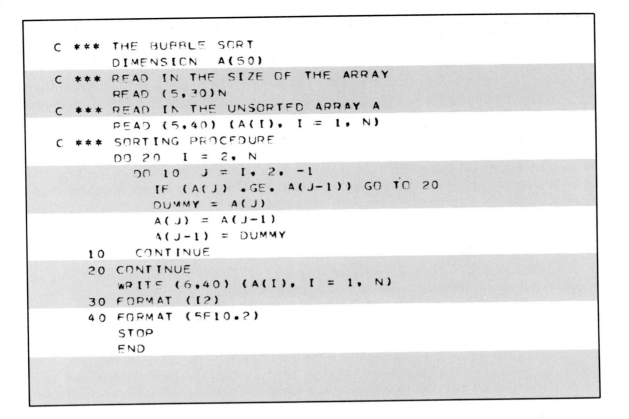

```
C  ***  THE BUBBLE SORT
        DIMENSION  A(50)
C  ***  READ IN THE SIZE OF THE ARRAY
        READ (5,30)N
C  ***  READ IN THE UNSORTED ARRAY A
        READ (5,40) (A(I), I = 1, N)
C  ***  SORTING PROCEDURE
        DO 20  I = 2, N
          DO 10  J = I, 2, -1
            IF (A(J) .GE. A(J-1)) GO TO 20
            DUMMY = A(J)
            A(J) = A(J-1)
            A(J-1) = DUMMY
10        CONTINUE
20      CONTINUE
        WRITE (6,40) (A(I), I = 1, N)
30      FORMAT (I2)
40      FORMAT (5F10.2)
        STOP
        END
```

The DATA used for this program is identical to that of the previous program and is keypunched in the same way as for the previous program since the READ and FORMAT statements for both programs are the same. The variable name DUMMY is used to switch elements and to avoid loss of memory of the real constant of one of the elements that is switched. Comment statements fully explain the program. The generated output of this program is the same as for the previous program.

In the figure below, the program procedure is illustrated through the use of the same example as for the first sorting program. When switches are made, the switches are made, the constants are underlined.

Illustrating the Second Sorting Program

	J-VALUES					
A(I)	2	3	4	5		
7	*1*	1	1	1	1	1
1	*7*	7	7	7	7	7
10		10	10	10	*9*	9
12			12	*9*	10	10
9				*12*	12	12
	1 comparison 1 switch	1 comparison no switch	1 comparison no switch	3 comparisons 2 switches		

Notice that 6 passes are made to accomplish the ordering. The use of the previous program resulted in $5^2 = 25$ passes. So, the second program is significantly more efficient than the first. Note also that there was no need for an additional array to store the ordered values.

3. Other Sorting Techniques

Sorting has traditionally been used for business data processing. Nevertheless, it is a tool that any good programmer should master for use in a wide variety of situations.

A very comprehensive coverage of sorting techniques can be found in "The Art of Computer Programming—Volume 3/Sorting and Searching", by Donald E. Knuth of Standford University, published by Addision Wesley Publishing Company. In this text the author points out that computer manufacturers estimate that over 25% of running time on their computers is currently being spent on sorting and that there are many installations in which sorting uses more than half of the computing time. This is perhaps why efforts and reserach have gone into the development of efficient sorting techniques. The sorting examples presented in this chapter clearly illustrate the difference between a poor and a good sorting technique (program #1 versus program #2), in terms of running time.

There are major trade-offs between different sorting techniques, with respect to running time versus programming time. For short lists, the inefficient but easy-to-program routines, such as the ones illustrated in this chapter are preferred. However, when the list is long one should think about sort-merge routines which require significantly less steps.

Different types of internal sorting techniques are discussed in Knuth's text. These are: the insertion sort (where items are considered one at a time, and each new item is inserted into the appropriate position relative to the previous sorted item), the exchange sort (where two adjacent items which are out of order are interchanged), the selection sort (where the smallest item that is located is separated from the rest, then the next smallest, and so on . . .), the enumeration sort (where each item is compared with each of the others and where counting the number of smaller keys determines the item's final position), special purpose sorting methods, etc. . . . The book discusses approximately 25 such sorting techniques.

A useful summary of sorting algorithms can be found in a book published by Prentice Hall: "Computer Numerical Methods", by Maurer and Williams.

Problem No. 1

You are required to write a program to perform some statistical analysis, as outlined below:

Read in the following data, showing the yield of corn which each of several farmers obtained. The yield is specified in bushels per acre:

35	29	32	31	33
33	38	26	29	32
32	37	32	36	32
33	31	30	32	30
33	27	34	35	30
34	36	34	31	32
32	34	32	31	31
30	33	32	30	33
34	32	31	34	32
31	32			

The output of your program should contain the following:

1. the data samples
2. the data samples arranged in order of increasing yields
3. a frequency table, i.e., the number of times each yield was reported
4. the range of the yield, which is the difference between the largest and the smallest yield
5. the mode value, which is the yield with highest frequency of occurrence.
6. the mean value which is the value at which the yields tend to center, and can be expressed as follows:

$$\overline{X} = \frac{\sum\limits_{i=1}^{N} X_i}{N} \quad \text{where} \quad \overline{X} \text{ is the sample mean}$$

$$\sum\limits_{i=1}^{N} X_i \text{ is the sum of all N values of X}$$

N is the sample size, or the number of values of X

7. the standard deviation, which is the measure of deviation from the mean and can be expressed as follows:

$$s = \sqrt{\frac{N \sum\limits_{i=1}^{N} X_i^2 - \left(\sum\limits_{i=1}^{N} X_i \right)^2}{N(N-1)}}$$

where s is the standard deviation
N is the sample size

$$\sum\limits_{i=1}^{N} X_i \text{ is the sum of the N values of X}$$

$$\sum\limits_{i=1}^{N} X_i^2 \text{ is the sum of the N values of } X^2.$$

8. graph of the frequency statistics, as obtained under #3.

Anything that is relevant to the problem may be added. In the development of the program, take the following requirement into consideration: the input and output statements should be developed in the main program, whereas routines should be written for parts 2, 3, 6, 7, and 8. Your program should be general enough to allow for statistical analysis for any sample size (maximum 500).

Problem No. 2

You are responsible for merging two arrays, array A and array B, into array C. Array A consists of M elements and array B consists of N elements.

Before you merge the two arrays into one array, C, order array A and B in increasing order by the use of a subroutine subprogram. To form the array C you cannot tack A and B together to form C and then do a sort. Neither can you assume that you can perform the merge by simply alternating entries from A and B into C.

To merge A and B to form C set up three pointers: one pointer (I) to mark your current position in A, a second pointer (J) to mark your current position in B and, finally, a third pointer (K) to mark your current position in C. Note that pointer I can never exceed M, and pointer J can never exceed N.

For many reasons one may want to have the capability of manipulating the real world and observing the effects of this manipulation without having to suffer the consequences of actual physical changes. This capability implies that the observer is able to construct a model which exhibits the properties of the real world.

The model need not necessarily be a duplication of the actual system. One merely has to try to create some operating function or model which can effect the same relationship between the inputs and outputs that the real world exhibits. This model is called a "simulation model" as it simulates reality. High-speed computers have stimulated the progress of the use of simulation models in many research areas.

We should know in advance the nature and form of the input. The nature of the system may indicate that a deterministic or a stochastic input environment exists. If the input is stochastic, then it is necessary to use a random number generator to generate random numbers which can then be used or transformed through a function to obtain the desired inputs. These inputs can now be "pushed" through the simulation model and, in a sense, the "reaction" of the model to these inputs can be observed through the analysis of the generated outputs.

1. The Random Number Generator

A random number generator is a process for generating uniformly distributed randon numbers over a given range. Its cumulative distribution function can, therefore, be expressed as follows:

$$F(X) = \begin{cases} 0, X \leq 0 \\ X, 0 < X < 1 \\ 1, X \geq 1 \end{cases}$$

The sequence of random numbers, X, can be generated in a number of ways: manual methods, library tables, analog computer methods (which yield truly random numbers), and digital computer methods.

The internal generation of random numbers by the use of a recurrence relation on a digital computer is used to generate random numbers in FORTRAN. Functions subprograms and/or scientific subroutine subprograms are used by all systems to generate such pseudorandom numbers. The names of the function subprograms and/or scientific subroutine subprograms very much depend on the computing system. Let us look at one such function, whose general form is:

RAN(v)

where: RAN is the name of a real function that generates random numbers between zero and one;

v is the function argument; it is a real variable that has a real constant assigned to it.

The argument is used for the storage of the random number seed. This argument is very useful when there is a need for generating separate, independent strings of random numbers. By explicitly defining the random number seeds, we are able to generate independent strings of random numbers. This is exhibited in the following three FORTRAN programs.

The seed value in Program #1 is 97 (B = 97); in Program #2 it is 87 (C = 87). Program #3 illustrates that independent strings of random numbers can be repeated by reusing the previously used seed values.

Program 1

```
      B = 97
      DO 20  I = 1, 20
        X = RAN(B)
        WRITE (6,10) X
10      FORMAT(3X,F10.7)
20    CONTINUE
      STOP
      END
```

Output

```
   0.1948187
   0.7324636
   0.6087399
   0.3225784
   0.1084520
   0.1884822
   0.0617231
   0.7132555
   0.6379123
   0.0487533
   0.6707162
   0.3922178
   0.3791931
   0.5383146
   0.8838675
   0.4093819
   0.7998590
   0.4358952
   0.0197126
   0.1336374
```

Program 2

```
      C = 87
      DO 20  I = 1, 20
        Y = RAN(C)
        WRITE (6,10) Y
10      FORMAT(3X,F10.7)
20    CONTINUE
      STOP
      END
```

Output

```
   0.7382552
   0.2836873
   0.3098873
   0.8806020
   0.3251120
   0.9191828
   0.9049597
   0.7541427
   0.2565036
   0.8607842
   0.3848133
   0.8257723
   0.1789809
   0.2928331
   0.7630803
   0.5237110
   0.9764307
   0.4605818
   0.0075878
   0.3635267
```

Program 3

Output

```
      B = 97
      C = 87
      DO 20  I = 1, 20
        X = RAN(B)
        Y = RAN(C)
        WRITE (6,10) X, Y
10    FORMAT(3X,F10.7,3X,F10.7)
20    CONTINUE
      STOP
      END
```

0.1948187	0.7382552
0.7324635	0.2836873
0.6087399	0.3098873
0.3225784	0.8806020
0.1084520	0.3251120
0.1884822	0.9191828
0.0617231	0.9049597
0.7132555	0.7541427
0.6379123	0.2565036
0.0487533	0.8607842
0.6707162	0.3843133
0.3922178	0.8257723
0.3791931	0.1789809
0.5383146	0.2928331
0.8838675	0.7630803
0.4093818	0.5337110
0.7998590	0.9764307
0.4358952	0.4605818
0.0197126	0.0075878
0.1336374	0.3635267

In the following three simulation examples, you will see how computer generated pseudo-random numbers can be transformed through appropriate functions to generate the desired stochastic inputs.

2. Simulating the Inebriated Individual Crossing a Bridge

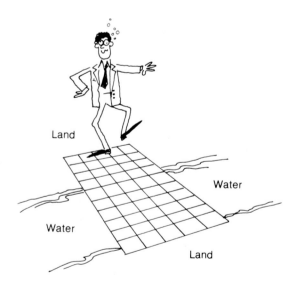

For he is a jolly good fellow!

Consider the drunken individual who is attempting to cross a bridge, which is 5 feet wide and 10 feet long. Assume that the individual is standing between the zero- and the first-foot mark in the middle of the bridge passway as illustrated on the previous page.

Each step the individual takes is a 1-foot step. Past records of our individual in his special condition show the following probability distribution for taking a 1-foot step in any direction:

Straight forward: 0.50

Straight backward: 0.10

Straight to the right: 0.20

Straight to the left: 0.20

In order to find the probability of the inebriate crossing the bridge, a simulation model is constructed which accomplishes the following:

(1) Simulate 1000 separate attempts that the person makes until he falls off the bridge, crosses the bridge, or backs off the bridge.
(2) Record (1000 times in total) the number of times he falls into the water, the number of times he crosses the bridge, and the number of times he backs off the bridge.
(3) Calculate the probability of crossing the bridge.

Programming Procedure

A detailed flowchart for this simulation appears on the following page. An explanation of the programming procedure with references to program statements within parentheses follows.

A random-number generator is used to simulate the set of steps of the inebriated individual. Most computers have at least one function that generates pseudo-random numbers. The one used here is called RAN(X), where X is a seed. The generated real constants, YFL, are between zero and 0.9999999, and these constants are rectangularly distributed. In the flowchart and the program, these real constants are converted to integer constants from one (1) to ten (10) through the following function:

$$K = 10.0*YFL + 1.0 \text{ (statement \#90)}$$

If K equals 1, 2, 3, 4, or 5, a forward step is taken, and I is incremented by 1 (statement #110).
When a forward step is made, the model checks whether the drunk is still on the bridge (statement #120). If I is greater than 10, then the drunk crossed the bridge, and the counter for crossing the bridge is increased by 1 (statement #130).

If K equals 6, a backward step is taken, and I is decreased by 1 (statement #150).
When a backward step is made, the model checks whether the drunk is still on the bridge (statement #160). If I is less than 1, then the drunk backed off the bridge and the counter for backing off the bridge is increased by 1 statement #170).

If K equals 7 or 8, a step to the right is taken and J is increased by 1 (statement #190).
When a step to the right is made, the model checks whether the drunk is still on the bridge (statement #200). If J is graeater than 5, then the drunk fell in the water and the counter for falling in the water is increased by 1 (statement #210).

If K equals 9 or 10, a step to the left is taken and J is decreased by 1 (statement #230).
When a step to the left is made, the model checks whether the drunk is still on the bridge (statement #240). If J is less than 1, then the drunk fell in the water and the counter for falling in the water is increased by 1 (statement #250).

When the drunk crosses the bridge, falls into the water, or backs off the bridge, this program places him again on the first footmark, in the middle of the bridge passway, until one thousand sets of passes have been generated (statements #260, #60, and #70). In order to calculate the probability of crossing the bridge, CROSS is divided by one thousand, which is the number of simulated runs (statement #270).

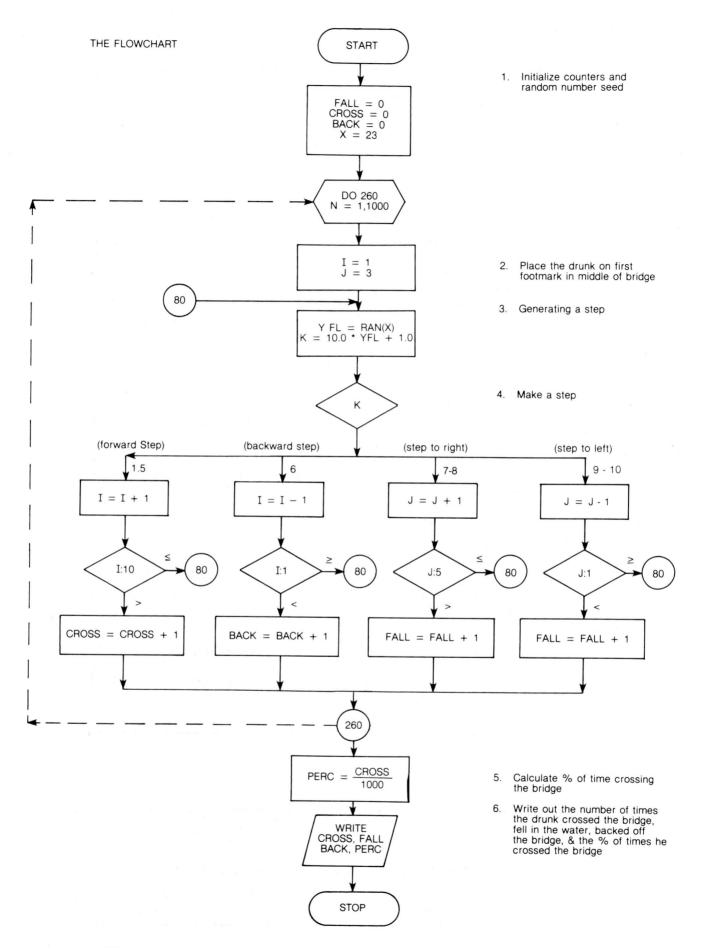

1. Initialize counters and random number seed

2. Place the drunk on first footmark in middle of bridge

3. Generating a step

4. Make a step

5. Calculate % of time crossing the bridge

6. Write out the number of times the drunk crossed the bridge, fell in the water, backed off the bridge, & the % of times he crossed the bridge

The FORTRAN Program

```
C *** SIMULATION OF DRUNK CROSSING THE BRIDGE
      INTEGER FALL, CROSS, BACK
   10 FALL = 0
   20 CROSS = 0
   30 BACK = 0
   40 X = 23
   50 DO 260  N = 1, 1000, 1
C ***      PLACEMENT OF DRUNK ON THE BRIDGE
   60    I = 1
   70    J = 3
C ***      GENERATING A STEP
   80    YFL = RAN(X)
   90    K = 10.0 * YFL + 1.0
  100    GO TO (110,110,110,110,110,150,190,190,230,230), K
C ***      A FORWARD STEP IS MADE
  110    I = I+1
  120    IF (I .LE. 10) GO TO 80
  130    CROSS = CROSS + 1
  140    GO TO 260
C ***      A BACKWARD STEP IS MADE
  150    I = I - 1
  160    IF (I .GE. 1) GO TO 80
  170    BACK = BACK + 1
  180    GO TO 260
C ***      A STEP TO THE RIGHT IS MADE
  190    J = J + 1
  200    IF (J .LE. 5) GO TO 80
  210    FALL = FALL + 1
  220    GO TO 260
C ***      A STEP TO THE LEFT IS MADE
  230    J = J - 1
  240    IF (J .GE. 1) GO TO 80
  250    FALL = FALL + 1
  260 CONTINUE
  270 PERC = FLOAT(CROSS) / 1000.0
  280 WRITE (6,300) CROSS, FALL, BACK
  290 WRITE (6,310) PERC
  300 FORMAT(1H1,//,2X,'SIMULATION PROBLEM',///,
      *        2X,'NUMBER CROSSINGS = ',I3,' NUMBER FALLS = ',
      *        I3,' NUMBER BACKING = ',I3)
  310 FORMAT(//,2X,'PROBABILITY OF CROSSING = ',F3.2)
      STOP
      END
```

The Output

```
SIMULATION PROBLEM


NUMBER CROSSINGS = 342 NUMBER FALLS = 500NUMBER BACKING = 158


PROBABILITY OF CROSSING =.34
```

3. Computation of π Through Simulation

The Monte Carlo technique is used here to calculate π (PI). Consider the circle which is inscribed inside a square, as illustrated in the figure below.

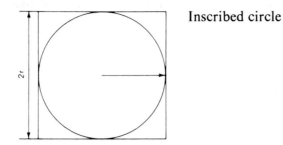

Inscribed circle

The area of the circle equals $\pi r^2 = Y$, where r is the radius, whereas the area of the square equals $(2r)^2 = X$, where 2r is its side's length. The ratio of the area of the square to the area of the circle, therefore is:

$$\frac{\text{Area of Square}}{\text{Area of Circle}} = \frac{X}{Y} = \frac{(2r)^2}{\pi r^2} = \frac{4r^2}{\pi r^2} = \frac{4}{\pi}$$

Therefore, π can be expressed as follows:

$$\pi = \frac{4Y}{X} = \frac{4 \text{ times the area of the circle}}{\text{the area of the square}}$$

So, in order to calculate π, one must be able to measure the areas of the circle and the square, or one must be able to calculate the ratio of the area of the circle to the area of the square. The following simulation technique, often referred to as the Monte Carlo method, will calculate that ratio.

Reconsider the above figure and inscribe the circle as in the figure below.

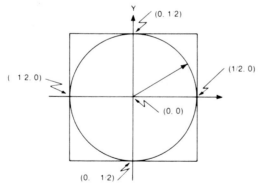

Inscribed circle reconsidered

Note that the radius is now equal to ½ and that the center of the circle coincides with the origin of the X-Y plane. If we can now devise a method whereby we can choose points at random which fall within the square, then 4 times the ratio of the number of these points which fall within the circle to the total number of points within the square equals π:

$$\pi = \frac{4 \text{ times number of points within circle}}{\text{total number of points in square}}$$

These points can be generated by the use of two random number genrerators, since each point is represented by an X-Y coordinate.

RAN(B) can be used to generate the X-coordinate and RAN(C) can be used to generate the Y-coordinate.

Note, however, that RAN(B) generates pseudo-random numbers between zero and one and that in our reconsidered inscribed circle, X lies between $-\frac{1}{2}$ and $+\frac{1}{2}$. Therefore the random numbers have to be scaled as follows:

$$-\tfrac{1}{2} < RAN(B) - .5 < +\tfrac{1}{2} \longrightarrow -\tfrac{1}{2} < X < +\tfrac{1}{2}$$

A similar scaling is necessary for the Y-coordinate:

$$-\tfrac{1}{2} < RAN(C) - .5 < +\tfrac{1}{2} \longrightarrow -\tfrac{1}{2} < Y < +\tfrac{1}{2}$$

The point that is thus defined by an X-Y coordinate:

$$(X,Y)(RAN(B) - .5, RAN(C) - .5)$$

will always lie within the square. It will also lie within the circle if it is within a distance (Z) of $\frac{1}{2}$ from the origin:

$$\text{If } Z = \sqrt{X^2 + Y^2} \simeq \sqrt{(RAN(B) - .5)^2 + (RAN(C) - .5)^2} < .5$$

This Monte Carlo procedure is used in the following FORTRAN program and is exhibited in the flowchart.

Programming Procedure

A detailed flowchart of this simulation appears on the next page. It reflects the following 6 steps:

1. Initialize variables and random number seeds.
2. Generate a point by defining its X-Y coordinates.
3. Calculate the distance from origin to the point with X-Y coordinates.
4. Locate the point: does it fall within the circle or is it outside the circle?
5. Calculate π.
6. Write the simulation run-number and the value of π.

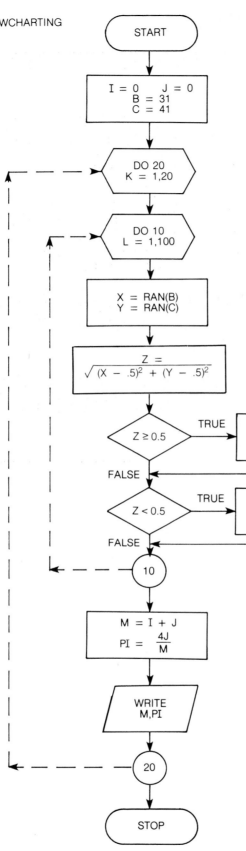

START

I = 0   J = 0
B = 31
C = 41

1. Initialize variables and random number seeds

DO 20
K = 1,20

DO 10
L = 1,100

X = RAN(B)
Y = RAN(C)

2. Generate a point by calculating X-Y coordinates

$$Z = \sqrt{(X - .5)^2 + (Y - .5)^2}$$

3. Calculate distance from origin to the point

4. Locate the generated point:

$Z \geq 0.5$ TRUE   I = I + 1   (if point is outside circle increment Icounter by 1)

FALSE

$Z < 0.5$ TRUE   J = J + 1   (if point is inside circle increment Jcounter by 1)

FALSE

10

M = I + J
$$PI = \frac{4J}{M}$$

5. Calculate π

WRITE
M,PI

6. Write simulation run and π

20

STOP

The Program

```
C *** CALCULATION OF PI
      I = 0
      J = 0
      B = 31.
      C = 41.
      WRITE (6,30)
C *** GENERATING POINTS AND FINDING THEIR LOCATION
      DO 20  K = 1, 20
         DO 10  L = 1, 100
C ***          CALCULATION OF TWO RANDOM NUMBERS
            X = RAN(B)
            Y = RAN(C)
C ***          CALCULATION OF DISTANCE AND LOCATION OF POINT
            Z = SQRT((X - 0.5) ** 2 + (Y - 0.5) ** 2)
            IF (Z .GE. 0.5) I = I + 1
            IF (Z .LT. 0.5) J = J + 1
   10    CONTINUE
         M = I + J
         PI = FLOAT(4 * J) / FLOAT(M)
         WRITE (6,40) M, PI
   20 CONTINUE
   30 FORMAT(1H1,5X,'ITERATION',5X,'PI',//)
   40 FORMAT(5X,I5,9X,F6.4)
      STOP
      END
```

The Output

ITERATION	PI
100	2.8400
200	2.8000
300	2.9333
400	2.9500
500	2.9760
600	2.9933
700	3.0229
800	3.0600
900	3.0844
1000	3.0840
1100	3.0691
1200	3.0833
1300	3.0862
1400	3.0714
1500	3.0773
1600	3.0800
1700	3.0847
1800	3.1000
1900	3.1074
2000	3.1000

4. Transportation Cost Analysis: A Simulation

The manager of a hypothetical company Widget, Inc., is interested in estimating the future cost of shipping a product via the most economical mode of transportation to each of his five distribution centers.

The future transportation costs are generated by simulating quantities, destination, and due dates for twenty orders every day over a 20-day period.*

In order to build "good will" within distribution channels, Widget, Inc., always ships via whatever form of transportation it takes to meet the time requirements of its distribution centers.

Problem Statement and Procedure

Since Widget, Inc., is a hypothetical company, most of the data is generated by the function RAN. This random number generator is used to generate for each order the following information:

1. destination of each order (DEST),
2. quantity of each order (QTY), and
3. due date of each order (TIME)

The generated data is manipulated by the program to come up with workable data, as follows:

1. Detination

There are five distribution centers: A, B, C, D, and E. The random-number generator generates real numbers between 0 and 1. Since there are five different destinations, these real numbers (0 to 1) are transformed to integer numbers from 1 to 5 (1 representing A, 2 representing B, 3 representing C, 4 representing D, and 5 representing E). The transformation function used is:

$$DEST = \frac{XFL*10.}{2.} + 1.$$

where: XFL: is the generated real random constant,

$\frac{XFL*10.}{2.} + 1.$ is a real expression

DEST: is an integer name for destination.
$(1 \leq DEST \leq 5)$

2. Quantity

The product can only be ordered in quantities of 20, 40, 60, 80, or 100 cases per shipment. In order to generate one of these cases for each order by the use of the random-number generator (which produces real numbers between 0 and 1), the following transformation functions are used:

$$IJ = \frac{ZFL*10.}{.2.} + 1.$$

QTY = IJ*20

where: ZFL: is the generated real random constant,

$\frac{ZFL*10.}{2.} + 1.$ is a real expression

IJ: is an integer name $(1 \leq IJ \leq 5)$.
QTY: is an integer name for quantity.
$(20 \leq QTY \leq 100)$

---

*It would be redundant to show the simulated output for all twenty days, so the simulated output for only three days is shown.

3. Due Date

As all dates are within 20 days, a random number is generated and transformed by the following function:

$$\text{TIME} = \frac{\text{YFL}*40.}{2.} + 1.$$

where: YFL: is the generated real random constant,

$\dfrac{\text{YFL}*40.}{2.} + 1.$ is a real expression

TIME: is an integer name for the date.

$(1 \leq \text{TIME} \leq 20)$

The input data consists of the distance in miles between Widget, Inc., and the five destinations (table 14.1), the cost for each mode of transportation per case and per mile combined with the different destinations (table 14.2), and the maximum number of days it takes for each mode to reach each destination (table 14.3).

Table 14.1 Miles (MILE)

To/From	Widget, Inc.
A	500
B	1000
C	1500
D	600
E	2000

Table 14.2 Unit Transportation Cost (COST(I,DEST))

Mode (I)/Destination (DEST)	A=1	B=2	C=3	D=4	E=5
Barge (1)(.005)	2.5	5.0	7.5	3.0	6.0
Rail (2)(.01)	5.0	10.0	15.0	6.0	12.0
Truck (3)(.015)	7.5	15.0	22.5	9.0	18.0
Air (4)(.03)	15.0	30.0	45.0	18.0	36.0

Table 14.3 Max. Number of Traveling Days (IDEST(I,DEST))

Mode (I)/Destination (DEST)	A=1	B=2	C=3	D=4	E=5
Barge (1)	4	6	8	4	17
Rail (2)	3	4	6	3	7
Truck (3)	2	2	2	2	2
Air (4)	1	1	1	1	1

Steps To Be Performed

1. Input the IDEST matrix, the cost matrix, the MILE array, and transportation mode (A1) array.
2. Generate the destination (DEST), due date (TIME), and order quantity (QTY).
3. Check on mode of transportation (I) to be used to maintain "good will" and to minimize transportation cost.
4. Calculate the transportation cost (OCOST=QTY*COST(I,DEST)).
5. Repeat steps 1 through 4 for 20 orders over 20 days and accumulate daily totals for mileage covered, cases shipped and shipping cost; then print out developed data.

Names Used

Program
Variable Names	*Definition*	*Mode*	*Dimension*
A1	An array where the different transportation modes are stored	alphanumeric	1
COST	The unit transportation cost	real	2
IDEST	Matrix indicating the maximum number of traveling days to each destination by each mode	integer	2
MA	Storage for the total number of cases shipped per day	integer	0
DEST	Destination of an order	integer	0
ME	Storage for the total number of miles traveled each day	integer	0
MILE	Array for storing the miles from Company to destination	integer	1
QTY	Order quantity: number of cases to be shipped	integer	0
TIME	Due date of an order	integer	0
OCOST	Total shipping cost of an order	real	0
T	Matrix for storing the daily shipping cost, miles covered, and cases sent	real	2

Flowcharting the Transportation Cost Case

1. Read in data, write daily heading, and initialize daily totals.

2. Generate destination, due date, and order quantity.

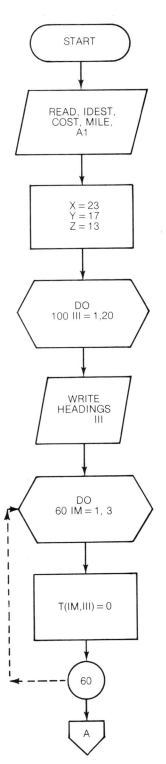

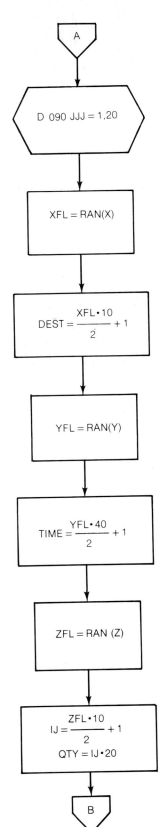

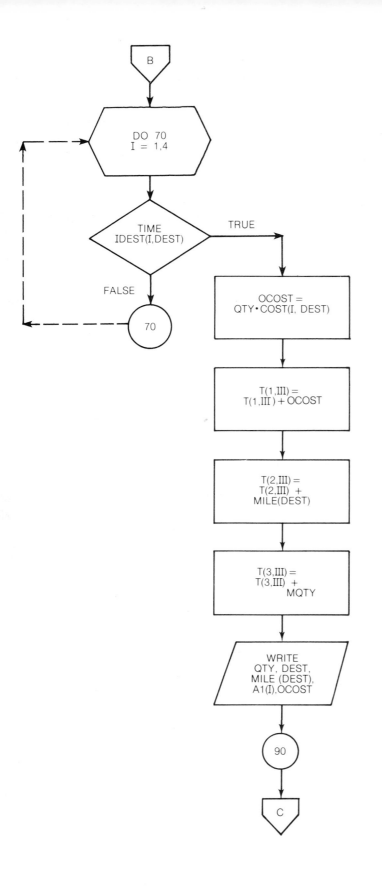

3–4. Calculate shipping cost, daily cost, daily mileage covered, and daily number of cases shipped. Write out order quantity, destination, mileage, mode, and shipping cost.

5. Write number of cases shipped daily, number of miles covered daily, and daily shipping cost.

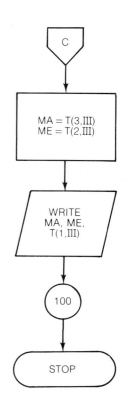

The FORTRAN IV Program

```
C *** TRANSPORTATION COST ANALYSIS - A SIMULATION
      INTEGER   DEST, QTY, TIME
      DIMENSION   IDEST(4,5), COST(4,5), MILE(5), A1(4), T(3,20)
   10 FORMAT(20I3,/,20F4.2,/,5I4,/,4A4)
   20 FORMAT(1H1,///,54X,'WIDGET INCORPORATED',38X,'PAGE',2X,I2,//,
     *          21X,'QUANTITY ORDERED',8X,'DESTINATION',8X,'MILES',
     *          8X,'MODE',10X,'COST')
   30 FORMAT(24X,I3,2X,'CASES',16X,I1,14X,I4,8X,A4,9X,'$',F8.2)
   40 FORMAT('0',6X,'***',1X,'DAILY TOTAL',1X,'***',7X,I5,2X,'CASES',
     *          18X,I6,2X,'MILES',16X,'$',F11.2)
C ***           READ IN DATA
      READ (5,10) ((IDEST(I,J), I=1,4), J=1,5),
     *            ((COST(L,M), L=1,4), M=1,5),
     *            (MILE(N), N=1,5), (A1(NN), NN=1,4)
C ***           INITIALIZE THE RANDOM NUMBER GENERATOR
      X = 23.
      Y = 17.
      Z = 13.
      DO 100  III = 1, 20
        WRITE (6,20)  III
        DO 60  IM = 1, 3
          T(IM,III) = 0
   60   CONTINUE
        DO 90  JJJ = 1, 20
C ***           GENERATE THE DESTINATION
          XFL = RAN(X)
          DES = ((XFL * 10.0) / 2.0) + 1.0
C ***           GENERATE THE DUE DATE
          YFL = RAN(Y)
          TIME = ((YFL * 40.0) / 2.0) + 1.0
C ***           GENERATE THE QUANTITY
          ZFL = FAN(Z)
          IJ = ((ZFL * 10.0) / 2.0) + 1.0
          QTY = IJ * 20
C ***           CALCULATE THE SHIPPING COST
          DO 70  I = 1, 4
            IF (TIME .GE. IDEST(I,DEST))  GO TO 80
   70     CONTINUE
   80     OCOST = QTY * COST(I,DEST)
C ***           CALCULATE THE DAILY SHIPPING COST,
C ***             MILES AND CASES SENT
          T(1,III) = T(1,III) + OCOST
          T(2,III) = T(2,III) + MILE(DEST)
          T(3,III) = T(3,III) + QTY
C ***           WRITE OUT DEVELOPED DATA
          WRITE (6,30) QTY, DES, MILE(DEST), A1(I), OCOST
   90   CONTINUE
        MA = T(3,III)
        ME = T(2,III)
        WRITE (6,40) MA, ME, T(1,III)
  100 CONTINUE
      STOP
      END
```

Input Format

Card #	Columns	Description	Format
1	1–60	IDEST(4,5)	20I3
2	1–80	COST(4,5)	20F4.2
3	1–20	MILE(5)	5I4
4	1–16	A1(4)	4A4

Data Input

004003002001006004003001008006005001004003002001014007006001

025005000750150005001000150030000750150022504500030006000900180006001200180036000

0500100015006001200

BOATRAILTRUK AIR

Program Output

```
                              WIDGET INCORPORATED                                    PAGE   1
        QUANTITY ORDERED         DESTINATION        MILES        MODE        COST
             20   CASES               1              500          AIR      $    300.00
             20   CASES               1              500          AIR      $    300.00
             20   CASES               1              500          AIR      $    300.00
             20   CASES               1              500          TRUK     $    150.00
             20   CASES               2             1000          RAIL     $    200.00
             60   CASES               1              500          BOAT     $    150.00
             20   CASES               3             1500          BOAT     $    150.00
            100   CASES               2             1000          AIR      $   3000.00
             60   CASES               3             1500          BOAT     $    450.00
             20   CASES               1              500          RAIL     $    100.00
             80   CASES               5             1200          BOAT     $    480.00
             40   CASES               1              500          BOAT     $    100.00
            100   CASES               2             1000          BOAT     $    500.00
             40   CASES               5             1200          BOAT     $    240.00
             20   CASES               5             1200          AIR      $    720.00
             20   CASES               3             1500          BOAT     $    150.00
             60   CASES               5             1200          AIR      $   2160.00
            100   CASES               4              600          BOAT     $    300.00
             40   CASES               3             1500          BOAT     $    300.00
             60   CASES               4              600          BOAT     $    180.00

*** DAILY TOTAL ***        920   CASES              18500   MILES              $     10230.00
```

```
                              WIDGET INCORPORATED                                    PAGE   9
        QUANTITY ORDERED         DESTINATION        MILES        MODE        COST
             20   CASES               5             1200          RAIL     $    240.00
             40   CASES               1              500          BOAT     $    100.00
             60   CASES               4              600          RAIL     $    360.00
             40   CASES               1              500          TRUK     $    300.00
            100   CASES               5             1200          AIR      $   3600.00
             20   CASES               3             1500          BOAT     $    150.00
             60   CASES               2             1000          BOAT     $    300.00
             40   CASES               4              600          BOAT     $    120.00
             40   CASES               3             1500          BOAT     $    300.00
             40   CASES               5             1200          BOAT     $    240.00
            100   CASES               5             1200          BOAT     $    600.00
             60   CASES               3             1500          BOAT     $    450.00
             60   CASES               3             1500          RAIL     $    900.00
            100   CASES               3             1500          RAIL     $   1500.00
             40   CASES               2             1000          BOAT     $    200.00
             80   CASES               3             1500          BOAT     $    600.00
             80   CASES               5             1200          AIR      $   2880.00
             60   CASES               4              600          BOAT     $    180.00
             60   CASES               2             1000          BOAT     $    300.00
             40   CASES               3             1500          AIR      $   1800.00

*** DAILY TOTAL ***       1140   CASES              22300   MILES              $     15120.00
```

```
                              WIDGET INCORPORATED
        QUANTITY ORDERED       DESTINATION      MILES      MODE      COST
            40   CASES              2            1000      BOAT    $   200.00
            40   CASES              2            1000      BOAT    $   200.00
            20   CASES              2            1000      BOAT    $   100.00
            20   CASES              3            1500      AIR     $   900.00
            60   CASES              2            1000      BOAT    $   300.00
           100   CASES              5            1200      AIR     $  3600.00
            40   CASES              4             600      BOAT    $   120.00
            60   CASES              4             600      BOAT    $   180.00
            60   CASES              1             500      BOAT    $   150.00
            20   CASES              2            1000      AIR     $   600.00
            20   CASES              3            1500      BOAT    $   150.00
            40   CASES              2            1000      BOAT    $   200.00
            20   CASES              1             500      BOAT    $    50.00
            40   CASES              4             600      BOAT    $   120.00
            80   CASES              5            1200      AIR     $  2880.00
            40   CASES              2            1000      BOAT    $   200.00
            40   CASES              1             500      BOAT    $   100.00
            60   CASES              1             500      BOAT    $   150.00
            20   CASES              1             500      AIR     $   300.00
            20   CASES              3            1500      BOAT    $   150.00

  *** DAILY TOTAL ***        840   CASES        18200   MILES     $   10650.00
```

Exercises

Problem #1

Simulate the game of tossing two dice and play that game 100 times. Record the outcomes of the simulated game in a file called GAME and make sure that each of the one hundred lines in that file contains two numbers, representing the two faces of the simulated game.

Problem #2

There is a casino and anyone can play against it. The maximum bet which is allowed by the house is 500 dollars. The rules for the game are as follows:

1. If the sum of points of the two dice faces which turn up in the first toss is 2 or 12, the player wins three times as much as he bet.
2. If double 4 (that is, if the first and the second die has the face with 4 points up), or double 5, or double 3, he wins twice as much as he bet.
3. If the sum of the two dice is 5 or 7, he wins as much as he bet.
4. If double 2 is up, he must toss the dice again. If this time the sum of the points on the two faces is 12 or 5 or 7 or 2, he wins as much as he bet; otherwise he loses.
5. In all other cases he loses.

Write a FORTRAN program that simulates this (no more than 20 games) and use the data that you have placed in file GAME when solving problem #1.

Your output must show for each game the amount of the bet, the outcome of the game, and the amount won or lost by the player.

Business Analysis Cases

1. Moving Averages of the Dow Jones Industrial Stocks

Patterns in time series vary widely, but can be classified under the following groups: averages, trends in the averages, cyclic effects, seasonal effects, and random variations. In most forecasting models, averages are meaningless, since trends, cycles, and seasonal patterns may prevail. A variation of simple averages is moving averages, which emphasize recent values and therefore estimate trend effects. The method of moving averages is useful also in isolating cyclical components and has the advantage of not needing any trend computing. In general, moving averages tend to lag a trend, raise the valleys, and depress the peaks of cyclic patterns.

When calculating moving averages, only data from more recent time periods are used. The amount of data used in calculating a moving average needs to be determined very carefully, since the magnitude of the lag and the smoothing of cyclic patterns depend on the amount of data used.

In this case the moving averages technique is applied to a series of 100 Friday closings of the Dow Jones Industrial Stocks in order to picture a general trend and cycle effect, if any.

Theory and Procedure

The following is the basis for applying the moving averages forecasting method to the Friday closings of the Dow Jones Industrial Stocks. The irregular fluctuations of these stocks in the past cannot be used, as such, for future stock estimates. Rather, one wishes to isolate continuing changes. So, we desire to separate the continuing from the temporary effects, which can be accomplished by taking a 10-week moving average. As the continuing influences—trends, for example—tend to steer the stock values of all Friday closings in the same direction, such influences will appear in the moving averages. The temporary influences, which raise the price of a stock today and lower it tomorrow, will not appear in the moving averages.

However, as the 10-week moving averages include data from 10 weeks before, a lag in the forecast occurs. The moving average will lag behind the current stock price level if there is a steady rise or fall in the stock price and will lag still further behind the future stock price level that it is trying to forecast.

The calculation procedure for the 10-week moving averages of the Dow Jones Industrial Stocks is as follows (DJIS):

1. Add the Friday closing prices of the DJIS for the first 10 consecutive weeks (week #1 through week #10).
2. Divide this sum by 10 to obtain the first moving average to predict or forecast for the 11th week.
3. Repeat the above 2 steps for weeks #2 through #11, #3 through #12, . . . , for weeks #92 through #101.

The program written here provides for a printout of the actual Friday closing prices and the predicted Friday closing prices.

Names Used

Program Variable Names	Definition	Mode	Dimension
AVDJIA	Average of 10 Friday closings of Dow Jones Industrial stocks	Real	1
DJIA	Sum of 10 Friday closings of Dow Jones Industrial stocks	Real	0
L	Integer referring to "week"	Integer	0
Y	Actual stock price of the Friday closing of Dow Jones Industrial stocks	Real	1

Flowcharting the Moving-Averages Technique

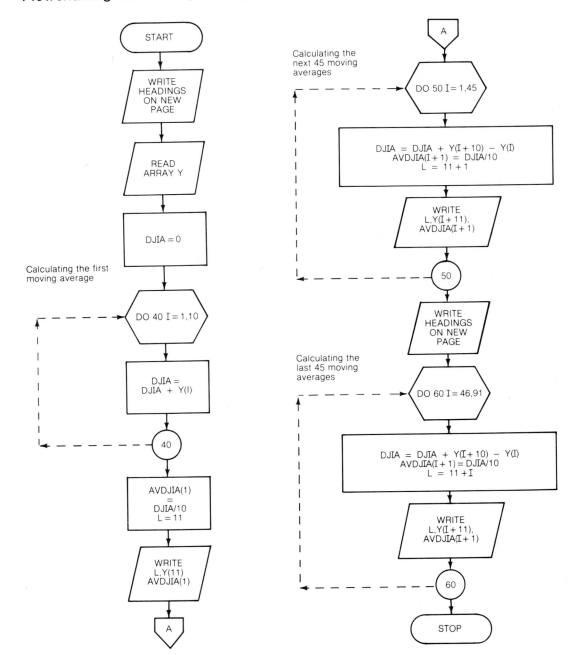

The FORTRAN IV Program

```
C *** DOW JONES INDUSTRIAL MOVING AVERAGES

      DIMENSION  AVDJIA(92), Y(101)
   10 FORMAT(1H1,//,20X,'WEEK',9X,'ACTUAL',20X,'PREDICTED',//)
   20 FORMAT(F6.2)
   30 FORMAT(20X,I3,10X,F6.2,20X,F6.2)
      WRITE (6,10)
C *** READING ALL 101 STOCK VALUES
      READ (5,20)  (Y(I), I = 1, 101)
      DJIA = 0.0
C *** CALCULATING THE FIRST 10-WEEKS MOVING AVERAGE
      DO 40  I = 1, 10, 1
         DJIA = DJIA + Y(I)
   40 CONTINUE
      AVDJIA(1) = DJIA / 10.0
      L = 11
      WRITE (6,30)  L, Y(11), AVDJIA(1)
C *** CALCULATING THE NEXT 45 10-WEEKS MOVING AVERAGES
      DO 50  I = 1, 45, 1
         DJIA = DJIA + Y(I+10) - Y(I)
         AVDJIA(I+1) = DJIA / 10.0
         L = 11 + I
         WRITE (6,30)  L, Y(I+11), AVDJIA(I+1)
   50 CONTINUE
C *** CALCULATING THE LAST 45 10-WEEKS MOVING AVERAGES
      WRITE (6,10)
      DO 60  I = 46, 91, 1
         DJIA = DJIA + Y(I+10) - Y(I)
         AVDJIA(I+1) = DJIA / 10.0
         L = 11 + I
         WRITE (6,30)  L, Y(I+11), AVDJIA(I+1)
   60 CONTINUE
      STOP
      END
```

Input Format

Card Number	Column	Variable Name	Content
1 through 101	1–6	Y	Stock value

Data Input

913.62	937.56
900.93	924.77
897.80	894.84
903.51	876.16
922.46	869.76
913.92	886.12
888.47	852.25
871.27	845.92
869.65	818.06
885.89	826.59
892.34	824.46
896.01	820.88
921.25	837.25
917.21	836.72
924.42	819.50
933.80	824.25
952.95	830.39
949.59	824.18
967.49	808.41
961.28	806.96
948.41	836.06
958.98	862.26
965.88	855.99
967.06	860.48
985.08	849.26
978.24	823.13
981.29	812.30
966.99	793.03
952.51	786.69
951.89	789.86
925.53	797.65
935.54	809.20
938.59	798.11
946.05	782.60
947.85	775.54
951.95	744.06
916.65	752.77
905.21	753.30
911.18	757.46
904.28	777.59
920.00	784.12
935.48	772.11
927.30	763.66
933.46	791.05
924.82	791.84
924.00	794.46
957.17	775.94
961.61	747.29
967.30	733.63
947.45	717.73
	702.22

Program Output

WEEK	ACTUAL	PREDICTED
11	892.34	896.75
12	896.01	894.62
13	921.25	894.13
14	917.21	896.47
15	924.42	897.84
16	933.80	898.04
17	952.95	900.03
18	949.59	900.48
19	967.49	914.31
20	961.28	924.09
21	948.41	931.63
22	958.98	937.24
23	965.88	943.53
24	967.06	948.00
25	985.08	952.98
26	978.24	959.05
27	981.29	963.49
28	966.99	966.32
29	952.51	968.06
30	951.89	966.56
31	925.53	965.63
32	935.54	963.34
33	938.59	960.99
34	946.05	958.26
35	947.85	956.16
36	951.95	952.44
37	916.65	949.81
38	905.21	943.34
39	911.18	937.17
40	904.28	933.03
41	929.00	928.27
42	935.48	927.72
43	927.30	927.71
44	933.46	926.58
45	924.82	925.32
46	924.00	923.02
47	957.17	920.22
48	961.61	924.28
49	967.30	929.92
50	947.45	935.53
51	937.56	939.84
52	924.77	941.60
53	894.84	940.53
54	876.16	937.28
55	869.76	931.55
56	886.12	926.05

WEEK	ACTUAL	PREDICTED
57	852.25	922.26
58	845.92	911.77
59	818.06	900.20
60	826.59	885.27
61	824.46	873.19
62	820.88	861.87
63	837.25	851.49
64	836.72	845.73
65	819.50	841.78
66	824.25	836.76
67	830.39	830.57
68	824.18	828.38
69	808.41	826.21
70	806.96	825.24
71	836.06	823.28
72	862.26	824.44
73	855.99	828.58
74	860.48	830.45
75	849.26	832.83
76	823.13	835.80
77	812.30	835.69
78	793.03	833.88
79	786.69	830.76
80	789.86	828.59
81	797.65	826.88
82	809.20	823.04
83	798.11	817.73
84	782.60	811.95
85	775.54	804.16
86	744.06	796.79
87	752.77	788.88
88	753.30	782.92
89	757.46	778.95
90	777.59	776.03
91	784.12	774.80
92	772.11	773.45
93	763.66	769.74
94	791.05	766.29
95	791.84	767.14
96	794.46	768.77
97	775.94	773.81
98	747.29	776.12
99	733.63	775.52
100	717.73	773.14
101	702.22	767.15
102	0.00	758.96

2. Goodness-of-Fit Test for the Random-Number Generator

You may recall from chapter 14 that the function which generates random numbers is called RAN. The hypothesis that RAN is a reliable random number generator is tested by means of a χ^2 test for goodness of fit.

Theory on the χ^2 Test for Goodness of Fit

The real sample values, as generated by RAN, fall between 0 and 1. The values are called random values because all numbers between 0 and 1 have an equal chance to occur when a number is generated.

To test this randomness, 1,000 numbers are generated and split arbitrarily into 20 classes, as follows:

class 1 contains all numbers between 0.00 and 0.04999 . . .

class 2 contains all numbers between 0.05 and 0.09999 . . .

class 3 contains all numbers between 0.10 and 0.14999 . . .

— — —

class 19 contains all numbers between 0.90 and 0.94999 . . .

class 20 contains all numbers between 0.95 and 0.9999 . . .

Since 1,000 random numbers are generated, it may be expected that for each of the 20 classes, 50 numbers will be generated. Fifty numbers is the theoretical frequency if RAN is a perfect random-number generator. In general, and quite acceptably, a variation from this theoretical frequency is expected. The relative total variation can be calculated as follows:

$$\sum_{I=1}^{20} \frac{(OBS(I) - 50)^2}{50}$$

where: OBS(I) is the observed frequency in class I
50 is the theoretical frequency.

This relative total variation is a χ^2 value, and a measure of the goodness of fit between the random numbers generated by RAN and the theoretical random frequencies (which the generated numbers are supposed to fit).

The larger the χ^2 value, the worse the fit. To decide whether the generated data constitute a sample that is randomly distributed, the calculated χ^2 value is compared to a tables χ^2 values at a significance level, α, with n degrees of freedom. The degrees of freedom equals the number of classes (20) minus one, and α is chosen at 5%. A 5% significance level means that 5% of the times one may reject randomness when indeed randomness occurs.

The χ^2 table value equals:

$$\chi^2_{(n=19,\alpha=.05)} = 30.14$$

If the calculated χ^2 value $\sum_{I=1}^{20} \frac{(OBS(I) - 50)^2}{50}$ is smaller than the theoretical $\chi^2_{(n=19,\alpha=.05)}$ value (30.14), then RAN is a good random number generator; otherwise, if the calculated χ^2 value is larger than the $\chi^2_{(n=19,\alpha=.05)}$, RAN does not generate random numbers.

Programming Procedure

The following basic steps are used to test the random-number generator:

STEP 1 Initialize all necessary arrays. These arrays are:
- the theoretical frequency array (ACT) to be initialized to 50
- the observed frequency array (OBS) to be initialized to 0
- the $[(OBS-50)^2]$ array (DIFSQ) to be initialized to 0
- the $[(OBS-50)^2/50]$ array (RDIFSQ) to be initialized to 0.

STEP 2 Initialize all necessary variables. These are:
- the calculated χ^2 value (CHICAL) to be initialized to 0
- the input argument of RAN(X) to be initialized to an arbitrary integer, say 13.

STEP 3 Generate all 1,000 numbers by calling RAN 1,000 times and by changing the new input argument of RAN to the old output argument each time a number is generated.

STEP 4 For each generated number, define the class to which it belongs by assigning to the integer class "J" the real expression.

$$FL*20+1.$$

where "FL" is the real output argument of RAN and is a constant between 0 and 1. After the class "J" is defined, augment the observed frequency of that class "J" by 1 unit.

STEP 5 For all 20 classes calculate:
- the squared difference between the observed and the actual frequency, divided by the actual frequency [RDIFSQ(I)].

STEP 6 Calculate the χ^2 value by adding the RDIFSQ(I) for all 20 classes.

STEP 7 Print out the appropriate table, containing:
- the observed frequency for all classes
- the actual frequency for all classes

Flowcharting the χ^2 Test for Random-Number Generator

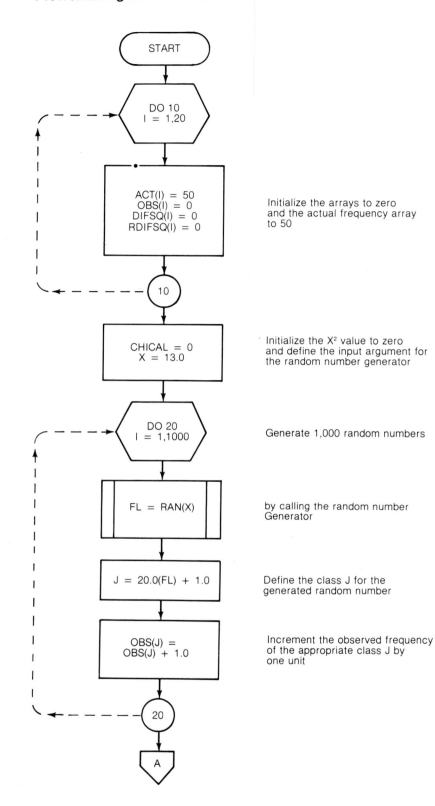

START

DO 10
I = 1,20

ACT(I) = 50
OBS(I) = 0
DIFSQ(I) = 0
RDIFSQ(I) = 0

Initialize the arrays to zero
and the actual frequency array
to 50

10

CHICAL = 0
X = 13.0

Initialize the χ^2 value to zero
and define the input argument for
the random number generator

DO 20
I = 1,1000

Generate 1,000 random numbers

FL = RAN(X)

by calling the random number
Generator

J = 20.0(FL) + 1.0

Define the class J for the
generated random number

OBS(J) =
OBS(J) + 1.0

Increment the observed frequency
of the appropriate class J by
one unit

20

A

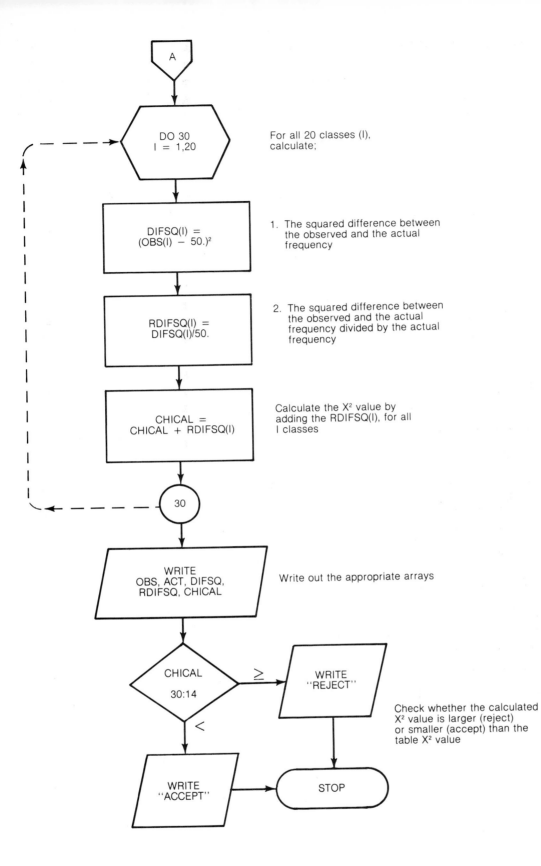

For all 20 classes (I),
calculate;

1. The squared difference between
   the observed and the actual
   frequency

2. The squared difference between
   the observed and the actual
   frequency divided by the actual
   frequency

Calculate the X^2 value by
adding the RDIFSQ(I), for all
I classes

Write out the appropriate arrays

Check whether the calculated
X^2 value is larger (reject)
or smaller (accept) than the
table X^2 value

```
C *** RANDOM NUMBER GENERATOR TEST

      DIMENSION  OBS(20), DIFSQ(20), RDIFSQ(20), ACT(20)
C *** INITIALIZE ALL ARRAYS, CHI SQUARE VALUE AND THE
C ***  SEED OF THE RANDOM NUMBER GENERATOR
      DO 10  I = 1, 20
         ACT(I) = 50
         OBS(I) = 0.
         DIFSQ(I) = 0.
         RDIFSQ(I) = 0.
   10 CONTINUE
      CHICAL = 0.
      X = 13.0
C *** GENERATING 1000 RANDOM NUMBERS, DEFINING THEIR
C ***  CLASS J AND ALL CLASS FREQUENCIES
      DO 20  I = 1, 1000
         FL = RAN(X)
         J = FL * 20.0 + 1.0
         OBS(J) = OBS(J) + 1.0
   20 CONTINUE
C *** CALCULATION OF CHI SQUARE VALUE
      DO 30  I = 1, 20
         DIFSQ(I) = (OBS(I) - 50.0) ** 2
         RDIFSQ(I) = DIFSQ(I) / 50.0
         CHICAL = CHICAL + RDIFSQ(I)
   30 CONTINUE
      WRITE (6,100) (OBS(J), ACT(J), DIFSQ(J), RDIFSQ(J), J=1,20), CHICAL
      IF (CHICAL .LT. 30.14) GO TO 40
         WRITE(6,110)
         GO TO 50
   40    WRITE(6,120)
   50 STOP
  100 FORMAT(1H1,//,25X,'TEST OF RAN  ',//,
     *          25X,'CHI-SQUARE VALUE IS 30.14',//,
     *          25X,'BREAKDOWN IN CLASSES',//,
     *          10X,'OBSERVED',3X,'ACTUAL',3X,'(OBS-ACT)**2',3X,
     *            '(OBS-ACT)**2/ACT',/,
     *          20(10X,F3.0,7X,F3.0,7X,F5.0,10X,F9.3,//),
     *          45X,F9.3,///,
     *          25X,'IF THE COMPUTED CHI IS GREATER',//,
     *          25X,'THAN THE TABLE CHI THEN REJECT',///)
  110 FORMAT(25X,'REJECT')
  120 FORMAT(25X,'ACCEPT')
      END
```

The Program Output

```
                    TEST OF RAN

              CHI-SQUARE VALUE IS 30.14

              BREAKDOWN IN CLASSES
```

OBSERVED	ACTUAL	(OBS-ACT)**2	(OBS-ACT)**2/ACT
65.	50.	225.	4.500
49.	50.	1.	0.020
59.	50.	81.	1.620
44.	50.	36.	0.720
48.	50.	4.	0.080
41.	50.	81.	1.620
46.	50.	16.	0.320
58.	50.	64.	1.280
48.	50.	4.	0.080
50.	50.	0.	0.000
46.	50.	16.	0.320
48.	50.	4.	0.080
44.	50.	36.	0.720
52.	50.	4.	0.080
52.	50.	4.	0.080
56.	50.	36.	0.720
37.	50.	169.	3.380
44.	50.	36.	0.720
47.	50.	9.	0.180
66.	50.	256.	5.120
			21.640

```
              IF THE COMPUTED CHI IS GREATER

              THAN THE TABLE CHI THEN REJECT

              ACCEPT
```

3. Network Analysis: PERT-Program Evaluation Review Technique

The PERT method is a management-oriented technique for the scheduling of a series of nonrepetitive jobs so that the entire project can be completed in the shortest amount of time. This method considers the series of interrelated activities and determines the optimum planning and scheduling of the activities to obtain the desired goal. Information can also be obtained to show what jobs could be delayed and yet still not slow down the completion of the total project. For the critical path analysis, the following information has to be obtained:

EARLY START AND EARLY FINISH

LATE START AND LATE FINISH

TOTAL SLACK FOR EACH JOB

This set of information is generated by the program and used in determining the critical path.

Setting Up the Network

The preliminary step before executing the PERT algorithm is to develop the network model representing the interrelationships between activities and the general flow of activities. This development can be accomplished as follows:

Step 1 Develop the logical sequence in which the activities have to be performed for completing the project. An activity is the performance of a specific task and, consequently, it is the effort of manpower and machinery resources.

Step 2 Draw the arrow diagram network using activities and events. An event is represented by a node, representing the occurrence of a checkpoint in time. This is the accomplishment of a task, rather than the performance of a task (activity). The event represents the start of activity(s) or the completion of an activity(s).

Step 3 Assign three times to each activity:
1. PT: the most pessimistic time
2. PRT: the most probabilistic time
3. OT: the most optimistic time

These times must be developed by qualified people—supervisors or foremen in charge of the project, engineers, and others. Then times will be used to calculate the expected times (EXPT) and the standard time deviation (STDD).

Step 4 Number the nodes in such a way that:
1. each job has a unique set of node numbers assigned to it
2. all activities entering a node have identical followers
3. all activities leaving a node have identical predecessors
4. a node represents the complete relationship between all entering and exiting jobs
5. they are in ordered sequence, such that the I node (beginning node) is smaller than the J node (ending node)

Example

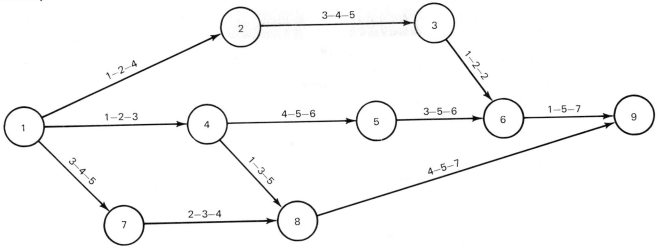

Node I	Location J	Job Description	PST.	Most Prob. Estimated Times	OPT.
1	2	order fixtures	1	2	4
1	4	excavation	1	2	3
1	7	Order trees and shrubs	3	4	5
2	3	manufacture furniture	3	4	5
3	6	deliver furniture	1	2	2
4	5	erect steel structure	4	5	6
4	8	back filling	1	3	5
5	6	masonry work	3	5	6
6	9	install furniture	1	5	7
7	8	plant trees and shrubs	1	3	5
8	9	final grading	4	5	7

PERT-Algorithm

The algorithm steps can be executed using the following procedure:

Step 1 Initialize data tables. This step involves loading the arrays which are required by the critical path algorithm. These data include: the starting (I) node and the ending (J) node for each job; the pessimistic (PT), most probable (PRT), and optimistic (OT) completion times for each job; and a job description (ALPHA) for each job within the project.

Step 2 Calculate the expected times for each activity (EXPT). Pert networks utilize a Beta Distribution for the development of the EXPT times. The Beta Distribution represents three specific points for each activity: PT (pessimistic time), PRT (most probable time), and OT (optimistic time).

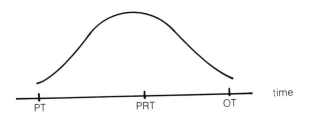

The pessimistic time is the minimum possible period of time in which an activity can be accomplished; it is that time in which an activity can be completed if everything goes exceptionally well. The assumption is made that an activity does not have more than 1 chance in 100 of being completed in that time. The optimistic time is the time required for an activity under adverse conditions. It is estimated that the activity would have no more than 1 chance in 100 of exceeding this amount of time. The most probable time estimate is the most realistic estimate of the time the activity might consume. It is assumed that this time would occur most often if the activity is repeated under the same conditions. Assuming a Beta Distribution of the time variable, the EXPT (expected) time for activity K can now be calculated as follows:

$$EXPT(K) = \frac{OT(K) + 4\,PRT(K) + PT(K)}{6}$$

the standard time deviation for activity K is

$$STDD(K) = \frac{OT(K) - PT(K)}{6}$$

Step 3   Calculation of the early start (ES) and early finish (EF) times. The early start time is that time at which an event can be started providing all events preceding it have been started and completed as early as possible. The simplest way of calculating the ES for all activities is to use the Forward Scan Rule as outlined here:

Give each node a BUCKET value: BUCKET(I)
Initialize these BUCKET(I)s to zero
Now for each activity K proceed as follows:
    BUCKET (JNODE)'←BUCKET(INODE) + EXPT(INODE,JNODE)
        iff BUCKET(JNODE)'≥BUCKET(JNODE)
    —assign (BUCKET(INODE) + EXP(INODE,JNODE)) to BUCKET(JNODE)
        if and only if (BUCKET(INODE) + EXP(INODE,JNODE)) is greater than
        the previous BUCKET(JNODE) value—
    ES(K) = BUCKET(INODE)'
After all ES(K)s are calculated, the EF(K)s can be calculated as follows for each activity K
    EF(K) = ES(K) + EXPT(K)

Step 4   Calculation of the late start (LS) and late finish (LF) times. The latest finish time is that time at which an event must be accomplished so as not to cause slippage in the project-completion date. The simplest way of calculating the LS for all activities is to use the Reverse Scan Rule as outlined here:

Give each node a BUCKET value: BUCKET(I)
Initialize the BUCKET(I)s to the project completion date
Now for each activity K, starting with the last activity, proceed as follows:
    BUCKET(INODE)'←BUCKET(JNODE)—EXPT(INODE, JNODE)
        iff BUCKET(INODE)'≤BUCKET(INODE)
    —assign (BUCKET(JNODE)—EXP(INODE,JNODE)) to BUCKET(INODE)
        if and only if (BUCKET(JNODE)—EXP(INODE,JNODE)) is smaller

than the previous BUCKET(INODE) value—

$$LS(K) = BUCKET(JNODE)' — EXPE(K)$$

After all LS(K)s are calculated, the LF(K)s can be calculated as follows for each activity K

$$LF(K) = LS(K) + EXPT(K)$$

Step 5 Calculation of the total slack (TOTSL) times. The total slack is a relationship between ES and LS and indicates how long an activity may be postponed without affecting the due date. It is calculated for each activity as follows:

$$TOTSL(K) = LS(K) — ES(K)$$

Step 6 Critical Activities. The critical activities are those activities which cannot be delayed in order to finish the job as early as possible. So, if TOTSL of an activity K is zero, then that Kth activity is a critical activity.

Names Used

Program Variable Names	Definition	Mode	Dimension
ALPHA	Activity Description	Alpha.	2
BUCKET	Bucket for each node	Real	1
EF	Early finish time	Real	1
ES	Early start time	Real	1
EXPT	Expected time	Real	1
I	Beginning node	Integer	1
J	Ending node	Integer	1
LF	Late finish time	Real	1
LS	Late start time	Real	1
N	Number of activities	Integer	0
NN	Number of the highest node	Integer	0
OT	Optimistic time	Real	1
PRT	Most probable time	Real	1
PT	Pessimistic time	Real	1
STDD	Standard time deviation	Real	1
TOTSL	Total slack time	Real	1

Flowcharting the PERT-Algorithm

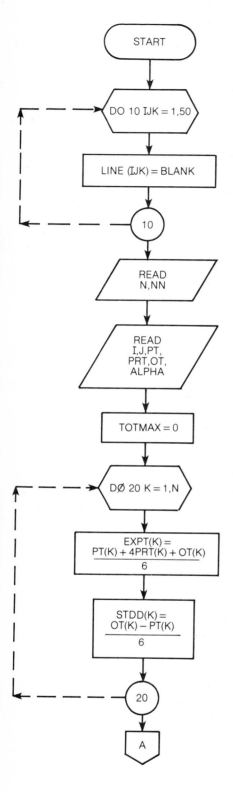

START

DO 10 IJK = 1,50

LINE (IJK) = BLANK

10

READ
N,NN

READ
I,J,PT,
PRT,OT,
ALPHA

TOTMAX = 0

DØ 20 K = 1,N

$$EXPT(K) = \frac{PT(K) + 4PRT(K) + OT(K)}{6}$$

$$STDD(K) = \frac{OT(K) - PT(K)}{6}$$

20

A

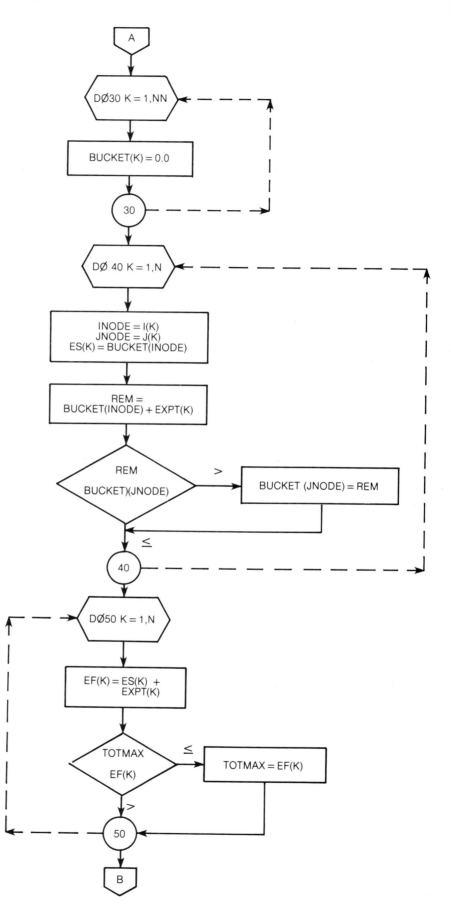

A

DØ30 K = 1,NN

BUCKET(K) = 0.0

30

DØ 40 K = 1,N

INODE = I(K)
JNODE = J(K)
ES(K) = BUCKET(INODE)

REM =
BUCKET(INODE) + EXPT(K)

REM
BUCKET)(JNODE)   >   BUCKET (JNODE) = REM

≤

40

DØ50 K = 1,N

EF(K) = ES(K) +
EXPT(K)

TOTMAX
EF(K)   ≤   TOTMAX = EF(K)

>

50

B

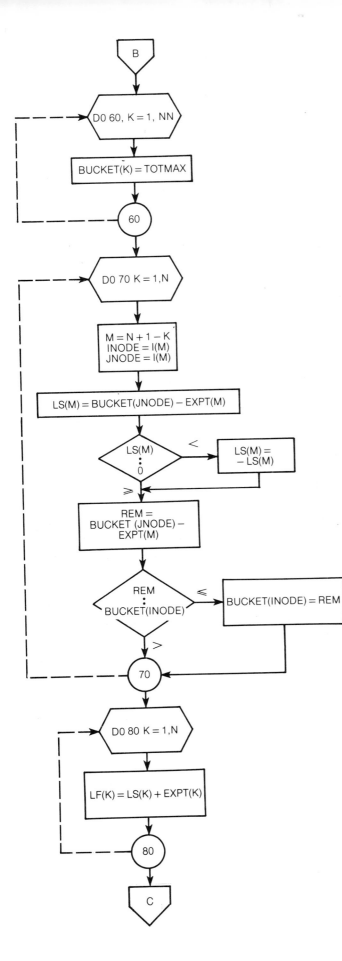

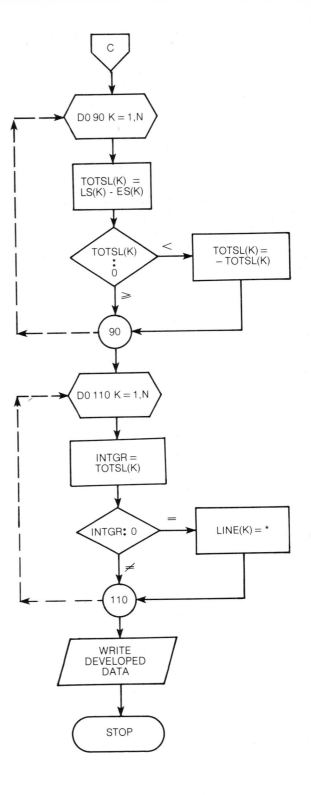

The FORTRAN IV Program

```
C *** PERT ANALYSIS

      INTEGER  ASK, BLANK
      REAL  LS(0050), LF(0050)
      DIMENSION  I(0050), J(0050), PT(0050), PRT(0050), OT(0050),
     *           ALPHA(04,0050), EXPT(0050), STDD(0050), TOTSL(0050),
     *           ES(0050), EF(0050), BUCKET(0050), LINE(0050)
      DATA  BLANK,ASK/1H, 1H*/
      DO 10  IJK = 1, 50
        LINE(IJK) = BLANK
   10 CONTINUE
C *** READ IN THE TOTAL NUMBER OF ACTIVITIES AND NODES
      READ(5,200) N, NN
      READ(5,210) (I(K), J(K), PT(K), PRT(K), OT(K),
     *            (ALPHA(L,K), L = 1, 4), K = 1, N)
      TOTMAX = 0.0
C *** CALCULATE THE EXPECTED TIMES AND THE STANDARD DEVIATION
C ***  OF EACH ACTIVITY
      DO 20  K = 1, N
        EXPT(K) = (PT(K) + (4.0 * PRT(K)) + OT(K)) / 6.0
        STDD(K) = (OT(K) - PT(K)) / 6.0
   20 CONTINUE
C *** INITIALIZE THE BUCKETS TO ZERO
      DO 30  K = 1, NN
        BUCKET(K) = 0.0
   30 CONTINUE
C *** FORWARD SCAN RULE FOR EARLY START
      DO 40  K = 1, N
        INODE = I(K)
        JNODE = J(K)
        ES(K) = BUCKET(INODE)
        REM = BUCKET(INODE) + EXPT(K)
        IF (REM .GT. BUCKET(JNODE))  BUCKET(JNODE) = REM
   40 CONTINUE
C *** EARLY FINISH IS EQUAL TO EARLY START PLUS EXPECTED TIME
      DO 50  K = 1, N
        EF(K) = ES(K) + EXPT(K)
        IF (EF(K) .GT. TOTMAX)  TOTMAX = EF(K)
   50 CONTINUE
C *** INITIALIZE THE BUCKETS TO TOTMAX
      DO 60  K = 1, NN
        BUCKET(K) = TOTMAX
   60 CONTINUE
C *** REVERSE SCAN RULE FOR LATE START
      DO 70  K =1, N
        M = N + 1 - K
        INODE = I(M)
        JNODE = J(M)
        LS(M) = BUCKET(JNODE) - EXPT(M)
        IF (LS(M) .LT. 0.0)  LS(M) = LS(M) * (-1.0)
        REM = BUCKET(JNODE) - EXPT(M)
        IF (REM .LE. BUCKET(INODE))  BUCKET(INODE) = REM
   70 CONTINUE
C *** LATE FINISH EQUALS LATE START PLUS EXPECTED TIME
      DO 80  K = 1, N
        LF(K) = LS(K) + EXPT(K)
   80 CONTINUE
```

```
C *** CALCULATION OF SLACK TIME
      DO 90  K = 1, N
         TOTSL(K) = LS(K) - ES(K)
         IF (TOTSL(K) .LT. 0.0)  TOTSL(K) = TOTSL(K) * (-1.0)
   90 CONTINUE
C *** DEFINE CRITICAL PATH
      DO 110  K = 1, N
         INTGR = TOTSL(K)
         IF (INTGR) 110, 100, 110
  100    LINE(K) = ASK
  110 CONTINUE
C *** PRINT OUT DEVELOPED DATA
      WRITE(6,220)
      WRITE(6,230) (I(K), J(K), (ALPHA(L,K), L = 1, 4), EXPT(K),
     *              STDD(K), ES(K), EF(K), LS(K), LF(K), TOTSL(K),
     *              LINE(K), K = 1, N)
      WRITE(6,240)
      STOP
  200 FORMAT(2I2)
  210 FORMAT(2I2,3F2.0,4A4)
  220 FORMAT(1H1,//,42X,'PERT ANALYSIS',///,
     *       12X,'ACTIVITY',10X,'JOB',9X,'EXPECTED',3X,'STANDARD',
     *        2X,'EARLY',2X,'EARLY',3X,'LATE',3X,'LATE',
     *        4X,'TOTAL',2X,'CRIT.',/,
     *        9X,'I NODE J NODE',4X,'DESCRIPT   ',7X,'TIME',4X,
     *        'DEVIATION',2X,'START',2X,'FINISH',2X,'START',2X,
     *        'FINISH',2X,'SLACK',2X,'PATH',//)
  230 FORMAT(11X,I2,5X,I2,4X,4A4,4X,F5.1,5X,F6.2,3X,F5.1,2X,F5.1,
     *        3X,F5.1,2X,F5.1,3X,F5.1,4X,A1)
  240 FORMAT(1H1)
      END
```

Data Format

Card Number	Column	Listname	Content
1	1–2	N	Number of activities
	3–4	NN	Number of nodes
2–12*	1–2	I	Beginning node
	3–4	J	Ending node
	5–6	PT	Pessimistic time
	6–7	PRT	Most probable time
	8–9	OT	Optimistic time
	10–25	ALPHA	Activity description

---

*The cards have to be ordered such that the INODES are in increasing sequence and such that the JNODE for activities with the same starting NODE are also in increasing sequence.

Data Input

```
11 9
    1 2 1 2 4ORD. FIXTURES
    1 4 1 2 3EXCAVATION
    1 7 3 4 5ORD. TREES SHRUBS
    2 3 3 4 5MANUF. FURNIT.
    3 6 1 2 2DELIVER FURNIT.
    4 5 4 5 6ERECT STRUC. STL.
    4 8 1 3 5BACK FILLING
    5 6 3 5 6MASONRY WORK
    6 9 1 5 7INSTALL FURNIT.
    7 8 2 3 4FINAL GRADING
    8 9 4 5 7PLT TREES, SHRUBS
```

Program Output

PERT ANALYSIS										
ACTIVITY I NODE	J NODE	JOB DESCRIPTION	EXPECTED TIME	STANDARD DEVIATION	EARLY START	EARLY FINISH	LATE START	LATE FINISH	TOTAL SLACK	CRIT. PATH
1	2	ORD. FIXTURES	2.2	0.50	0.0	2.2	3.8	6.0	3.8	
1	4	EXCAVATION	2.0	0.33	0.0	2.0	0.0	2.0	0.0	*
1	7	ORD. TREES$SHRUB	4.0	0.33	0.0	4.0	4.3	8.3	4.3	
2	3	MANUF. FURNIT.	4.0	0.33	2.2	6.2	6.0	10.0	3.8	
3	6	DELIVER FURNIT.	1.8	0.17	6.2	8.0	10.0	11.8	3.8	
4	5	ERECT STRUC. STL	5.0	0.33	2.0	7.0	2.0	7.0	0.0	*
4	8	BACK FILLING	3.0	0.67	2.0	5.0	8.3	11.3	6.3	
5	6	MASONRY WORK	4.8	0.50	7.0	11.8	7.0	11.8	0.0	*
6	9	INSTALL FURNIT.	4.7	1.00	11.8	16.5	11.8	16.5	0.0	*
7	8	FINAL GRADING	3.0	0.33	4.0	7.0	8.3	11.3	4.3	
8	9	PLT TREES,SHRUBS	5.2	0.50	7.0	12.2	11.3	16.5	4.3	

Three Case Proposals

In this final chapter, you are encouraged to develop flowcharts, write programs, and run programs with data for three case proposals. These cases are a **payroll case,** an **asset depreciation case,** and a **marketing case.** Each case is fully explained, and data is supplied so that you can execute your own programs.

1. CASE STUDY #1 The Payroll Case

The purpose of this case is to prepare the payroll register and paychecks for Carson & Sons, Inc., a small manufacturing concern located in Cincinnati, Ohio, for the one-week pay period that ended July 30, 1980. The employee's earnings for the period are also posted to his individual pay record kept by the company.

The input data used for this case consists of the employee's name, his state of residence, the number of dependents he claims, his hourly rate of pay, the number of hours he worked that period, and his cumulative earnings for the year to date. It is assumed that this company has twenty employees and, therefore, twenty data cards are used (one per employee).

The output for this program consists of the company's payroll register which shows the earnings, deductions, taxes owned, and amount paid out for each employee; the checks and stubs that will be given to the employees; and the current postings to the individual pay records kept for each employee in order to update his cumulative year-to-date earnings.

Procedure
The following calculations must be made to determine the employee's net pay for the period:

1. Determine the gross earnings:
   a) 40 hours is considered a regular work week.
   b) if the employee worked 40 hours or less, multiply his hours worked times his hourly rate to determine gross pay.
   c) if the employee worked more than 40 hours, multiply his hourly rate by 40 to determine his regular pay for the period; then subtract 40 from the total hours worked to determine his overtime hours; then multiply his hourly rate times 1.5 to determine his overtime rate; then multiply his overtime hours by his overtime rate to determine his overtime pay. Gross pay will then be equal to overtime pay plus regular pay.
2. Determine the necessary deductions that consist of the following:
   a) Federal Income Tax (using standard procedure)—the amount deducted is equal to 18% of the difference between the individual's gross pay and $13 multiplied by the number of dependents claimed (i.e., 18 [gross pay − $13x]) where x = the number of dependents.

b) State Income Tax—if the employee is a resident of Kentucky, this is equal to 4% of his gross pay; if he is a resident of Indiana it is equal to 2% of his gross pay; Ohio has a progressive state tax, 1.5%, is used here.

c) Local Tax—the local tax for the particular area where the company is located is equal to 1% of the person's gross pay.

d) FICA (Federal Insurance Contributions Act) Tax—this is equal to 6.13% of the employee's gross pay up to the point where his cumulative earnings for the year (1980) equal $22,900 if the employee's cumulative earnings for the year already exceed $22,900 he is no longer required to pay this tax; if his earnings for the current pay period will put him over the $22,900 mark, he is only required to pay tax on that portion that is still under $22,900 (The amount of tax withheld is the employee's contribution to the federal program of old-age, survivors, and disability insurance.)

e) Union Dues—this is a constant amount equal to $3.50 per week.

f) Hospital Insurance—this is a constant figure equal to $5.40 per week.

The deductions just calculated (2a-f) should now be added together and the total subtracted from the employee's gross pay to determine his net pay.

There are also a few taxes the employer must pay. These include:

1. FICA tax—the employer is required to pay for each employee an amount equal to the amount the employee pays; this is equal to the same figure determined in 2d.

2. State Unemployment Tax—the employer must pay 2.2% of the gross pay of each employee up to the point where the employee's cumulative earnings for the year equals $6000.00; if the employee's cumulative earnings for the year exceed $6000.00, no tax is required; if the employee's gross earnings for the period will put him over the $6000.00 mark only the portion under $6000.00 is taxed. (The tax paid is a part of the Social Security program. It is used to provide relief to those who become unemployed as a result of economic forces beyond their control.)

The employee's gross pay for the period must also be added to his cumulative earnings for the year to date in order to keep this figure current for future use (in calculating future payrolls).

Data Format
The following data format is suggested:

Card Number	Column	Listname	Content
1	1–2	M	Number of employees
2–21	1–20	XNAME1—XNAME5	Employee's name
	21–24	RES	State of residence
	25	DEP	Number of dependents
	26–29	RATE	Rate per hour
	30–31	HRS	Number of hours worked
	32–38	EARN	Last week's cumulative earnings

purchased the Fth day of the 1980 fiscal year, the depreciation value is:

$$\left(1-\frac{F}{365}\right)\frac{U}{\frac{U(U+1)}{2}}(C-S)$$

In case the asset was not purchased during the 1980 fiscal year and has not ended its useful life during the 1980 fiscal year, the sum-of-the-years-digits depreciation formula becomes:

$$\left(\frac{F}{365}\right)\frac{U+1-H+G}{\frac{U(U+1)}{2}}(C-S)+\left(1-\frac{F}{365}\right)\frac{U-H+G}{\frac{U(U+1)}{2}}(C-S)$$

Finally, if the asset has ended its useful life during the 1980 fiscal year, the final depreciation value is:

$$C-S-A. = Cost-Salvage-Accumulated\ Depreciation$$

Data Format

Card Number	Column	Variable Name	Content
1 through 20	1–5	L	Machine Number
	7–10	N	Machine Name
	13–16	F	Date Purchased
	17–19	G	Year Purchased
	21–30	C	Cost of Asset
	31–37	S	Salvage Value of Asset
	42–44	U	Life of Asset
	46	M	Depreciation Method
	49–59	A	Accumulated Depr.

Data Input

L	N	F	G	C	S	U	M*	A
1001	BLDG	001	1970	500,000	0	40	1	125,000.00
1002	MACH	182	1977	20,000	4,000	10	1	4,000.00
1003	MACH	235	1977	15,600	1,500	15	1	334.79
1004	MACH	326	1979	50,000	5,000	5	1	961.64
1005	MACH	053	1980	4,400	200	2	1	0
1006	BLDG	001	1973	200,000	0	20	2	106,239.00
1007	MACH	077	1975	30,000	1,000	6	2	25,601.00
1008	MACH	212	1977	55,000	5,000	10	2	22,731.00
1009	MACH	133	1977	2,200	20	3	2	2,152.25
1010	MACH	120	1980	25,000	3,000	8	2	0
1011	MACH	001	1977	18,000	3,000	5	3	12,000.00
1012	MACH	182	1976	20,000	0	4	3	19,002.73
1013	BLDG	273	1979	100,000	5,000	10	3	4,318.00
1014	MACH	001	1980	6,000	0	3	3	0
1015	MACH	080	1980	12,000	2,000	6	3	0
1016	MACH	343	1978	3,500	150	2	1	1,775.00
1017	MACH	261	1980	45,200	3,000	3	2	0
1018	BLDG	017	1980	150,000	0	15	2	0
1019	MACH	001	1978	26,400	2,500	5	3	19,916.00
1020	MACH	214	1979	84,800	6,000	4	1	8,150.00

*1: straight line
2: double-declining balance
3: sum-of-the-years-digits

3. CASE STUDY #3   Analysis of an Advertisement

A questionnaire has been developed and answerd by 100 people for a LARK Cigarette Advertisement. The information derived from the completed questionnaires is transferred to 80-column cards which are analyzed by the computer. A program must be designed that will analyze and summarize the responses to the questions asked in the questionnaires. Some of the information sought are answers to questions such as:

1. How many people who now smoke have seen the advertisement previously?
2. How many people read the logo of the advertisement?
3. How many people only read the headlines?
4. How many people only looked at the people shown in the advertisement?

Case Introduction

This case has application in the field of marketing, particularly in the area of advertising and promotion. Advertisers too often expend considerable time, money, and effort in the preparation of a particular advertising campaign. After it has been launched, however, they fail to do any follow-up studies to try to ascertain the effectiveness and end accomplishments of the campaign. Usually, they just assume that their advertising is effective in its performance.

It is becoming increasingly apparent, however, that post-advertising analysis is very important. Through such efforts the advertiser can not only discover interesting and critical data about his past advertising but, more importantly, he can also obtain valuable information that may then be applied toward developing his future advertising campaigns. In this manner, the advertiser is able to profit from his mistakes.

For this case, a single-page magazine advertisement is selected for testing. In order to accomplish the testing, a questionnaire is developed to be administered at random to 100 different people. The computer must then do the rest of the work by tallying the answers on the questionnaire. Ten different cross-tallies are selected, since they would provide us with interesting and important information. The computer must also tally these.

Questionnaire

1. Your sex: Male _____ Female _____
2. Your age: Under 20 _____ 20–29 _____ 30–39 _____ 40–49 _____
            50–59 _____ 60–69 _____ 70–79 _____ 80 or over _____
3. Your marital status single _____ married _____
                        divorced _____ widowed _____
4. Your present vocation: (Check only one category.) student _____ housewife _____
   teacher _____ secretary _____ laborer _____ salesman(woman) _____ manager
   other professional _____ retired _____
5. Have you ever smoked cigarettes?   Yes _____ No _____
   (If your answer to question 5 was "No," please skip to question 13.)
6. Do you now smoke cigarettes?   Yes _____ No _____
   (If your answer to question 6 was "No," please skip to question 10.)
7. How many cigarettes do you smoke per day?
   1–5 _____ 6–10 _____ 11–20 _____ 21–30 _____ 31–40 _____ more than 40
8. What brand of cigarettes do you now smoke?
   Camel _____ Kent _____ L&M _____ Marlboro _____ Pall Mall _____
   Salem _____ Tareyton _____ Winston _____
9. Is your current brand: (Check one in each of the following categories.)
   Tobacco: regular _____   or   menthol _____
   Length: standard _____   or   kings _____
   Filter: nonfilter _____   or   filter _____

10. Have you ever smoked Lark cigarettes?   Yes _____ No _____
     If your answer to question 10 was "No," skip to question 13.)
11. Did you like Lark cigarettes?   Yes _____ No _____
12. Do you now smoke Lark cigarettes?   Yes _____ No _____

(*Instructions to Interviewer:* At this time, present to the interviewee a copy of the advertisement to be tested. Proceed with the following questions.)

13. Have you ever seen this advertisement before now?   Yes _____ No _____
     (If your answer to question 13 was "No," please skip to question 20.)
14. Did you read the headline?   Yes _____ No _____
15. Did you look at the people pictured?   Yes _____ No _____
16. Did you read the first copy block?   Yes _____ No _____
17. Did you read the second copy block?   Yes _____ No _____
18. Did you look at the logo?   Yes _____ No _____
19. Did you like this advertisement?   Yes _____ No _____
20. Do you think this is an effective ad?   Yes _____ No _____

End of Questionnaire.
Thank your for your cooperation.

Coding of Questionnaire Results

In order to transfer the information of the completed questionnaires to 80-column cards, the questionnaire results are coded as follows:

1. Sex:
   (1)—male
   (2)—female

2. Age:
   (1)—under 20
   (2)—20–29
   (3)—30–39
   (4)—40–49
   (5)—50–59
   (6)—60–69
   (7)—70–79
   (8)—80 or over

3. Marital status:
   (1)—single
   (2)—married
   (3)—divorced
   (4)—widowed

4. Present vocation:
   (1)—student
   (2)—housewife
   (3)—teacher
   (4)—secretary
   (5)—laborer
   (6)—salesman(woman)
   (7)—manager
   (8)—other professional
   (9)—retired

5. Ever smoked cigarettes:
   (1)—yes
   (2)—no

6. Now smoke cigarettes:
   (0)—na
   (1)—yes
   (2)—no

7. Number cigarettes now smoked per day:
   (1)—1–5 (light)
   (2)—6–10 (light to medium)
   (3)—11–20 (medium)
   (4)—21–30 (medium to heavy)
   (5)—31–40 (heavy)
   (6)—more than 40 (very heavy)
   (0)—na

8. Brand now smoked:
   (0)—na
   (1)—Camel
   (2)—Kent
   (3)—L&M
   (4)—Marlboro
   (5)—Pall Mall
   (6)—Salem
   (7)—Tareyton
   (8)—Winston
   (9)—Other brand

9. Characteristics of current brand:
   (0)—na
   (1)—regular, standard, nonfilter
   (2)—regular, standard, filter
   (3)—regular, kings, nonfilter
   (5)—menthol, standard, nonfilter
   (6)—menthol, standard, filter
   (7)—menthol, kings, nonfilter
   (8)—menthol, kings, filter

10. Ever smoked Lark:
    (0)—na
    (1)—yes
    (2)—no

11. Liked Lark:
    (0)—na
    (1)—yes
    (2)—no

12. Now smoke Lark:
    (0)—na
    (1)—yes
    (2)—no

13. See advertisement:
    (1)—yes
    (2)—no

14. Read headline:
    (0)—na
    (1)—yes
    (2)—no

15. Looked at people:
    (0)—na
    (1)—yes
    (2)—no

16. Read first copy block:
    (0)—na
    (1)—yes
    (2)—no

17. Read second copy block:
    (0)—na
    (1)—yes
    (2)—no

18. Looked at logo:
    (0)—na
    (1)—yes
    (2)—no

19. Liked advertisement:
    (0)—na
    (1)—yes
    (2)—no

20. Effective advertisement:
    (1)—yes
    (2)—no

Information Sought

Besides tallying the answers for each question the computer will seek to answer the following questions:

Question	Related Ad. Ques.	Code
1. How many men now smoke cigarettes?	1	1
	6	1
2. How many women now smoke cigarettes?	1	2
	6	1
3. How many people who now smoke have seen ad previously?	6	1
	13	1
4. How many people who now smoke think ad effective?	6	1
	20	1
5. How many people read the heading only?	14	1
	15	2
	16	2
	17	2
	18	2

6. How many people read the logo only?	14	2
	15	2
	16	2
	17	2
	18	1
7. How many people looked at the people pictured only?	14	2
	15	1
	16	2
	17	2
	18	2
8. How many people read the headline and logo only?	14	1
	15	2
	16	2
	17	2
	18	1
9. How many people read headline, logo, and looked at people only?	14	1
	15	1
	16	2
	17	2
	18	1
10. How many people looked at and read entire advertisement? (i.e., read headline, looked at people, read first copy block, read second copy block, and looked at logo)	14	1
	15	1
	16	1
	17	1
	18	1

Solution Procedure

The following steps are taken to prepare the input for the computer:

STEP 1 Collect all answered questionnaires.

STEP 2 Code the answers to all questions.

STEP 3 Transfer the coded results of the questionnaire to data cards as follows:
100 cards: one per questionnaire
20 key punched columns per card: one for each coded answer.

These 100 data cards can now serve as input to a computer program that will

1. tally all questions
2. tally all 10 selected cross-tallies.

```
1111120000000011122111
11211126211211222221
23271147320020000001
1436120000002C000001
11452000000011122121
11141151620011222222
24431162512212122211
24322000000020000002
23281134111211111111
14431146411120000001
22141200000011212121
12351117820011112211
12472000000020000002
23292000000020000002
22381152712212222212
11221121312211211122
12441142411211222211
23161200000011122221
24381164220020000002
15412000000020000001
26331200000011122112
27251119711120000001
28172000000020000001
12191138811220000002
14211157612212222222
16321200000012222211
18432000000020000001
21342000000011122212
13452000000020000002
25461200000011111111
17271146520020000002
11282000000011222212
22192000000012122211
14121133420012122222
26362000000020000002
25241124120020000001
16212000000020000001
25221200000020000002
24231124411120000002
18141143511211222212
11151167720011111211
22362000000020000001
13471200000011222211
27482000000020000001
24391119620020000002
14271200000012222222
13252000000011212121
13232000000011122112
15112000000020000001
17141200000011111122
11112000000011122111
11211126211211222221
23271147320020000001
14361200000020000001
11452000000011122121
11141151620011222222
24431162512212122211
```

```
24322000000020000002
23281134111211111111
14431146411120000001
22141200000011212121
12351117820011112211
12472000000020000002
23292000000020000002
22381152712212222212
11221121312211211122
12441142411211222211
23161200000011122221
24381164220020000002
15412000000020000001
26331200000011122112
27251119711120000001
28172000000020000001
12191138811220000002
14211157612212222222
16321200000012222211
18432000000020000001
21342000000011122212
13452000000020000002
25461200000011111111
17271146520020000002
11282000000011222212
22192000000012122211
14121133420012122222
26362000000020000002
25241124120020000001
16212000000020000001
25221200000020000002
24231124411120000002
18141143511211222212
11151167720011111211
22362000000020000001
13471200000011222211
27482000000020000001
24391119620020000002
14271200000012222222
13252000000011212121
13232000000011122112
15112000000020000001
17141200000011111122
```

1. Processing Group

PROCESS Any processing function; defined operation(s) causing change in form, value, or location of information.

2. Decision Group

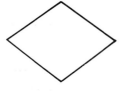

DECISION A decision or switching-type operation that determines which of a number of alternative paths to follow.

3. Input/Output Group

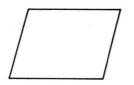

INPUT/OUTPUT General I/0 function; information available for processing (input), or recording of processed information (output).

PUNCHED CARD Input/output function in card medium (all varieties).

DOCUMENT Output on paper medium.

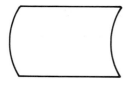

ONLINE STORAGE Input/output using any kind of online storage—magnetic tape, drum, disk.

MANUAL INPUT   Information input by online keyboards, switch settings, pushbuttons.

TERMINAL, INTERRUPT   A terminal point in a flowchart—start, stop, halt, delay, or interrupt; may show exit from a closed subroutine.

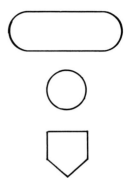

CONNECTOR   Exit to, or entry from, another part of the chart.

PAGE CONNECTOR

5. Linkage Group

ARROWHEADS and FLOWLINES   In linking symbols, these show operations sequence and dataflow direction.

COMMUNICATION LINK   Function of transmitting information by a telecommunication link.

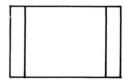

6. Predefined Process Group

PREDEFINED PROCESS   One or more named operations or program steps specified in a subroutine or another set of flowcharts.

7. Preparation Group

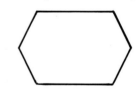

PREPARATION   Instruction modification to change program—set a switch, modify an index register, initialize a routine.

8. Comment Group

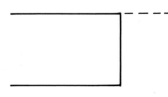

COMMENT   Additional descriptive clarification, comment. (Dotted line extends to symbols as appropriate.)

Arithmetic Assignment Statement (p. 44)

Variable Name = Arithmetic Expression

Variable Name: Integer
      Real

Arithmetic Expression: Constants
        Variable Names
        Operators $(+,-,*,/,**)$

Arithmetic IF Statement (p. 99)

$IF(e)n_1,n_2,n_3$

e: arithmetic expression

n_1,n_2,n_3: are statement numbers

n_1: if the arithmetic expression is negative, then control transfers to n_1

n_2: if the arithmetic expression is zero, then control transfers to n_2

n_3: if the arithmetic expression is positive, then control transfers to n_3

Character Declaration Statement (p. 54)

$$CHARACTER *w \; a_1*v_1,a_2*v_2,...$$

*w: maximize size of character constants

*v: optional maximum size of specific character constant

Computed GO TO Statement (p. 102)

$GO \; TO \; (n_1,n_2,n_3,...n_m),i$

$n_1,n_2,n_3,...n_m$: are statement numbers

i: is an integer variable name

n_1: if the variable name i is one, then transfer is made to n_1

n_m: if the variable name i is m, then transfer is made to n_m

Common Statement (p. 227)

COMMON v_1,v_2,v_3
COMMON w_1,w_2,w_3

v_i: are variable names to share common storage location with w_1

Data Statement (p. 241)

DATA list/$d_1,d_2,d_3,...d_n$/,list/$d_1,k_2*d_3,.../$

list: contains the name of the variables to receive values

$d_1,d_2,d_3,...d_n$: are the values of the variables in the list

k: if used, it is an integer constant

Dimension Statement (p. 154)

DIMENSION v,v,v

v: variable names followed by parentheses, enclosing 1, 2, 3, up to 7 integer constants, giving the maximum size of each subscript (with optional beginning and ending subscript)

DO Loop (p. 129)

DO n i$=m_1m_2,m_3$

n: statement number, which is the end of the range of the DO loop—terminal statement

i: an integer or real variable name

m_1,m_2,m_3: unsigned integer constants, OR nonsubscripted, unsigned integer variables

m_1: initial value

m_2: test value

m_3: increment

Implied DO loop (p. 172)

READ(i,n)((A(I,J),I$=m_1,m_2,m_3$),J$=m_1,m_2,m_3$)
WRITE(i,n)((A(I,J),I$=m_1,m_2,m_3$),J$=m_1,m_2,m_3$)

i: symbolic unit number of an input/output device

n: number of format statement

m_1,m_2,m_3: unsigned integer constants, OR nonsubscripted, unsigned integer variables

Double Precision Declaration Statement (p. 235)

DOUBLE PRECISION $a_1,a_2,a_3,...$

a_1: the variable names $a_1,a_2,a_3,...$are declared to be double precision

End Statement (p. 83)

END

Format Statement (p. 60)

n FORMAT($S_1,S_2,S_3,...S_n$)

n: statement number that is referenced by an associated I/O statement

S: the format specifications

Specifications:	nx:	skip spaces
	/:	skip card or line
	1H1:	go to the next printing page
	nFa.b:	Floating-point specification
	nEw.d:	Real E specification
	nIa:	Integer specification
	nAw:	alphanumeric specification
	wH:	Hollerith specification

Function Statement (p. 221)

FUNCTION $v(a_1, a_2, \ldots a_n)$

v: function variable name

a_i: input arguments

Halt Statements (p. 83)

CALL EXIT
STOP
PAUSE
PAUSE n

Implicit Statement (p. 240)

IMPLICIT type (letter, letter,...), type (letter,...),....

type: declaration statement such as INTEGER, REAL, LOGICAL, etc.

letter: letters of the alphabet with which variable names begin

Integer Declaration Statement (p. 234)

INTEGER $a_1, a_2, a_3, \ldots$

a_i: the variable names $a_1, a_2, a_3, \ldots$ are declared to be integer

Logical Declaration Statement (p. 240)

LOGICAL $a_1, a_2, a_3, \ldots$

a_i: the variable names $a_1, a_2, a_3, \ldots$ are declared to be logical

Logical IF Statement (p. 105)

IF(e)S

e: a logical expression

S: is an executable statement, to be executed if e is true

Fortran 77 Logical IF statement structures (p. 115)

The IF-THEN structure:
```
IF(e) THEN
    S
END IF
```

The IF-THEN-ELSE structure:
```
IF(e) THEN
    S
ELSE
    S
END IF
```

The IF-THEN-ELSE-IF structure:
```
IF(e) THEN
    S
ELSE IF(e) THEN
    S
    ELSE IF(e) THEN
        S
        .......
        .......
        .......

END IF
```

Read Statement (p. 59)

READ(i,n,END=m)<list>

i: symbolic unit number of an input device

n: number of that format statement which applies to the particular input record to be used

m: statement number to which control is transferred at end of file. This is an optional entry.

<list>: ordered series of variable names separated by commas

Fortran 77 variations of the READ statement (p. 59)

READ(FMT=n,UNIT=i)<list>
READ(i,*)optional format spec <list>

Real Declaration Statement (p. 235)

REAL $a_1,a_2,a_3,...$

a_i: the variable names $a_1,a_2,a_3,...$ are declared to be real

Return Statement in a Function or Subroutine (p. 220)

RETURN
RETURN i

i: integer constant

Subroutine Call Statement (p. 224)

CALL $n(a_1,a_2,a_3,...a_m)$

n: subroutine name

a_i: input/output real arguments

Subroutine Statement (p. 224)

SUBROUTINE $n(a_1,a_2,a_3,...a_m)$

n: subroutine name

a_i: input/output dummy arguments

Unconditional GO TO Statement (p. 97)

GO TO n

n: Is the statement number to which control is passed

Write Statement (p. 60)

WRITE(i,n)<list>

i: symbolic unit number of an output device

n: number of that format statement which applies to the particular output record to be used

<list>: ordered series of variable names separated by commas

Fortran 77 variations of the WRITE statement (p. 77)

WRITE(FMT=n,UNIT=i)<list>
WRITE(i,*)optional format specs<list>
WRITE(i,v)<list>
        where: v: specification character variable

Flowchart	Page Number
1. The Payroll Example	29
2. Computing the Tuition for One Student	31–33
3. Monthly Payments of a Car Loan	34
4. Homeowner's Real Estate Tax	35
5. Checking the Logical Flow	37
6. The One-Year-Investment Problem	84
7. The Compounded-Interest-Investment Problem	86
8. The Gross-Profit and Net-Profit Problem	88
9. The Straight-Line-Depreciation Problem	90
10. The EOQ Problem	92
11. Calculation of Wages	98
12. Federal Tax Example	100
13. The Salary Increase Problem	103
14. Calculation of Gross Pay	108
15. The Accumulated Purchase Value	110
16. Measuring the Profitability of Investment in Assets	113
17. Sum of Integers from 1 to 100	131–33
18. Calculation of Wages (with DO loop)	138
19. Range of Sales Volume	140
20. The Break-even Analysis	150
21. A Queuing Problem	143
22. Generating Market Statistics	158
23. The Mail Order Example	163
24. Manipulation of Loop Indexes	174
25. The Mail Order Example with Price Breaks	176
26. Calculating the Monthly Payment of a Loan (Subscript)	190
27. Updating the Inventory Stock	194
28. Term Revolving Credit Plan	199
29. Savings Accumulation—Single-Premium Life Insurance	206
30. Main and Function Subprogram	221
31. Main and Subroutine Subprogram	224–26
32. Computing the Balance in Customers' Checking Accounts	237
33. The Selection Sort	245
34. The Bubble Sort	248
35. Crossing a Bridge: A Simulation	256
36. Computation of π Through Simulation	260
37. Transportation Cost Analysis: A Simulation	265
38. Moving Averages of the Dow Jones Industrial Stocks	271
39. Goodness-of-Fit Test for the Random-Number Generator	278
40. Network Analysis: PERT-Program Evaluation and Review Technique	286

The IBM 29 Card Punch

In order to enter instructions and data into the computer, many systems require that the information first be keypunched onto standard 80-column cards. This is accomplished through the use of a card or keypunch machine. The IBM 29 card punch machine is the one most commonly used.

Components of the IBM 29 Card Punch

The eighty-column cards move through four stations during the keypunching operation: they leave the CARD HOPPER to move via the PUNCHING STATION under the PUNCHING HEAD to the READING STATION, and from there they travel under the READING HEAD into the CARD STACKER. For this to happen, the MAIN line SWITCH must be ON.

MAIN OFF/ON SWITCH   The main line is located at knee height under the keyboard. The purpose of this switch is to turn the machine ON and OFF.

CARD HOPPER   The card hopper can hold about 500 cards for continuous punching. Cards should be placed so that the nine (9)-edge is down and the face of the card is toward you. If the cards are placed correctly in the hopper, they can then be fed automatically into the punching station one at a time.

PUNCHING STATION AND PUNCHING HEAD   The punching station receives the cards from the hopper and can hold a maximum of two (2) cards: while one card is under the punching head being punched, the other is held in the station. After 80 columns of the former card pass under the punching head, the latter card is registered under the punching head, ready to be punched.

READING STATION, READING HEAD, AND BACK SPACE KEY   A punched card passes from under the punching head into the reading station, and from there will move under the reading head as a new card passes under the punching head. The movement of the card under the reading head and of the card under the punching head is synchronized columnwise. If so desired, the information from the card moving under the reading head may then be transmitted onto the card moving under the printing head.

The backspace key is located under the reading station. Depressing this key backspaces the cards under the reading head and the punching head simultaneously.

STACKER   The stacker receives and stores all the cards that come from the reading station. Its capacity is the same as that of the card hopper.

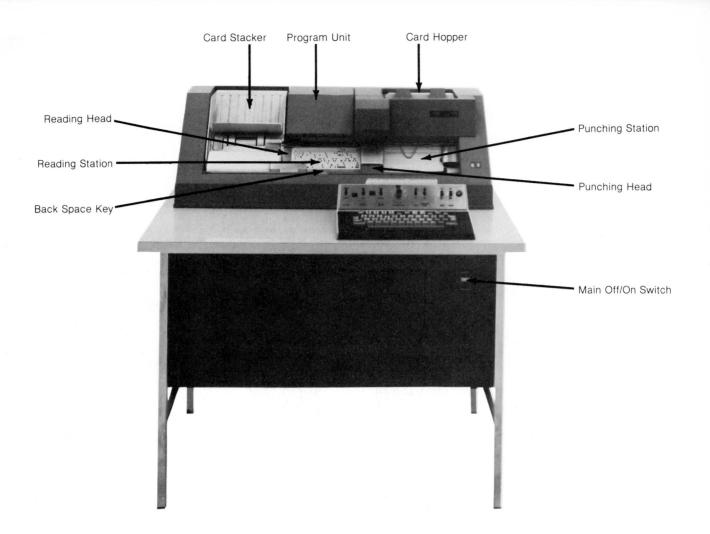

Card Stacker   Program Unit   Card Hopper

Reading Head

Punching Station

Reading Station

Punching Head

Back Space Key

Main Off/On Switch

PROGRAM UNIT   When punching certain repetitive operations the program unit can be used to automate this operation. The automated control can be accomplished by the use of a program card or, as it is also called, a drum card.*

There are three types of keys: the spacing key, punching keys, and functional keys.

1. The Spacing Key

If you wish to skip a column or columns on an eighty-column (80) card the SPACE BAR must be depressed.

2. Punching Keys

Keys #1–#34 are the punching keys and are used to enter the appropriate punches in the columns of an eighty (80)-column card. Because the keyboard is in alphabetic shift, depressing any of these 34 keys will produce the keypunching of the lower key characters. The upper key characters can be punched by simultaneously depressing the NUMERIC key (#35) and the appropriate punching key.

3. Functional Keys

Keys #35–#47 are functional keys.

---

*A detailed description of this unit and its control cards can be found in Carl Feingold, *Introduction to Data Processing 3d* ed. (Dubuque, Iowa: Wm. C. Brown Company Publishers, 1980), pp. 641–49.

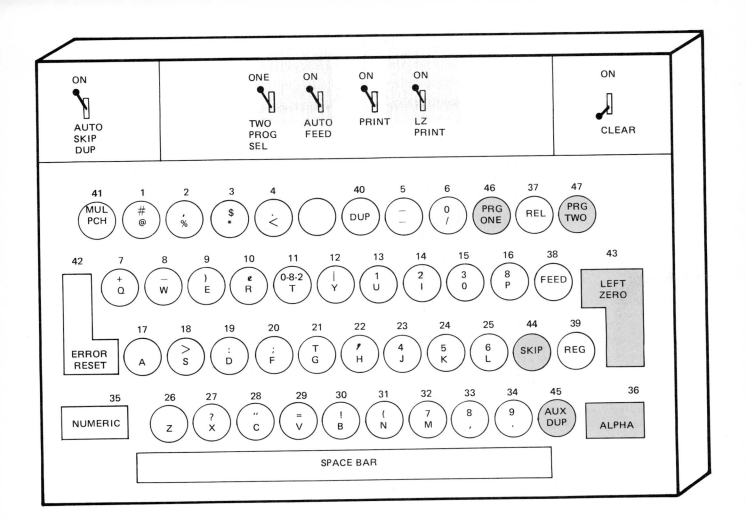

NUMERIC Key #35   Because the keyboard is in alphabetic shift, this key must be depressed to shift into the upper key characters. When, simultaneously depressing the NUMERIC key and a punching key, the upper key character will be punched.

ALPHA Key #36   A program or drum card (see program unit) can be used to switch the keyboard from alphabetic mode to numeric mode. If this is done, then the ALPHA key must be depressed to shift into the lower key characters. When simultaneously depressing the ALPHA key and a punching key, the lower key character will be punched.

REL Key #37   This is the release key. If the AUTO FEED toggle switch is ON, depressing this key causes the following four actions to take place (see the figure on p. 310):

1. If there is a card in the READING STATION, that card then moves into the CARD STACKER.
2. If there is a card under the PUNCHING HEAD, that card then moves into the READING STATION where it is positioned under the READING HEAD.
3. If there is a card in the PUNCHING STATION, that card is then registered in the PUNCHING STATION under the PUNCHING HEAD.
4. If there is a card in the CARD HOPPER, that card is then fed from the HOPPER into the PUNCHING STATION. If the AUTO FEED toggle switch is OFF, then no card is fed from the CARD HOPPER into the PUNCHING STATION. The other three events will occur however.

FEED Key #38   If no card is registered under the PUNCHING HEAD, depressing this key causes the following to occur (see the figure on p. 310).

1. If there is a card in the READING STATION, that card then is registered in that READING STATION under the READING HEAD.
2. If there is a card in the PUNCHING STATION, that card then is registered in that PUNCHING STATION under the PUNCHING HEAD.
3. If there is a card in the CARD HOPPER, that card then is fed from the HOPPER into the PUNCHING STATION.

REG Key #39   This is the Card Register key. When there is a need to insert cards manually into the READING STATION, then this key can be used to register these cards under the READING HEAD and PUNCHING HEAD.

DUP Key #40   This is the Duplicate key. Depressing this key causes keypunched characters on the card that passes under the READING HEAD to be duplicated in corresponding columns on the card passing under the PUNCHING HEAD.

MUL PCH Key #41   This is the Multiple punch key. If you wish more than one character in the same card column, you must then keep the MUL PCH key down until all characters are punched.

ERROR RESET Key #42   If during keypunching the machine blocks because you hit two keys simultaneously, you can unblock the keypunching by depressing the ERROR RESET key and continue keypunching.

Keys #43–#47   These keys require a drum or program card to be operative and are therefore not discussed here.

Instructions for the use of the IBM 29 Card Punch

1. Sit down at the IBM 29 card punch and turn on the MAIN power SWITCH.
2. Prepare your toggle switches: place the AUTO SKIP DUP, AUTO FEED and PRINT switches in the ON position.
3. You are now ready to place a deck of unkeypunched cards in the CARD HOPPER. As indicated before, you must make sure that the 9-edge of the card is down and that the face of the card is toward you.
4. Depress the FEED key: a card slides down from the CARD HOPPER into the PUNCHING STATION.
5. Depress the FEED key again: a second card slides down from the CARD HOPPER into the PUNCHING STATION and the previous card registers under the PUNCHING HEAD.
6. Keypunch all necessary information on the cards by using keys #1–35. Use key #35 simultaneously for characters shown on the upper half of the punching keys. The SPACE BAR must be used if you wish to leave a card column blank.
7. Depress the RELease key when you have finished punching a card, so that you can get ready to punch a new card.
8. Repeat steps 6 and 7 for continuous punching until you have finished.
9. To remove cards from the PUNCHING and READING STATION hold the right-hand toggle switch—the CLEAR switch—in the ON position.
10. Now remove your cards from the CARD STACKER and check them for keypunching errors. If you detect errors, repunch the card. Suppose that in punching a given card, errors have been made in columns 5, 10, 15, and 20; you may then want to use the DUPlicate key to aid you in correcting these errors as follows:

—manually insert the card that contains the errors into the READING STATION and a blank into the PUNCHING STATION;

—depress the REGister key to register the two cards under the READING HEAD and the PUNCHING HEAD respectively;

—depress the DUPlicate key to duplicate the card that goes under the READING HEAD onto the card that goes under the PUNCHING HEAD. Release the DUPlicate key when columns 5, 10, 15, and 20 are encountered and depress the punching keys to insert the correct entries in these columns. The column indicator, which can be seen through the window in the PROGRAM UNIT, must guide you during the duplicating and correcting operation.

11. When you have finished your job, remove blank cards from the CARD HOPPER: gather all keypunched cards from the CARD STACKER; clean up your keypunch station, and switch OFF the MAIN power SWITCH.

File Processing

Throughout this FORTRAN text, we have used cards for input data and the line printer for printing out the results. However, other devices can be used for input and/or output of information, such as paper and magnetic tape, disks, drums, terminals, plotters, and others. In general, a file can be represented as shown in the figure below.

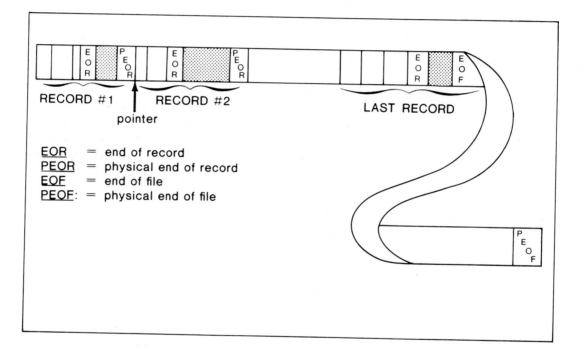

RECORD #1   RECORD #2   LAST RECORD

pointer

EOR   = end of record
PEOR = physical end of record
EOF   = end of file
PEOF: = physical end of file

A file is a named collection of all occurrences of a given type of logical record. Records in a file may have the same number of data items or they may have varying numbers of data items. Since the collection of records may take up less space than the actual size of the file, one must distinguish between the physical end of the file (PEOF) and the end of all records or the end of the file (EOF). A physical record often contains multiple segment or data items. Since the length of a record is determined by the system programmer, or may be fixed, the actual end of a recorder (EOR) is often different from the physical end of a record (PEOR). A pointer is used to locate the next data element of a record under consideration.

Examples of records are: the inventory records in an inventory file, students' records in a student file, etc. The elements of an inventory record may be the identification (ID), amount of stock on hand, vendor's address, lead time, safety stock, reorder point, etc. Most likely, in such a type of inventory file all records have the same number of data items. The elements of a student record may be the student average, courses taken and grades received. In such a file, the records may exhibit a varying number of data items.

1. Reading from and Writing on Tape

As in reading cards or writing on the line printer, it is necessary to specify an appropriate logical unit number in the READ or WRITE statement to designate tape input and output. In the following example the tape unit is specified by the logical unit number 12.

```
      DIMENSION NAME(4)
      READ(12,10)NAME,PRICE,AMOUNT
   10 FORMAT(4A4,F8.2,F8.0)
```

In this particular example, a tape record is read that contains 32 characters of data. The following set of statements will write out the above information in two records.

```
      WRITE(16,20)NAME,PRICE,AMOUNT
   20 FORMAT(5X,4A4,/,5X,F8.2,4X,F8.0)
```

In the above two examples, FORMAT statements are used to carefully control the reading and writing of records. Such control is not always desirable, especially when different input/output (I/O) devices are used to supplement the computer's memory. If one wishes to use I/O devices as an extension of the computer's memory, then it is natural to store data in a form similar to the one used to store data in memory cells. This is accomplished with the aid of unformatted I/O statements. When unformatted I/O statements are used, the computing system will define the form of data storage. The unformatted I/O statements are similar to the formatted, except that there is no reference to a format statement and no format statement, as follows:

```
      DIMENSION NAME(4)
      READ(12)NAME,PRICE,AMOUNT
```

and

```
      WRITE(16)NAME,PRICE,AMOUNT
```

2. Sequential Files

Magnetic tape stores information sequentially. This means that, in order to obtain information from a particular record, it will be necessary to read all preceding records.

In order to illustrate the updating of a sequential file, consider the following inventory system. This system consists of a master file and a transaction file.

The master file contains, for each inventory item, an inventory identification number, quantity on hand, and unit price.

The Transaction file contains information on the daily transactions. For each transaction that took place, information on that transaction is recorded consisting of the inventory identification number, quantity sold (−) or quantity placed in inventory (+). At the end of each day, the content of the transaction file can be merged with the contents of the master file via a FORTRAN program to create a new master file. This is shown in the following figure.

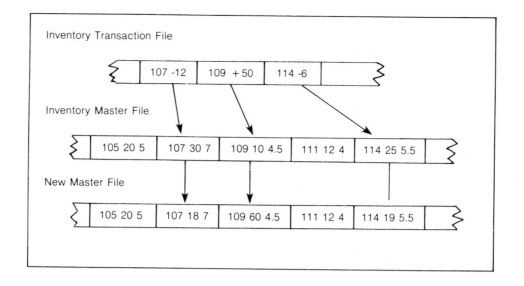

It is apparent from figure above that the ordering of records in the transaction and master files enables the updating of the master file.

The updating of this inventory system is shown in the following flowchart.

Three statements can be used to manipulate sequential files. These are:

END FILE i
BACKSPACE i
REWIND i

where i is the unit number referencing the file.

An end-of-file marker can be placed on a tape by the use of the END FILE statement. In order to backtrack one record on a file, the BACKSPACE statement is used, and the REWIND statement repositions the unit to its first record.

3. Direct Files

The major disadvantage of a sequential file is that a particular record on a file can be processed only after all its preceding records have been read. This problem can be overcome by the use of direct access files. A direct access file is a data file that is not necessarily read or written sequentially. Reading from or writing to a direct access file is done after first setting a pointer to the appropriate location of the file.

Records on magnetic tape cannot be directly accessable, however records on magnetic disk can. As opposed to sequential files, direct access files must be defined by the use of the DEFINE statement.

The general form of the DEFINE statement is as follows:

DEFINE i(r,w,f,v)

where: i: is the unit reference number
   r: indicates the total number of records in the file
   w: is an integer constant that identifies the size of the record. The size is either given in terms of characters (if read in or written out unformatted.)
   f: identifies whether the record is read in or written to with or without format. It is either L, E or U. L means that formatted or unformatted input-output will be used; E means that only formatted input-output will be used and U means that only unformatted input-output will be used.
   v: is an integer variable that will take on the value of the latest record number read in or written to.

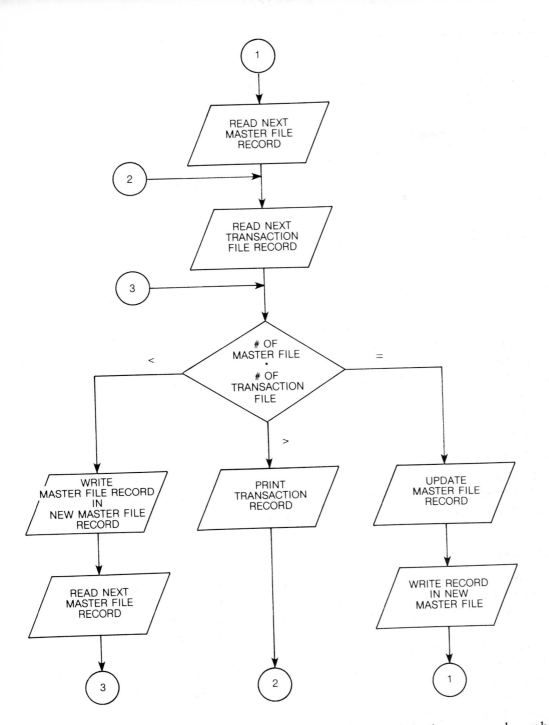

v is an integer variable that will take on the value of the latest record number read in or written to.

So, a file referenced with the unit number 17 that contains 50 records, consisting of 100 characters per record that can be read with format control, is defined as follows:

DEFINE 17(50,100,E,ID)

Similar statements as for sequential access files can now be used to process direct access files. The only difference is that the programmer must identify which record must be read or written.

The general form of the read or write statement for direct access files is as follows:

READ(i'r#,n)<list>
READ(i'r#)<list>   unformatted
WRITE(i'r#,n)<list>
WRITE(i'r#)<list>   unformatted

where: i: is the unit reference number
        r#: is the record number
        n: is the format statement number
        <list> is a list of variable names

For example, the following statements

    DEFINE 77(100,25,E,IKE)
    READ(77'12,20)CAP,TIME,INT
20 FORMAT(5X,F8.2,I3,F5.2)

reads three variables according to format statement number 20 out of the 12th record from unit number 77. These three variables will be assigned to CAP, TIME, and INT respectfully.

Index

A format
  input, 63
  output, 70
Abacus, 3
Accumulator, 3
Adding machine, 3
Addition, 46
Aikens, 3
ALGOL, 4
Alphanumeric Specification, 3, 70
Analog computer, 4
Analytical engine, 3
Arithmetic expression, 44
Arithmetic IF, 99
  DO loop, 134
  flowchart symbol, 99
Arithmetic rules, 45
Arithmetic statement function, 219
Arithmetic unit, 8
Arrays. *See* Subscripted variables
Assembler, 4
Assignment statement, 19, 44
  double precision, 236
  integer, 51
  logical, 240
  real, 51

Babbage, 3
BASIC, 4, 6
Binary number system, 3
Built-in functions, 217

CAL, 6
CALL EXIT statement, 19, 83
CALL statement, 19, 225
Card punch, 309
Carriage control, 73
Central processing unit, 8
Central storage, 8
CHARACTER statement, 54
  assignments, 53
  constant, 53
COBOL, 4
Coding, 17
Comment cards, 17

Comment field, 17
Comment symbol, 23
COMMON statement, 227
Compiler, 4, 14
Computed GO TO, 102
  flowchart, 102
Computers
  four generations of, 3
  history, 3
Concatenation, 54
Conditional transfer, 105, 115
Connectors, 23, 28
Constants, 46
  double precision, 236
  fixed, 46
  floating, 46
  integer, 46
  logical, 106, 240
  real, 46
Continuation field, 17
CONTINUE statement, 19, 134
Control cards, 16
Control statement, 16
Control unit, 8
Counter, DO, 129, 134
  increment, 129, 134
  initialize, 131, 134
  test, 131, 134
CPU, 8
CTSS, 6

D exponent, 236
D format, 236
DATA statement, 241
Debugging, 17
Decision symbol, 23, 27
Declaration statement
  COMMON, 227
  CHARACTER, 53
  DIMENSION, 19, 154, 169
  DOUBLE PRECISION, 235
  EQUIVALENCE, 205
  IMPLICIT, 240
  INTEGER, 45, 234
  LOGICAL, 240
  REAL, 45, 235
Difference engine, 3

Digital computer, 4
DIMENSION statement, 19, 154, 169
Direct access files, 316
Division, 46
DO loop, 129
  CONTINUE, 19, 134
  inner loop, 135
  rules, 134
DO statement, 19, 129
  counter, 129, 134
  examples, 134
  flowcharting symbol, 131
  general form, 129
  increment, 129, 134
  index, 129, 134
  initial value, 129, 134
  nested, 135
  range, 130
  rules, 134
  test value, 129, 134
  with logical IF, 134
Double precision arithmetic, 236
  assignment, 236
  constants, 236
  examples, 236
  expressions, 236
  I/O, 236
  variables, 236
DOUBLE PRECISION
  statement, 46, 235

Eckert, 3
EDVAC, 3
END statement, 19, 83
ENIAC, 3
Executable statements, 17
Exponentiation, 46
Expression,
  arithmetic, 44–46
  double-precision, 236
  integer, 49
  logical, 106, 240
  real, 49
Extended precision. *See* Double-precision

F format
    input, 62
    output, 67
Files,
    Direct access, 316
    Sequential access, 315
File processing, 314
Fixed-point. *See* Integer
Floating-point. *See* Real
Flowchart, 23
    arrowhead, 23, 28
    connectors and terminal
      symbols, 23, 28
    decision symbol, 23, 27, 99,
      102, 106
    flow direction, 28
    input/output symbol, 23–24,
      59
    list of flowcharts, 323
    page connector, 23, 28
    predefined process, 23, 30, 216
    preparation symbol, 23, 30,
      131
    processing symbol, 21–22, 44
    program, 24
    starting symbol, 23
    systems, 24
Format—I/O
    alpha numeric character, 63,
      70
    double precision, 236
    extra specifications, 77
    hollorith, 72
    implied decimal, 75
    integer, 61, 67
    logical, 240
    punched decimal, 76
    real, 62, 67
    repetition, 76
    rescanning, 77
    rules, 75
    skip cards, 64
    skip lines, 68
    skip spaces, 64, 66
    statement, 19, 60
    summary, 78
    tab, 75
FORTRAN, 77
    arithmetic assignment, 53
    control statements, 115
    DO loop, 144
    input/output, 77
    subprogram, DIMENSION,
      227
    subscripted variables, 180
FUNCTION subprogram, 220
    arguments, 220
    calling, 221
    examples, 222
    name, 220
    rules, 220
    statement, 19

GO TO statement, 19, 97
    computed, 102
    unconditional, 97
GPSS, 4
Greek computer, 3

H format
    input, 73
    output, 72
Halt statements, 83
Harvard Mark I, 3
High-level language, 4, 14
Hollorith field, 72
    specification, 73

I format
    input, 61
    output, 67
IAS computer, 3
Identification field, 17
IF statement
    arithmetic, 99
    logical, 105
    THEN ELSE, 115
IMPLICIT statement, 240
Implied DOs, 155, 171
Increment, DO, 129, 134
Index of DO, 129, 134
Initial value of DO, 129, 134
Input-Output, 59
    alpha numeric characters, 63,
      70
    arrays, 154
    double precision, 236
    format, 60
    hollorith, 72
    integer, 61, 67
    logical, 240
    real, 62, 67
    skip, 64, 66, 68
    statement, 19
    symbol, 23–24, 59
    tab, 75
Input unit, 8
Integer
    arithmetic, 49
    assignment, 49
    constants, 45
    declaration, 45, 234
    expression, 49
    function, 220
    I/O, 61, 67
    magnitude, 46
    overflow example, 235
    subscripted variables, 153
    variables, 45
INTEGER statement, 19, 234
Interactive processing, 6
Interrupt symbol, 4

JOSS, 6

Kelvin, 4
Key-punched card, 3
Key words, 19

L format, 240
Label field, 17
Language
    high level, 4
    low level, 4
Leibnitz, 3
Library functions, 217
Linkage editor, 14
LISP, 6
Load module, 14
Logical
    assignment, 240
    checking logical flow, 36
    constants, 106
    examples, 240
    expressions, 106, 240
    flowchart, 106
    IF statement, 105, 134
    I/O, 240
    operators, 106
    variables, 240
Logical IF, 105
    flowchart symbol, 106
    in DO loop, 134
LOGICAL statement, 240
Lord Kelvin, 4
Low level language, 4

MAC, 6
Machine language, 4
Main program, 221, 224
Main storage, 8
Mathematical functions, 217
Maughly, 3
Memory, 8
Mixed mode
    arithmetic, 49
    exponentiation, 50
    expressions, 49
Mnemonics, 4
Monitor system, 22
Multiplication, 46

Nonexecutable statements, 17

Object program, 14
Operators, 46
    addition, 46
    arithmetic, 46
    assignment, 46
    concatenation, 54
    division, 46
    exponentiation, 46
    logical, 106
    multiplication, 46
    relational, 106
    subtraction, 46
Organization of computer, 8

Output. *See* Input-Output
Output page, 65
Output unit, 8

Page connector, 23, 28
Parameter, 219
Parantheses,
   expressions, 47
   formats, 76
Pascal, 3
PAUSE statements, 83
PL/I, 4
Predefined processing symbol, 23,
    30, 216
Preparation symbol, 23, 30
Priority of operators, 47
Processing a job, 14
Processing symbol, 23–24
Program flowchart, 24
    rules, 82, 118, 145, 187, 228
Pseudocode, 23

Random number generator, 252
Range of DO, 130
READ statement, 19, 59
   flowchart symbol, 23, 24, 59
Real
   arithmetic, 49
   assignment statement, 49
   constants, 46
   declaration, 45, 235
   expressions, 49
   input/output, 62, 67
   magnitude, 46
   subscripted variables, 153
   variables, 45
REAL statement, 19, 235

Relational operators, 106
RETURN statement, 222
RPG, 4

Sequential access files, 315
SIMSCRIPT, 4
Simulation, 252
Single precision. *See* Real
Skip specifications
   cards, 64
   lines, 68
   spaces, 64, 66
Slash format, 64
Sorting, 244
Source program, 14
   statements, 17
Specifications, 45, 54, 234
Starting symbol, 23
Statement field, 17
Stonehenge, 3
STOP statement, 19, 83
Storage unit, 8
Structured programming, 23
Subprogram, 216
   function, 220
   subroutine, 223
SUBROUTINE statement, 19,
   224
   arguments, 224
   examples, 226
Subscripted variables, 152
   expressions, 153
   form of subscripts, 153
   integer, 153
   I/O, 154, 170
   one-dimensional, 152
   real, 151
   two-dimensional, 167

Subscripts, 152, 153
Subtraction, 46
Symbolic name, 45
Symbolic unit number, 59
Syntax error, 17
Systems flowchart, 24

Tab specification, 75
Tape, 315
Terminal symbol, 23, 28
Test vlue of DO, 129, 134
Time sharing, 4–5
Transfer statements, 97
   arithmetic, 99
   computed GO TO, 102
   conditional, 115
   GO TO, 97
   logical IF, 105, 115
   unconditional, 97
Type declaration. *See* Declaration
   statements

Variable dimensions, 228
Variables, 24, 28, 30, 44–45
   double-precision, 235
   integer, 45, 234
   logical, 240
   real, 45, 235
Von Newman, 3

WRITE statement, 19, 60
   flowchart symbol, 23–24, 59

X format specification, 66